Housing and Building Control Act 1984

AUSTRALIA
The Law Book Company Ltd.
Sydney : Melbourne : Brisbane

CANADA AND U.S.A.
The Carswell Company Ltd.
Agincourt, Ontario

INDIA
N. M. Tripathi Private Ltd.
Bombay
and
Eastern Law House Private Ltd.
Calcutta and Delhi
M.P.P. House
Bangalore

ISRAEL
Steimatzky's Agency Ltd.
Jerusalem : Tel Aviv : Haifa

MALAYSIA : SINGAPORE : BRUNEI
Malayan Law Journal (Pte.) Ltd.
Singapore

PAKISTAN
Pakistan Law House
Karachi

Housing and Building Control Act 1984

with annotations by

ANDREW ARDEN LL.B., *Barrister*

and

CHARLES CROSS M.A., LL.B., *Barrister*

LONDON
SWEET & MAXWELL
1984

Published in 1984 by
Sweet & Maxwell Limited of
11 New Fetter Lane, London,
and printed in Great Britain
by The Eastern Press Limited
of London and Reading

ISBN 0 421 33080 5

© Sweet & Maxwell
1984

HOUSING AND BUILDING CONTROL ACT 1984*

(1984 c.29)

ARRANGEMENT OF SECTIONS

PART I

DISPOSAL OF PUBLIC SECTOR DWELLING-HOUSES AND RIGHTS OF SECURE TENANTS

Right to buy

Right to a shared ownership lease

Other provisions with respect to disposals

Other rights of secure tenants

Miscellaneous

Supplemental

* Annotations by Andrew Arden LL.B., Barrister, and Charles Cross M.A., LL.B., Barrister.

An Act to make further provision with respect to the disposal of, and the rights of secure tenants of, dwelling-houses held by local authorities and other bodies in England and Wales; to amend the law of England and Wales relating to the supervision of building work, the building regulations, sanitation and buildings and building control; and for connected purposes. [26th June 1984]

COMMENCEMENT
Ss.42(2), 56(2), 57(2) and 58; so far as they relate to the amendments of s.69 of the Health and Safety at Work etc. Act 1974, s.64 and Sched. 11; and so far as they relate to the repeals of s.67 of the Public Health Act 1936 and s.62(3) of the 1974 Act, s.65 and Pt. II of Sched. 12, will come into force on such day as the Secretary of State may by order appoint. The whole of Pts. I and IV, and the balance of Pts. II and III come into force on August 26, 1984.

EXTENT
The Act does not extend to Scotland or Northern Ireland.

PARLIAMENTARY DEBATES
Hansard: H.C. Vol. 44, col. 174; Vol. 45, col. 160; Vol. 51, col. 442; Vol. 58, col. 542; Vol. 61, col. 875; H.L. Vol. 446, col. 840; Vol. 447, cols. 453 and 468; Vol. 448, cols. 1162 and 1179; Vol. 449, cols. 146, 433 and 1372; Vol. 450, cols. 10, 27 and 801, Vol. 451, col. 1017, Vol. 453, cols. 156 and 171.
This Bill was considered by Standing Committee B (July 12 to November 11, 1983).

PART I

DISPOSAL OF PUBLIC SECTOR DWELLING-HOUSES AND RIGHTS OF SECURE TENANTS

GENERAL NOTE TO PART I
This Part of the Act contains the "housing" provisions, and is largely a "Housing (Amendment) Act" expanding upon, and refining, the provisions of the Housing Act 1980 and, in particular, Part I, Chapter 1 of that Act (the "right to buy"). Given the innovatory quality of the right to buy, it had certainly to be anticipated, even at the time it was passing into law, that a *technical* amendment Act would be required. This Act, however, contains what are principally substantive amendments

"Approximately 630,000 houses and flats were sold between April 1979 and September 1983 by local authorities and new towns in Great Britain, some 400,000 of them under the right to buy . . . In addition, housing associations sold about 40,000 dwellings . . ." (Sir George Young, December 21, 1983; *Hansard*, H.C. Vol. 51, col. 428 (oral answers)). It is accepted that the overwhelming majority of sales are of houses, and the government intend to make it more widely known that tenants of flats have the right to a long lease (Standing Committee B, July 28, 1983, col. 221) although the new Act takes no initiatives in this direction.

Instead, the thrust of the legislation is general expansion of tenants' rights to buy (or of the "theology of the right to buy": Lord Bellwin, February 28, 1984, *Hansard*, H.L. Vol. 448, col. 1230). The central features may be described as follows.

The right to buy is now to apply even where the landlord does not own the freehold (s.1). It was estimated "that this provision will benefit some 50,000 secure tenants of public leasehold property . . ." (Lord Bellwin, January 30, 1984, *Hansard*, H.L. Vol. 447, col. 454 (second reading)). Tenants will be entitled to leases of five days' less than their landlord's interests, although this extension of right to buy will not apply at all if the landlord's interest at the date of service of the notice claiming the right to buy is less than 21 years (in the case of a house) or less than 50 years (in the case of a flat).

More dwellings for the disabled have been brought within the right to buy, and there is a general extension, but subject to defined exceptions, to tenants of county councils (s.2) An attempt to extend the right to buy in relation to dwellings for the disabled led to a reaction in the House of Lords, resulting in only limited changes unlikely to increase, and possibly with the result of reducing, the number of such dwellings available for sale (*ibid.*).

The residential qualification for exercise of the right to buy has been reduced from three years to two (s.3). The minimum discount has been reduced by only one per cent. to reflect the three year to two year reduction (33 per cent. to 32 per cent.), but the maximum discount increased from 50 per cent. to 60 per cent. (A similar increase was effected in relation to *voluntary* sales on July 5, 1983 by amendment to the General Consents). Children succeeding to their parents' tenancies will now be entitled to discounts as of right, rather than under discretion. There is a new formula for limiting discounts available to "second-time purchasers" (*ibid.*).

The definition of periods to be taken into account when determining residential qualification, and when determining discount, have been harmonised, and expanded, in particular by inclusion of periods of occupation with a wider range of public or quasi-public landlord (*ibid.*).

The circumstances in which discount may have to be repaid have been reduced (s.5). The procedures which the landlord must follow during the exercise of a right to buy have been tightened up, to allow less room for delay, while the corresponding tenants' obligations have been slackened, allowing them much greater freedom and time than hitherto before there is any risk of cancellation of the transaction (s.6). The Secretary of State's powers of intervention have been considerably enlarged, and he now enjoys a power to grant assistance to those having difficulty exercising the right to buy, including by way of legal advice, assistance and representation (ss.9–11).

One major innovation is the creation of a "right to a shared ownership lease" (ss.12–17, s.37) which arises when a tenant (*a*) seeks a mortgage from the landlord or the Housing Corporation, and (*b*) is not entitled to a mortgage amounting to the whole of the purchase price (plus specified related costs). The shared ownership lease starts at a 50 per cent. slice of the equity, with a right to buy further shares, and a right to mortgage for initial and subsequent purchases. Subsequent tranches of equity will be at "later" values.

Other new rights for public sector occupants (or those who buy from the public sector) include a service charge protection similar to that enjoyed by tenants in blocks of flats, relating to leases and freeholds of houses on estates where continuing services are to be provided (s.18). Secure tenants, who remain as such (*i.e.* who do not buy) gain rights: to exchange (s.26), to carry out repairs (pursuant to a scheme to be drawn up) (s.28), and to information about district heating charges (also pursuant to a scheme yet to be drawn up) (s.29). The tenants of charitable housing associations, not within the right to buy, will be within a scheme to be drawn up which will give them the right to a "premium" with which to buy in the private sector, equivalent to the discount to which they would otherwise have been entitled (s.35).

Leaving aside a number of relatively minor provisions, concerning both voluntary and mandatory sales, and secure tenants, attention may finally be drawn to amendments governing assignments between secure tenants, designed to limit their capacity for use in right to buy avoidance (s.26); and to new provisions governing disposals by local authorities, similarly designed to prevent right to buy avoidance (s.22).

ABBREVIATIONS

In the annotations to Pt. I the following abbreviation is used:
1980 Act: Housing Act 1980.

Right to buy
Extension to certain cases where landlord does not own freehold

1.—(1) The provisions of this section and of Schedule 1 to this Act shall have effect for the purpose of extending the right to buy conferred by Chapter I of Part I of the Housing Act 1980 (in this Part of this Act referred to as "the 1980 Act") to certain cases where the landlord does not own the freehold of the dwelling-house.

(2) In section 1(1) of the 1980 Act (right to acquire freehold or long lease) for paragraphs (*a*) and (*b*) there shall be substituted the following paragraphs—

"(*a*) if the dwelling-house is a house and the landlord owns the freehold, to acquire the freehold of the dwelling-house;

(*b*) if the landlord does not own the freehold or (whether or not the landlord owns it) the dwelling-house is a flat, to be granted a lease of the dwelling-house; and".

(3) At the end of section 2(3) of the 1980 Act (exceptions to right to buy) there shall be inserted the words "or has an interest sufficient to grant a lease in pursuance of this Chapter—

(*a*) where the dwelling-house is a house, for a term exceeding 21 years commencing with the relevant time;

(*b*) where the dwelling-house is a flat, for a term of not less than 50 years commencing with that time."

(4) The amendments made by this section and Schedule 1 to this Act (except paragraph 10) shall not apply where the landlord's notice under section 5(1) of the 1980 Act was served before the commencement date.

DEFINITIONS

"commencement date": s.66.
"dwelling-house": s.38 and 1980 Act s.3.
"flat": s.38 and 1980 Act s.3.
"house": s.38 and 1980 Act s.3.
"relevant time": s.38 and 1980 Act s.3.
"right to buy": s.38 and 1980 Act s.1.

GENERAL NOTE
1980 Act
The right to buy as initially enacted by the 1980 Act applied only where the landlord held a freehold interest in the property: 1980 Act, s.2(3). If a house (as defined; see 1980 Act, s.3) the right to buy is a right to a freehold; if a flat (*ibid*) to no more than a long lease (the length of which is determined by 1980 Act, s.17 and Sched. 2, the latter now as amended by Sched. 1, below).

Main Changes
The amendment contained in subs.(2) of this section leaves the position unchanged in relation to houses where the landlord owns the freehold, but adds to the class entitled to a lease the tenants of both houses and flats, where the landlord has an interest sufficient to grant a lease of specified length (as to which see notes to subs.(3) below).

Exempt from the operation of this extension is property where the interest superior to that of the authority is the Crown; see notes to Sched. 1, para. 9, below. In outline, the exemption will *not* apply (and the right will therefore be available) if either the Crown consents to the grant, or no consent to the grant is or would be required under the terms of the lease.

Sched. 1 contains amendments to the 1980 Act reflecting these changes; the terms of the lease are defined by the 1980 Act as so amended. These provisions are considered in detail in the notes to Sched. 1 below. The lease will be of 125 years, *unless* either (*a*) the landlord's interest is of less than 125 years and five days, in which case the grant is to be for a period expiring five days before the expiry of the landlord's interest; or (*b*) the lease is of a flat in a building in which a previous lease under the right to buy has already been granted, in which case the grant may be for a shorter period, coterminous with the earlier grant.

The principal, and perhaps surprising (but not unanticipated; see Sched. 11, para. 2, below which amends the Leasehold Reform Act 1967) side-effect of the provision for leases (at what will certainly be a low rent; see 1980 Act, Sched. 2, para. 11, as substituted by Sched. 1, para. 10 below) of *houses* (but not flats) is that the tenant will acquire the right, after three years (*N.B.* not two) as long leaseholder, to enfranchise under the Leasehold Reform Act 1967.

The right will be exercisable not merely against the (public sector) landlord, but also against the (possibly (indeed probably) private sector) freeholder; see the 1967 Act, s.5 and Sched. 1. Landlords affected by the present Act could not themselves enfranchise because as legal, corporate or "artificial" persons they cannot fulfil the residential qualifications of the 1967 Act, s.1 (see, *e.g. Duke of Westminster* v. *Oddy*, *The Times*, March 27, 1984, C.A.).

This benefit will be available even though the lease itself may not be for more than 21 years; see Sched. 11, para. 2 below. The benefit will not be available at all, however, where the landlord is a housing association, and the freeholder is a body of persons or a trust established for charitable purposes; *ibid.*

Another intervention in the private sector is effected by Sched. 1, para. 11, below, adding a new para. 19A to 1980 Act, Sched. 2. In substance, the new para. 19A voids provisions in leases (including those granted by private landlords) which would prevent or inhibit the grant of subleases under the right to buy as now extended, or which would prevent or inhibit the sub-lessee's rights to further dispose of the sub-lease.

Subs. (2)

The right to buy is now a right to the freehold of a house, of which the landlord owns the freehold, and otherwise (*i.e.* when the relevant property is a flat, or a house where the landlord does not own freehold) to a lease

Subs. (3)

The 1980 Act (s.2, and Sched. 1 of that Act; see further notes to s.2 below) specifies the exceptions to the right to buy. While s.2(3) of the 1980 Act formerly excluded *all* cases where the landlord did not own the freehold, it is now to exclude only those cases where the landlord does not have a sufficient interest to grant a lease. *Sufficient interest* means, in the case of a house, an interest sufficient to grant a term exceeding 21 years commencing with the relevant time; in the case of a flat the term is to be of not less than 50 years commencing with the relevant time. *Relevant time* is defined in the 1980 Act s.3(5) as the date on which the tenant's notice claiming the right to buy is served.

Subs. (4)

When a secure tenant serves notice on a landlord claiming to exercise the right to buy, the landlord must normally reply within four weeks, either admitting the right, or denying the right and stating the reasons why the right is denied; see 1980 Act s.5(1). In those circumstances in which reliance is placed by the tenant on time spent with another landlord (for the purposes of qualifying for the right to buy) the period is extended to eight weeks; see 1980 Act, s.5(1) and (2).

By virtue of this subsection, the extension of the right to a long lease does not apply if the landlord has already served notice, denying the tenant's right to buy, under s.5, of the 1980 Act before the commencement of this Part of the Act. There is, however, nothing to stop such a tenant serving a new notice claiming the right once this Part comes into force (although the purchase price may be higher because of the delay).

If a tenant's claim is still unanswered when this Part comes into force, the tenant will benefit from these amendments. It would not seem open to a landlord to argue that the amendments do not apply in a case in which the s.5 notice *ought* to have been served prior to commencement, but has not been; this would be to raise the landlord's own wrong.

Variation of circumstances in which right does not arise

2.—(1) Subsection (5) of section 2 of the 1980 Act (exceptions to the right to buy) shall be omitted and for paragraphs 1 and 2 of Part I of Schedule 1 to that Act (circumstances in which the right to buy does not arise) there shall be substituted the following paragraph—

"1.—(1) The dwelling-house either forms part of, or is within the curtilage of, a building to which sub-paragraph (2) below applies or is situated in a cemetery and (in either case) the dwelling-house was let to the tenant or to a predecessor in title of his in consequence of the tenant or predecessor being in the employment of the landlord or of a body specified in sub-paragraph (3) below.

(2) This sub-paragraph applies to a building if the building or so much of it as is held by the landlord—

(*a*) is held mainly for purposes other than housing purposes; and
(*b*) consists mainly of accommodation other than housing accommodation;

and in this sub-paragraph 'housing purposes' means the purposes for which dwelling-houses are held by local authorities under Part V of the 1957 Act or purposes corresponding to those purposes.

(3) The bodies referred to in sub-paragraph (1) above are—
  (*a*) a local authority;
  (*b*) a development corporation;
  (*c*) an urban development corporation within the meaning of Part XVI of the Local Government, Planning and Land Act 1980;
  (*d*) the Commission for the New Towns;
  (*e*) a county council;
  (*f*) the governors of an aided school; and
  (*g*) the Development Board for Rural Wales."

(2) For paragraphs 3 and 4 of that Part of that Schedule there shall be substituted the following paragraphs—

"3. The dwelling-house has features which are substantially different from those of ordinary dwelling-houses and which are designed to make it suitable for occupation by physically disabled persons and either—
  (*a*) the dwelling-house has had those features since it was constructed or, where it was provided by means of the conversion of a building, since it was so provided; or
  (*b*) the dwelling-house is one of a group of dwelling-houses which it is the practice of the landlord to let for occupation by physically disabled persons and a social service or special facilities are provided in close proximity to the group of dwelling-houses wholly or partly for the purpose of assisting those persons.

3A. The landlord or a predecessor of the landlord has carried out, for the purpose of making the dwelling-house suitable for occupation by physically disabled persons, one or more of the following alterations, namely—
  (*a*) the provision of not less than 7·5 square metres of additional floor space;
  (*b*) the provision of an additional bathroom or shower-room;
  (*c*) the installation of a vertical lift.

3B. The dwelling-house is one of a group of dwelling-houses which it is the practice of the landlord to let for occupation by persons who are suffering or have suffered from a mental disorder (within the meaning of the Mental Health Act 1983) and a social service or special facilities are provided wholly or partly for the purpose of assisting those persons.

4. The dwelling-house is one of a group of dwelling-houses which are particularly suitable, having regard to their location, size, design, heating systems and other features, for occupation by persons of pensionable age and which it is the practice of the landlord to let for occupation by such persons, or for occupation by such persons and physically disabled persons, and special facilities are provided wholly or mainly for the purpose of assisting those persons which consist of or include either—
  (*a*) the services of a resident warden; or
  (*b*) the services of a non-resident warden, a system for calling him and the use of a common room in close proximity to the group of dwelling-houses."

(3) For paragraph 5 of that Part of that Schedule there shall be substituted the following paragraph—

"5.—(1) The Secretary of State has determined, on the application of the landlord, that the right to buy is not to be capable of being exercised with respect to the dwelling-house; and he shall so determine if, and only if, he is satisfied that the dwelling-house—
  (*a*) is particularly suitable, having regard to its location, size,

design, heating system and other features, for occupation by persons of pensionable age; and

(b) was let to the tenant or to a predecessor in title of his for occupation by a person of pensionable age or a physically disabled person (whether the tenant or predecessor or any other person).

(2) An application for a determination under this paragraph shall be made within four weeks or, in a case falling within section 5(2) of this Act, eight weeks of the service of the notice claiming to exercise the right to buy."

(4) The amendments made by subsections (1) and (3) above shall not apply where the tenant's claim to exercise the right to buy was made before the commencement date; and the amendment made by subsection (2) above shall not apply where the landlord's notice under section 5(1) of the 1980 Act was served before that date.

DEFINITIONS
    "commencement date":s.66.
    "development corporation": s.38 and 1980 Act s.50.
    "dwelling-house": s.38 and 1980 Act s.3.
    "local authority": s.38 and 1980 Act s.50.
    "right to buy": s.38 and 1980 Act s.1.

GENERAL NOTE
1980 Act
    S.2 and Sched. 1, of the 1980 Act set out the circumstances in which the right to buy is not available, even to a secure tenant. (The right is, of course, only available generally to *secure* tenants, *i.e.* not to all public sector tenants.) Sched. 1 is in two parts. Pt. I details the circumstances in which the right does not arise, Pt. II details those circumstances in which the right cannot be exercised, creating classes of absolute exclusion, referable to the property, and of qualified exclusion referable to the tenant (see also s.16(9) of the 1980 Act which entitles a landlord to refuse to complete if the tenant is in four or more weeks' arrears of rent).

Main Changes
    This section contains amendment to the above mentioned provisions. Subs. (1) reflects, and relates to, the amendments made by s.36 below, bringing into security most tenants and licensees of county councils, and some tied occupiers. (Hitherto, occupiers of county council accommodation were only within security if the property in question was provided by the county council in the exercise of its reserve housing powers under the Local Government Act 1972). But although brought within security, some of them are not to enjoy the right to buy; see notes to subs. (1) below.
    The more contentious provisions are those contained in subs. (2) (reducing the class of accommodation occupied by the disabled which qualifies as exempt from the right to buy). The subsection also deals with sheltered accommodation for the mentally handicapped and for the elderly. Also contentious in its passage through Parliament, but less so in the end result, are the provisions of subs. (3), which deal with single dwellings for the elderly. While the government's intention was to increase the number of such dwellings available for sale, successful opposition in the House of Lords has in fact limited the changes, and some would say *tightened up* the exemption, leaving less such properties within the right.

Subs.(1)
    Under the 1980 Act (Sched. 1, Pt. 1, para. 1) local authority accommodation held *other* than under Part V of the Housing Act 1957 (the general housing power) was exempt from the right to buy. Under the 1980 Act s.2(5), however, the Secretary of State reserved the power to specify classes of such accommodation to which the right to buy would be extended, and did so by S.I. 1983 No. 672, for all such accommodation, but with certain exceptions. With the substitution under subs. (1) of this Act of a new para. 1 of the 1980 Act Sched. 1, Pt. 1, the power has become otiose and is accordingly repealed. (See, however, s.30 below introducing a different—in definition and intent—power to extend the right to buy).
    The effect of this substitution is to end the exemption of non-Part V stock altogether, and thus prima facie to bring all local authority stock within the right to buy. Sched. 1, Pt. 1,

para. 2 of the 1980 Act extended an analogous exemption to development corporations, the Commission for the New Towns and the Development Board for Rural Wales (land held for purposes not corresponding to Part V) and this exemption, too, is repealed by substitution, with the same substantive effect of bringing such stock prima facie within the right to buy.

In addition to these people, who may be described as occupying other than conventionally provided housing some conventionally provided housing is occupied other than on conventional lettings, *e.g.* service occupancies.

Until the repeal of Sched. 3, para. 3 of the 1980 Act by s.36, below, tenancies (and licences, *cf.* s.48 of the 1980 Act) were not *secure* if the terms of the tenancy provided for termination on the tenant ceasing to be employed by the landlord, *and* the property was held by the landlord for the purposes of its functions under the Education Act 1944 or any of the enactments specified in Sched. 1 of the Local Authority Social Services Act 1970, *and* the property formed part of, or was within the curtilage of, a building held for such purposes, *e.g.* caretakers or wardens. The repeal of para. 3 brings these lettings into security and, again, prima facie within the right to buy.

Finally, by way of prelude, and as noted above, while county councils have hitherto been outside the definition of a landlord whose tenants are secure, for the purposes of the 1980 Act which has left their tenants outside both security and right to buy, they are now brought in by s.36 below. Their tenants, too, have accordingly acquired security and, prima facie, the right to buy.

The cumulative effect of these amendments has been to define a new class of occupier, apparently within right to buy, and the purpose of subs. (1) is to take some of them back out again. (See also Sched. 3, para. 2 of the 1980 Act and new paras. 2A–2C, added by s.36 below, leaving certain other tied occupiers outside of security altogether, *i.e.* not just out of right to buy. Note, too, that although brought within security and then excluded from the right to buy, new grounds for possession have been added to the 1980 Act, Sched. 4 applicable to such occupiers; see below, s.25.)

Those still excluded from right to buy are the occupiers of property forming part of, or within the curtilage of, a building held by the landlord mainly for non-housing purposes, *i.e.* not for the purposes for which local authorities hold accommodation under Part V of the Housing Act 1957. The building must be one which consists mainly of non-housing accommodation. The exclusion will only apply, however, if the dwelling-house was let to the tenant, or his predecessor in title, in consequence of employment with the landlord, or with one of the other landlords who benefit from this provision (thus permitting landlords to house one another's employees). The same exemption applies where what is occupied is a dwelling-house in a cemetery (within the meaning of s.214 of the Local Government Act 1972; see the 1980 Act s.50(1), as amended by the 1984 Act, Sched. 11, para. 24, below).

Subs. (2)
Paras. 3, 3A: para. 3 of Pt. 1 of Sched. 1 of the 1980 Act excluded from the right to buy a dwelling-house with "features which are substantially different from those of ordinary dwelling-houses and which are designed to make it suitable for occupation by physically disabled persons".

In *Freeman* v. *Wansbeck District Council* (1983) 10 H.L.R. 54 CA, it was held that the introduction of an indoor downstairs lavatory was not a feature substantially different from the features of ordinary dwelling-houses, even though introduced by use of powers contained in the Chronically Sick and Disabled Persons Act 1970 for the benefit of the daughter of the tenants, who suffered from spina bifida. The word "designed" refers to the architectural process, and does not mean "intended". The Court of Appeal also held that when determining what constitutes the features of ordinary dwelling-houses, comparison should not be limited to other dwelling-houses in the same locality. Illustrations of appropriate special features included ramps, widened doors, lifts, and cooking surfaces at special heights.

By the present section, under new paras. 3 and 3A, the disablement exclusion is altered in three different ways. The first two ways concern single dwellings. (*i.e.* not in groups of sheltered accommodation for the disabled; see further below) and the third concerns dwellings which are in groups. (See also, but somewhat separately, (*a*) para. 4, concerning lettings of sheltered accommodation designed for the *elderly* to them *and* disabled persons; and (*b*) para. 5, introduced by subs. (3), below, concerning the letting of a single property designed for the *elderly* to or for a *disabled* person.)

To deal first with single dwellings, they may be excluded from right to buy in two different ways. First of all, under new para. 3, the existing exclusion (substantially different features designed to make suitable for occupation by the physically disabled) remains if the dwelling was *constructed* with those features, including as construction for this purpose a dwelling produced by conversion. This limb, then, does not include *alterations* to existing dwellings. The features will, of course, have to be those of the order discussed in *Freeman*.

Secondly, however, under new para. 3A, single dwellings will be excluded if the landlord, or a predecessor to the landlord, has carried out one or more of the specified three alterations, namely additional floor space, additional bathroom or shower-room, or installation of a lift.

Dwellings for the disabled may, nonetheless, be excluded, even if they do not fall within these single dwelling "construction or alteration" classes, if they are within the third class of disabled persons' dwellings, that is to say they are part of a group of "sheltered" dwellings with *Freeman* features; see new para. 3(*b*).

To qualify, (i) the individual unit must be one of a group; (ii) the dwelling must have features of the class discussed in *Freeman*, designed to make suitable for occupation by the physically disabled (whether by construction or subsequent alteration); (iii) it must be the practice of the landlord to let the group for occupation by the physically disabled; and (iv) a "social service or special" facility must be provided in "close proximity to the group of dwelling-houses". Furthermore, that facility must be "wholly or partly for the purpose of assisting" the disabled occupants.

This definition of what constitutes "sheltered accommodation" is modelled on, but is not identical to (*cf.* "wholly or partly for the purpose of assisting" with "only or main purpose of assisting") that formerly used to exclude elderly people's sheltered accommodation from the right to buy; see Sched. 1, Pt. 1, para. 4 of the 1980 Act (as unamended). It would seem that the allocation and adaptation of a single unit on an estate, or even one unit in each block on an estate, will not qualify as "one of a group" of dwelling-houses. Such properties would only be excluded if they qualify as "constructed" with, or altered to incorporate, special features, *i.e.* as if single units.

On the other hand, it is not necessary that an entire estate, or block, be for the disabled, so that units in developments for a range of special purposes will not necessarily fail to qualify under this heading. There must be something, however, susceptible to description as a "group" of which the property in issue is one.

Para. 3B: Turning to the mentally handicapped, there is, of course, no requirement for physical adaptation of property, nor for warden facilities, although only grouped accommodation will qualify, and there must be a social service or special facility provided "wholly or partly" to assist the occupants.

Para. 4: Under para. 4, of Pt. 1 of Sched. 1 of the 1980 Act, exempt from the right to buy were dwelling-houses in a group which it was the practice of the landlord to let for occupation by persons of pensionable age, and with social service or other special facilities in close proximity in order to assist such people.

The substitution of new para. 4 requires that a group of dwelling-houses is "particularly suitable" for occupation by the elderly, having regard to location, size, design, heating systems and other features, *in addition to* the former test of "practice of the landlord". Furthermore, the special facilities must include either a resident warden or, in the absence of a resident warden, a non-resident warden, *plus* a system for calling him, *plus* the use of a common room in close proximity to the group of houses. A small number of houses designed or adapted for the elderly, but on an otherwise conventional estate, would seem unlikely to qualify because of the need for the warden facility.

Subs. (3)

Para. 5: In addition to the provisions of former para. 4, there were the provisions of para. 5 of Pt. 1 of Sched. 1 of the 1980 Act. These exempted from the right to buy dwelling-houses designed or specially adapted for occupation by persons of pensionable age . . . [which] it is the practice of the landlord to let . . . only for occupation by such persons." Para. 5 was, accordingly, aimed mainly at single dwellings.

The provisions of para. 5 did not enjoy an easy passage through Parliament in 1980. They emerged as a compromise measure between a successful, non-government amendment in the House of Lords and the wishes of the government, during the all-night sitting which preceded the final passage of the 1980 Act. Had there been no such compromise, the Act might not have been passed in the then sitting.

One reflection of the hour and haste of passage is contained in the following "tongue-twister". Under a "normal" right-to-buy, the landlord is obliged to admit or deny an entitlement within four weeks (eight if the tenant relies on a period of occupation with another landlord): 1980 Act s.5. These dwellings for the elderly, however, were only exempt if within *six* weeks of service of notice claiming right-to-buy, the landlord had applied to the Secretary of State for—and the Secretary of State had issued—a determination that the conditions set out in the penultimate paragraph were fulfilled. The 1980 Act did not explain how a landlord could reply within four weeks, denying an entitlement to buy, on the basis of an application it had six weeks to make (with the Secretary of State having no prescribed time in which to respond).

As for the substance of the application itself, the Secretary of State was bound to determine that the right was not to be exercisable if satisfied that the property was designed or specially adapted for occupation by persons of pensionable age, and that it was the practice of the landlord to let it only for occupation by such persons.

New para. 5 contains a more precise test for when the Secretary of State is to be satisfied that the right is not to be exercisable. The property must be particularly suitable, having regard to location, size, design, heating system and "other features" for occupation by those of pensionable age. The Secretary of State must also be satisfied that it was let to the tenant, or predecessor in title, for occupation by one such person, or by a physically disabled person. "Other features" will presumably be covered in the guidance which is to be issued by Circular, after consultation with the local authority associations and other interested bodies (see *Hansard*, H.L. Vol. 453, col. 160 (June 19, 1984)).

The application for determination is to be made within either four or eight weeks, depending on which period governs requirement to reply to the would-be purchaser, which cures the first technical difficulty described in relation to the old para. 5 (the "six-week" point). The second difficulty (that the landlord must also *reply* within four or eight weeks whilst the Secretary of State has no prescribed time in which to make his determination) is overcome not by the new para. 5, but by an amendment contained in Sched. 11, para. 8. This has the effect of requiring a landlord to notify a tenant, in the reply to the tenant's claim, if an application has been made for a determination, and provides that an admission of right to buy is without prejudice to a successful determination.

Subs. (4)

The amendments concerning (a) non-Part V, tied housing, and (b) single dwellings for the elderly, do not take effect if the tenant's claim under s.5 of the 1980 Act had been made before the commencement date (*cf.* notes to s.1(4) above) although, of course, and at risk of a higher purchase price, an application may be withdrawn and reissued. The other amendments do not take effect if the landlord's reply under s.5 of the 1980 Act had been served before that date.

Further periods to count for qualification and discount

3.—(1) For subsections (3) to (7) of section 1 of the 1980 Act (determination of qualifying period) there shall be substituted the following subsections—

"(3) The right to buy does not arise unless the period which, in accordance with Part I of Schedule 1A to this Act, is to be taken into account for the purposes of this subsection is a period of not less than two years.

(4) Where the secure tenancy is a joint tenancy the condition in subsection (3) above need be satisfied with respect to one only of the joint tenants."

(2) For subsection (1) of section 7 of the 1980 Act (discount) there shall be substituted the following subsections—

"(1) A person exercising the right to buy is entitled to a discount equal, subject to the following provisions of this section, to the following percentage of the price before discount, that is to say—

(*a*) if the period which, in accordance with Part I of Schedule 1A to this Act, is to be taken into account for the purposes of discount is less than three years, 32 per cent.; and

(*b*) if that period is three years or more, 32 per cent. plus one per cent. for each complete year by which that period exceeds two years, but not together exceeding 60 per cent.;

and where joint tenants exercise the right to buy, that Part of that Schedule shall be construed as if for the secure tenant there were substituted that one of the joint tenants whose substitution will produce the largest discount.

(1A) There shall be deducted from the discount any amount which, in accordance with Part II of Schedule 1A to this Act, falls to be so deducted."

(3) In subsection (2) of that section after the words "31st March 1974" there shall be inserted the words "(or such later date as may be specified in an order made by the Secretary of State)".

(4) Subsections (5) to (11) of that section and section 15 of that Act (children succeeding parents) shall be omitted.

(5) After Schedule 1 to the 1980 Act there shall be inserted, as Schedule 1A, the Schedule set out in Schedule 2 to this Act.

(6) The amendments made by this section shall not apply—

    (*a*) for the purposes of section 1(3) of the 1980 Act where the landlord's notice under section 5(1) of that Act was served before the commencement date; or

    (*b*) for the purposes of discount where the notice under section 10(1) of that Act was served before that date.

DEFINITIONS

"commencement date": s.66.
"right to buy": s.38 and 1980 Act s.1.
"secure tenancy": s.38 and 1980 Act ss.27, 28.

GENERAL NOTE

1980 Act and Main Changes

The principal purpose of this section is to reduce from three to two years the minimum period of qualification to exercise the right to buy. (When three years was introduced in the 1980 Act, amendments to the Leasehold Reform Act 1967 altered from five to three years the qualifying period under that Act: although sympathy for a similar reduction was expressed during the passage of the present Act, no similar amendment has been made.) It was thought that some 250,000 tenants fell within the 2–3 year band (Standing Committee B, July 26, 1983, col. 171).

It is, of course, well known that the right to buy is exercisable at a price granting to the tenant a discount on the value of the property, reflecting years of public sector occupation. Those exercising the right after two years will obtain a minimum discount reduced from 33 per cent. to 32 per cent. (with a three year qualification remaining at 33 per cent. as before). One per cent. is added for each additional year of qualification, but to a new maximum of 60 per cent. (in place of 50 per cent.). It was thought that there were some 400,000 tenants with more than 20 years' tenancy, who could benefit from this extension (Standing Committee B, July 26, 1983, col. 173).

The present section introduces, through Pt. I of a new Sched. 1A to the 1980 Act, found in Sched. 2 to this Act, a uniform means of calculating qualification to exercise right to buy, and of calculating the discount. The harmonisation of the two approaches effectively extends the class of those qualifying to buy (*e.g.* by permitting time spent in the armed forces to count towards qualification for exercise as well as discount). The qualification of children who succeed their parents as secure tenants was already thus harmonised, but only arose (for either purpose) at the discretion of the landlord; see s.15 of the 1980 Act. Their position, too, has been absorbed into Pt. I of the new Sched. 1A and now arises as of right. Pt. 1 of the new Sched. 1A is considered in greater detail in the notes to Sched. 2 below.

However, the section has a subsidiary purpose, and Sched. 1A has a Pt. II. The subsidiary purpose is to alter the basis of discount available to "second-time" purchasers. At present, someone who exercises the right to buy for the second time is not allowed to take into account, either in relation to qualification (1980 Act s.1) or discount (1980 Act s.7) time before the previous purchase. This does not apply to earlier voluntary sales, nor did it prevent the second-time purchaser acquiring for a second time—33 per cent. for three years' occupation. On the other hand, an earlier discount may not have reflected the fullness of years preceding the previous purchase, if the discount was limited by cost floors; further, some part of the earlier discount may have been clawed back (*cf.* notes to s.5 below).

The new s.7(1A) of the 1980 Act requires the deduction of the amounts described in the new Sched. 1A, Pt. II, of that Act, which are described in the notes to Sched. 2 of this Act below. The purpose is to ensure that what the second-time purchaser gains and loses reflects the actual financial advantage of the previous purchase.

Subs. (3)

This relates to "cost floors", *i.e.* amounts below which a discount is not to reduce purchase price; see Ministerial Letter of October 3, 1980.

Subs. (4)

The repeals are of material now all replaced by 1980, Sched. 1A (see Sched. 2 below).

Subs. (6)

When a secure tenant serves notice on a landlord claiming to exercise the right to buy, the landlord must normally reply within four weeks, either admitting the right, or denying the right and stating the reasons why the right is denied: 1980 Act s.5(1). In those circumstances in which reliance is placed by the tenant on time spent with another landlord (for the purposes of qualifying for the right to buy) the period is extended to eight weeks: 1980 Act s.5(1), (2).

Under s.10 of the 1980 Act, as unamended by this Act (see further Sched. 11, para. 10, below) once the tenant has claimed to exercise the right to buy, and that right has been established (*i.e.* by admission under s.5, or otherwise, *e.g.* by county court action under the 1980 Act s.86) the landlord must serve a notice on the tenant describing the property, purchase price and terms of conveyance or grant. There are a number of other details which must be contained within the s.10 notice; see the 1980 Act s.10(2), (3). The s.10 notice had to be served, under the unamended 1980 Act, "as soon as practicable". It must now normally be served within eight weeks of a s.5 notice, or 12 weeks if an offer of a lease (Sched. 11, para. 10, below).

By virtue of this subsection, the amendments introduced, and described in the General Note to this section, which harmonise and substantively alter qualification to buy, and to discount, will not take effect: (a) as to qualification to buy if the landlord's notice under s.5 of the 1980 Act had been served before the commencement date of this Act; or (b) as to discount if the notice under s.10 of the 1980 Act had been served before that date.

As with s.1(4) (see notes thereto above) and s.2 in neither case would it seem to be open to a landlord to argue that the amendments do not apply in a case in which the appropriate notice *ought* to have been served prior to commencement, but has not been: this would be to raise the landlord's own wrong. It will be more difficult, however, to show that a s.10 notice ought to have been served prior to commencement (when no defined time limits applied, *cf.* Sched. 11, para. 10, below) than that a s.5 notice ought to have been served.

Inclusion of land let with or used for purposes of dwelling-house

4.—(1) For the avoidance of doubt it is hereby declared that in Chapter I of Part I of the 1980 Act "dwelling-house" has the meaning given by section 50(2) of that Act as extended by section 3(4) of that Act.

(2) In subsection (2) of section 3 of the 1980 Act (land used for purposes of dwelling-house) after the words "by virtue of" there shall be inserted the words "subsection (4) below or".

(3) For subsection (4) of that section there shall be substituted the following subsections—

"(4) There shall be treated as included in a dwelling-house any land which is or has been used for the purposes of the dwelling-house if—

(*a*) the tenant, by a written notice served on the landlord at any time before he exercises the right to buy, requires the land to be included in the dwelling-house; and

(*b*) it is reasonable in all the circumstances for the land to be so included.

(4A) A notice under subsection (4) above may be withdrawn by a written notice served on the landlord at any time before the tenant exercises the right to buy."

(4) Where, after the service of the notice under section 10(1) of the 1980 Act, a notice under section 3(4) of that Act is served or withdrawn, the parties shall, as soon as practicable after the service or withdrawal of that notice, take all such steps (whether by way of amending, withdrawing

or re-serving any notice or extending any period or otherwise) as may be requisite for the purpose of securing that all parties are (as nearly as may be) in the same position as that in which they would have been if the notice under section 3(4) had been served or withdrawn before the service of the notice under section 10(1).

DEFINITIONS
"dwelling-house": s.36 and 1980 Act s.3.
"right to buy": s.38 and 1980 Act s.1.

GENERAL NOTE
1980 Act
Under the 1980 Act s.3(4), as unamended, there shall be treated as included in the dwelling-house any land used for the purposes of the dwelling-house which the landlord and the tenant agree to include. Under s.50(2)(*b*) of that Act "land let together with a dwelling-house shall be treated as part of the dwelling-house unless the land is agricultural land exceeding two acres . . ." Land let together with the dwelling-house, other than agricultural land of more than two acres, is statutorily part of the dwelling-house, while land used for the purposes of the dwelling-house is merely discretionarily part of the dwelling-house.

Main Changes
The present section contains a declaration to the effect of the last paragraph, *i.e.* that s.50(2)(*b*) land is automatically included, and then extended by s.3(4): subs. (1). Subs. (2) introduces a new s.3(4), replacing (*a*) land used, (*b*) added by agreement, with (i) land which is or has been used, (ii) added if the tenant requests its inclusion, and it is reasonable in all the circumstances for the land to be so included.

A request may be made—or withdrawn—at any time before the exercise of the right to buy, *i.e.* before completion, and if the request is made or withdrawn after the s.10 offer notice has been served, the parties are to take such steps as are necessary to put themselves in the same position as if request or withdrawal had taken place before the service of the s.10 notice: subs. (3). Similar wording is used in s.32 below.

A dispute on reasonableness of request for inclusion can be resolved by reference to the county court; see s.86 of the 1980 Act.

Repayment of discount on early disposal

5.—(1) In subsection (1) of section 8 of the 1980 Act (repayment of discount on early disposal) for the words "disposal falling within subsection (3)" there shall be substituted the words "relevant disposal which is not exempted by subsection (3A)".

(2) For subsection (3) of that section there shall be substituted the following subsections—

"(3) A disposal is a relevant disposal for the purposes of this section if it is—

    (*a*) a further conveyance of the freehold or an assignment of the lease; or

    (*b*) the grant of a lease or sub-lease for a term of more than twenty-one years otherwise than at a rack rent,

whether the disposal is of the whole or part of the dwelling-house; and for the purposes of paragraph (*b*) above it shall be assumed that any option to renew or extend a lease or sub-lease, whether or not forming part of a series of options, is exercised, and that any option to terminate a lease or sub-lease is not exercised.

(3A) A relevant disposal is exempted by this subsection if—

    (*a*) it is a disposal of the whole of the dwelling-house and a further conveyance of the freehold or an assignment of the lease and the person or each of the persons to whom it is made is a qualifying person;

(*b*) it is a vesting of the whole of the dwelling-house in a person taking under a will or on an intestacy;

(*c*) it is a disposal of the whole of the dwelling-house in pursuance of an order under section 24 of the Matrimonial Causes Act 1973 or section 2 of the Inheritance (Provision for Family and Dependants) Act 1975;

(*d*) the property disposed of is acquired compulsorily or by a person who has made or would have made, or for whom another person has made or would have made, a compulsory purchase order authorising its compulsory purchase for the purposes for which it is acquired; or

(*e*) the property disposed of is land included in the dwelling-house by virtue of section 3(4) or 50(2) of this Act.

(3B) For the purposes of subsection (3A)(*a*) above a person is a qualifying person in relation to a disposal if he—

(*a*) is the person or one of the persons by whom it is made;

(*b*) is the spouse or a former spouse of that person or one of those persons; or

(*c*) is a member of the family of that person or one of those persons and has resided with him throughout the period of twelve months ending with the disposal.

(3C) Where there is a relevant disposal which is exempted by subsection (3A)(*d*) or (*e*) above—

(*a*) the covenant required by subsection (1) above shall not be binding on the person to whom the disposal is made or any successor in title of his; and

(*b*) that covenant and the charge taking effect by virtue of subsection (4) below shall cease to apply in relation to the property disposed of."

(3) In subsection (4) of that section for the words "specified in" there shall be substituted the words "falling within".

(4) After that subsection there shall be inserted the following subsection—

"(4A) The landlord may at any time by written notice served on a body falling within subsection (5) below postpone the charge taking effect by virtue of subsection (4) above to any legal charge securing any amount advanced or further advanced to the tenant by that body."

(5) For subsection (5) of that section there shall be substituted the following subsections—

"(5) The bodies referred to in subsection (4)(*b*) and (4A) above are—

(*a*) the Housing Corporation;

(*b*) any building society;

(*c*) any body falling within paragraphs 6 to 9 of the Schedule to the Home Purchase Assistance and Housing Corporation Guarantee Act 1978; and

(*d*) any body specified or of a class or description specified in an order made by the Secretary of State with the consent of the Treasury.

(5A) Before making an order under subsection (5) above varying or revoking an order previously made, the Secretary of State shall give an opportunity for representations to be made on behalf of any body which, if the order were made, would cease to be a body falling within that subsection."

(6) In subsection (8) of that section for the words "disposal falling within subsection (3) above" there shall be substituted the words "relevant disposal which is not exempted by subsection (3A) above)".

(7) Where any conveyance or grant executed in pursuance of Chapter I of Part I of the 1980 Act before the commencement date contains the covenant required by section 8(1) of that Act, then, as from that date, that covenant shall have effect with such modifications as may be necessary to bring it into conformity with the amendments made by this section.

DEFINITIONS

"commencement date": s.66.
"dwelling-house": s.38 and 1980 Act s.3.
"relevant disposal": subs. (2), introducing a new 1980 Act s.8(3).

GENERAL NOTE

1980 Act

Conveyances and grants under the right to buy are subject to a covenant, to be a charge on the dwelling-house, and binding on successors in title, the effect of which is to require repayment to the former landlord of a percentage of the discount applied to the purchase, on a subsequent disposal within five years: 1980 Act s.8. The repayment is of the full discount, reduced by 20 per cent. for each full year of occupation between conveyance (or grant) and disposal: 1980 Act s.8(2).

In outline, disposals requiring repayment were any further conveyance of freehold or assignment of lease, or the grant of a lease or sublease for a term of more than 21 years other than at a rack rent, and whether the disposal was of the whole or merely part of the dwelling-house: 1980 Act s.8(3), as unamended. Disposals in pursuance of an order under s.24 of the Matrimonial Causes Act 1973 (property transfer on divorce) or under s.2 of the Inheritance (Provision for Family and Dependants) Act 1975, or a disposal by will or on intestacy, were, however, exempt: *ibid.* The creation of mortgages were similarly exempt (1980 Act s.8(7)). Provision was made governing priority of the charge: 1980 Act s.8(4), (5).

Main Changes

This section substantively alters s.8 of the 1980 Act. While retaining the repayment requirement at its existing level, it extends the range of disposals exempt from its operation; see notes to subs. (2), below. It also slightly extends the circumstances in which the charge created by the requirement may take priority after mortgages; see notes to subs. (4) below. The amendments are to apply to conveyances and grants preceding the commencement of this Act; see notes to subs. (7) below.

Subs. (2)

The new s.8(3) reproduces the old s.8(3), without the exemptions it formerly contained. The exemptions are now to be found in the added s.8(3A). Before turning to the exemptions to be found in the added s.8(3A), however, it should be noted that the words at the end of the new s.8(3) ("and for the purposes of . . . is not exercised") are new. Their purpose was described thus:

". . . it would be possible for a tenant who has bought his home under the right to buy to get round the discount clawback provisions by granting a lease for less than 21 years with an option to renew, which would take the total period above 21 years.

The object of these amendments is to stop that loophole which they do, in effect, by providing that for the purpose of asserting whether a lease is for more than 21 years, it shall be assumed that any option to extend or renew the lease is exercised, and that any option to terminate the lease is not exercised. Anyone granting a lease for less than 21 years with an option to extend or renew will therefore be caught by the discount clawback provisions." (Lord Bellwin, *Hansard*, H.L. Vol. 450, col. 804 (April 5, 1984)).

To this extent only, then, the discount provisions have been tightened up. Otherwise, the intent is to liberalise. This is achieved by the added s.8(3A), classifying the disposals which will *not* attract recoupment of discount. The first group (subs. (3A)(*a*), taken together with the new (3B)) permits family disposals, *e.g.* between spouses or former spouses. The second and third groups (subs. (3A)(*b*) and (*c*)) reproduce the existing exemptions.

The fourth group (subs. (3A)(*d*)) permits purchase by a public authority, enjoying compulsory purchase powers, whether or not the purchase is in fact compulsory or by agreement, and whether or not the purchase is for the authority themselves or on behalf of another body, *e.g.* a local authority buying for a housing association.

The fifth group (subs.(3A)(*e*)) although apparently insignificant, is a substantive gain for purchasers. The repayment requirement is activated by a disposal of all or part only of the dwelling-house; see 1980 Act s.8(3), as set out in subs. (2) above. This exemption permits the disposal of "land included . . . by virtue of s.3(4) or 50(2) of" the 1980 Act. As to s.3(4) and s.50(2) of the 1980 Act see s.4 and the notes there to, above. These added lands may now be disposed of without requiring repayment of discount.

In the case of either fourth or fifth group disposals, the repayment covenant itself will not bind the purchaser, or a later successor in title, and the covenant and the consequential charge cease to apply in relation to the property disposed of: see the new s.8(3C).

Subss. (4), (5)

1980 Act: Under the 1980 Act as unamended, the repayment covenant results in a charge on the property, having priority immediately behind (*a*) a mortgage granted by the former landlord under the "right to a mortgage" (see 1980 Act s.9) by leaving some of the purchase price outstanding; (*b*) a mortgage granted by one of a specified schedule of bodies (including the Housing Corporation, which fulfills the duty to provide a mortgage where the landlord is a housing association, any building society, or bodies specified in relation to the Home Purchase Assistance and Housing Corporation Guarantee Act 1978) for the purpose of enabling the exercise of the right to buy; and (*c*) any *further* advance by one of those bodies (1980 Act s.8(4), as unamended).

Only initial advances, and a further advance by the body which made the initial advance, thus take priority over the repayment requirement.

Changes: The purpose of subs. (4) of this section is to permit building societies to take over local authority mortgages, and permit the authority to postpone the repayment requirement to take effect behind what would otherwise be a disposal activating it (Standing Committee B, November 1, 1983, col. 424).

An unmentioned side-effect is to permit further advances, *e.g.* to permit improvements or alterations, from a body *other* than that which granted the initial advance (although as building societies are generally unhappy with second mortgages, this will not be a common occurrence).

Subs. (5) will permit extension of the class of bodies which may grant mortgages and retain priority over the repayment of discount requirement, by order of the Secretary of State. (If an order is to have the effect of removing a body from the class thus specified, it is only to be laid after providing that body with an opportunity to make representations.)

Subs. (7)

Without requiring formal amendment of each such covenant, this subsection treats all covenants in conveyances and grants preceding the commencement of this Act as having effect as modified to conform with the changes wrought by this section, and to apply to all future conveyances and grants.

Notice to complete by landlord

6.—(1) In subsection (1) of section 16 of the 1980 Act (completion) for the words from "matters" to "dwelling-house" there shall be substituted the words "relevant matters".

(2) For subsection (2) of that section there shall be substituted the following subsections—

"(2) Subject to subsections (2A) and (3) below, the landlord may at any time serve on the tenant a written notice—

    (*a*) requiring him—

        (i) if all relevant matters have been agreed or determined, to complete the transaction within a period stated in the notice;

        (ii) if any relevant matters are outstanding, to serve on the landlord within that period a written notice to that effect specifying those matters; and

(*b*) informing the tenant of the effect of this subsection and of subsections (2A), (3), (6) and (6B) below;

and the period stated in a notice under this subsection shall be such period (not less than 56 days) as may be reasonable in the circumstances.

(2A) A notice under subsection (2) above shall not be served at any time if, at that time—

(*a*) any requirement for the determination or re-determination of the value of the dwelling-house by the district valuer has not been complied with;

(*b*) any proceedings for the determination of any other relevant matter have not been disposed of; or

(*c*) any relevant matter stated to be outstanding in a written notice served on the landlord by the tenant has not been agreed in writing or determined."

(3) In subsection (3) of that section for the words "three months", in each place where they occur, there shall be substituted the words "nine months".

(4) For subsection (6) of that section there shall be substituted the following subsections—

"(6) If the tenant does not comply with a notice under subsection (2) above, the landlord may serve on him a further written notice—

(*a*) requiring him to complete the transaction within a period stated in the notice; and

(*b*) informing him of the effect of subsection (6B) below;

and the period stated in a notice under this subsection shall be such period (not less than 56 days) as may be reasonable in the circumstances.

(6A) At any time before the end of the period stated in a notice under subsection (6) above (or that period as extended under this subsection), the landlord may by a written notice served on the tenant extend (or further extend) that period.

(6B) If the tenant does not comply with a notice under subsection (6) above the notice claiming to exercise the right to buy shall be deemed to be withdrawn at the end of the period stated in the notice under that subsection or, as the case may require, that period as extended under subsection (6A) above."

(5) In subsection (7) of that section for the words "subsection (6)" there shall be substituted the words "subsection (6B)" and in subsection (9) of that section for the words "subsection (2)" there shall be substituted the words "subsection (6)".

(6) After subsection (11) of that section there shall be inserted the following subsection—

"(12) In this section 'relevant matters' means matters relating to the grant and to the amount to be left outstanding or advanced on the security of the dwelling-house."

(7) Subsection (6B) of section 16 of the 1980 Act shall apply in relation to a notice under subsection (2) of that section served before the commencement date as it applies to a notice under subsection (6) of that section served after that date.

DEFINITIONS
"commencement date": s.66.
"dwelling-house": s.38 and 1980 Act s.3.
"relevant matters": subs. (6), adding 1980 Act s.16(12).
"right to buy": s.38 and 1980 Act s.1.

General Note

1980 Act

Under the pre-1984 Act position, once the right to buy had been claimed and established, the landlord is bound to make the appropriate grant to the tenant "as soon as all matters relating to the grant and to the amount to be left outstanding or advanced on the security of the dwelling-house have been agreed or determined" (1980 Act s.16(1), as unamended). If the tenant did not take all the necessary steps to complete the transaction, the landlord was entitled to serve notice requiring him to do so within a period of not less than 28 days: *ibid.* s.16(2).

Such notice could not be served less than: (*a*) three months after the tenant's time to exercise the right to a mortgage (see 1980 Act s.9) had elapsed, without the right being sought: (*b*) if the tenant is not entitled to defer completion (see further below), three months after notification of mortgage rights under 1980 Act s.12(4); or (*c*) if the tenant is entitled to defer completion (see further below), either two years after notice claiming the right to buy, or three months after notification of mortgage rights under s.12(4), whichever was the later: *ibid.* s.16(3).

The right to defer completion arises if the right to a mortgage (see 1980 Act s.9) has been claimed, and the tenant's personal entitlement means that he will receive less than a 100 per cent. mortgage (plus certain other specified sums, see notes to s.12, below), and, within three months of the service of the s.12(4) notification of mortgage rights, he has claimed the right to defer completion and paid a £100 deposit in pursuance thereof; *ibid.* s.16(4). Either the landlord, or a county court on application, may extend the three month period for claiming right to defer: *ibid.* s.16(5).

If the tenant did not comply with the notice from the landlord requiring completion, within the time specified, the notice claiming the right to buy was treated as withdrawn, and no further such notice could be served for a period of 12 months: *ibid.* s.16(6). The landlord is not bound to complete the transaction—even if he had served notice requiring the tenant to complete—if the tenant is more than four weeks in arrears with the rent or any other payment due from him as tenant: *ibid.* s.16(9).

Main Changes

The new section sets out to extend the time tenants have to complete transactions, both by preventing landlords serving notices to complete for longer periods (see notes to subs. (3) below) and by specifying a longer minimum time in such notices to complete (see notes to subs. (2) below). In addition, the new section limits the circumstances in which such notices to complete can be served; see notes to subs. (2) below.

The new section also introduces a further step in the proceedings, by way of preliminary or "warning" notice to complete (see notes to subs. (2) below) followed by a final notice (see notes to subs. (4) below). The new section eliminates the 12 month bar on further applications (*ibid.*) and to this extent applies to notices served before as well as after the Act's commencement (see notes to subs. (7).

Subs. (1)

The amendment wrought by this subsection is technical, removing to a definition of "relevant matters" (to be found in subs. (6)) the same phrase that formerly appeared in 1980 Act s.16(1).

Subs. (2)

S.16(2) of the 1980 Act gave the landlord the right to serve a notice to complete within a stated period to be not less than 28 days. The new subs. (2) and (2A) introduce instead a preliminary notice requiring completion, if all relevant matters have been agreed or determined, or requiring notification back to the landlord, in writing, of what matters are considered outstanding, *i.e.* not agreed or determined.

It would seem that the question of whether or not all relevant matters have been agreed or determined is one for tenants, not landlords. Notices tell the tenant to complete, or to specify reasons (unagreed or undetermined relevant matters) why not, as distinct from the landlord choosing which class of notice is appropriate (completion or statement of unagreed or undetermined relevant matters).

The notice must specify a period for "response", *i.e.* completion or statement, which period is now to be not less than 56 days. The notice must also inform the tenant of its effect, and of the effect of s.16(2A), (3), (6) and (6B); all of which are considered below in these notes.

The new subs. (2A) prevents service of the preliminary notice if one of three sets of circumstances applies. First of all, no notice may be served if there is a requirement for determination or redetermination of value by a district valuer, which has not been complied with. Determinations and redeterminations are dealt with in the 1980 Act by s.11. Secondly, no preliminary notice may be served if proceedings for the determination of any other relevant matter have not been disposed of. Thirdly, no preliminary notice may be served if a relevant matter considered by the tenant to be unagreed or undetermined has been the subject of a written notice served by him on the landlord.

Subs. (3)
The subsection extends from three months to nine months the existing periods during which no notice to complete (and, now, a preliminary notice to complete; see notes to last subsections above) can be served; see the General Note to this section.

Subs. (4)
If the tenant does not comply with the preliminary notice, *i.e.* within the time specified (not less than 56 days) and neither completes nor states in writing what the outstanding relevant matters are, the landlord can serve a further, and final notice, requiring completion, also in a time to be specified, being not less than 56 days. This notice must warn the tenant of the effect of non-compliance. The effect of non-compliance is contained in the new s.16(6B) and is no more than that the notice claiming to exercise the right to buy is deemed to have been withdrawn. The tenant can recommence proceedings to buy, forthwith if he wishes, although there is, of course, the prospect of a rise in the value of the property.
Under s.16(6A), as added by this subsection, the landlord has and retains the power to extend the time specified in this notice.

Subs. (7)
The operation of this subsection in relation to notices to complete served before the commencement of this Act means that the former one-year time lapse before any new notice claiming the right to buy might be served has been dispensed with.

Terms of conveyance or grant

7.—(1) Schedule 2 to the 1980 Act (conveyance of freehold and grant of lease) shall have effect, and shall be deemed always to have had effect, as if in paragraph 5 after the words "Subject to" there were inserted the words "paragraph 5A below and" and after that paragraph there were inserted the following paragraph—
  "5A. Any provision of the conveyance or lease shall be void in so far as it purported to enable the landlord to charge the tenant any sum for or in connection with the giving of any consent or approval."
  (2) For the avoidance of doubt it is hereby declared—
    (*a*) that nothing in paragraph 8 of that Schedule shall be taken as affecting the operation of paragraph 5 of that Schedule; and
    (*b*) that the burdens specified in paragraph 9 of that Schedule do not include burdens created by the conveyance.
  (3) For paragraphs 16 and 17 of that Schedule there shall be substituted the following paragraphs—
  "16. A provision is not void by virtue of paragraph 15 above in so far as it requires the tenant to bear a reasonable part of—
    (*a*) the costs of carrying out repairs not amounting to the making good of structural defects;
    (*b*) the costs of making good any structural defects falling within paragraph 17 below; or
    (*c*) where the lease acknowledges the right of the tenant and his successors in title to production of the relevant policy, the costs of insuring against risks involving such repairs or the making good of such defects.
  17.—(1) A structural defect falls within this paragraph if the notice under section 10 of this Act—
    (*a*) informed the tenant of its existence; and

(*b*) stated the landlord's estimate of the amount (at current prices) which would be payable by the tenant towards the cost of making it good.

(2) A structural defect falls within this paragraph if the landlord does not become aware of its existence earlier than 10 years after the lease is granted."

(4) Nothing in subsection (1) above shall entitle any person to recover a sum paid by him for or in connection with a consent or approval given before the commencement date; and the amendment made by subsection (3) above shall not apply when the notice under section 10(1) of the 1980 Act was served before that date.

DEFINITIONS

"commencement date": s.66.

GENERAL NOTE

This section contains miscellaneous amendments to Sched. 2 of the 1980 Act, which governs the terms of conveyances and grants under the right to buy.

Subs. (1)

Subject to the more detailed provisions of Sched. 2, a conveyance or grant "may include such covenants and conditions as are reasonable in the circumstances . . ." (1980 Act Sched. 2, para. 5). This amendment renders void any attempt to incorporate in the conveyance or lease a provision which enables the landlord to charge the tenant for consents or approvals that might be needed in connection with its terms. The amendment is to be treated as if it had always had effect, although (subs. (4)) not so as to entitle recovery by someone who has paid such a sum.

Subs. (2)

The purpose of this "declaration" is to prevent any argument that: (*a*) Sched. 2, para. 8, limits the general requirement that the conveyance or grant may include such covenants and conditions as are reasonable in the circumstances; see 1980 Act Sched. 2, para. 5; or (*b*) that Sched. 2, para. 9 permits the creation by the conveyance of *new* burdens in relation to the upkeep or regulation for the benefit of any locality of any land, buildings, structure, works, ways or watercourse, outside the para. 5 requirement (as to (*b*); see Standing Committee B, October 27, 1983, cols. 311 *et seq.*).

The provisions are intended to be delaratory, or "for the avoidance of doubt" rather than novel. The provision in (*a*) was at the request of the local authority associations (see *Hansard*, H.L. Vol. 448, col. 1251 (February 28, 1984)).

Subs. (3)

1980 Act: Under the 1980 Act, Sched. 2, paras. 15–17, the charges which a landlord may impose on a tenant who takes a long lease in relation to repairs are limited. Subject to para. 16, the tenant cannot be made to pay for the costs of discharging, or insuring against, what might be called "basic" repairs (*i.e.* repairs to the structure and exterior of the dwelling-house and building in which it is situated, including drains, gutters and external pipes, and repairs to other property which the tenant has rights over, *e.g.* common parts: 1980 Act, Sched. 2, para. 15, taken together with *ibid.*, para. 13(1)(*a*) and (*b*)).

Para. 16, as unamended, however, and despite the apparently sweeping terms of para. 15, excluding this wide range of repairs, adds back in, *i.e.* permits charging for, a "reasonable part" of the costs of repairs not amounting to structural defects, and of the costs of insuring their discharge, and of the cost of structural repairs within para. 17. Structural defects fell within para. 17 if *either* the landlord notified the tenant of their existence before the lease was granted, *or* the landlord did not become aware of them until 10 years after the lease was granted. The effect of this was that the landlord could pass on structural defect costs only if they were and remained latent for 10 years, or else the tenant had had ample prior notice; the landlord was left with structural defect costs which appeared soon after (*i.e.* within 10 years of) the grant.

Changes: The amendment by way of substitution of a new para. 16 only enables insurance charges to be passed on if the lease, in turn, permits the tenant to call for production of the insurance policy. With access to such policy, the tenant will usually be able to persuade a mortgagee not to require further insurance; without it, mortgagees will usually impose such a requirement, so that the tenant has to pay for two lots of insurance: (*a*) that required by their own mortgagee; and (*b*) that required by the landlord. The amendment does not apply if the s.10 offer notice was served before commencement of the Act: subs. (4).

The amendment brought about by the substitution of a new para. 17 requires prior notification of a structural defect for which the tenant may have to bear charges as early as the s.10 offer notice, and such notice must be accompanied by the landlord's estimate at then current prices of what the tenant's share of the costs will be. The alternative class of structural defect for which tenants can be made to pay—those which are and remain latent for the first ten years of the lease—is unchanged. The amendment does not apply if the s.10 notice was served before the commencement of the Act: subs. (4).

The purpose of this amendment is to overcome the problem which had emerged of notification of structural defects between the determination of value by a district valuer and completion, or after the expiry of the opportunity to seek such a valuation (Standing Committee B, October 27, 1983, cols. 302 *et seq*.). By requiring notification in the s.10 notice, the tenant is put on guard against acceptance of what may otherwise seem a "fair price".

Dwelling-houses in National Parks and areas of outstanding natural beauty etc.

8.—(1) In subsection (1) of section 19 of the 1980 Act (dwelling-houses in National Parks and areas of outstanding natural beauty etc.) for the words "and his successors in title" there shall be substituted the words "(including any successor in title of his and any person deriving title under him or any such successor)".

(2) In subsection (2) of that section for the words "his successors in title" there shall be substituted the words "a successor in title of his" and for the words "disposal falling within subsection (8) below" there shall be substituted the words "relevant disposal which is not exempted by section 8(3A) of this Act".

(3) In subsection (4) of that section for the words "disposal falling within subsection (8) below unless" there shall be substituted the words "relevant disposal which is not exempted by section 8(3A) of this Act unless in relation to that or a previous such disposal" and for the words "(or his successor in title)" there shall be substituted the words "(or his successor in title or the person deriving title under him or his successor)".

(4) In subsection (6) of that section for the words from "it would realise" onwards there shall be substituted the words "the interest to be reconveyed or surrendered would realise if sold on the open market by a willing vendor on the assumption that any liability under the covenant required by section 8(1) of this Act would be discharged by the vendor".

(5) For subsection (7) of that section there shall be substituted the following subsection—

"(7) If the landlord accepts the offer mentioned in subsection (4) above, the consideration shall be reduced by such amount (if any) as, on a relevant disposal made at the time that the offer was made and not exempted by subsection (3A) of section 8 of this Act, would fall to be paid under the covenant required by subsection (1) of that section; and no payment shall be required in pursuance of that covenant."

(6) Subsection (8) of that section shall be omitted.

(7) For subsection (11) of that section there shall be substituted the following subsection—

"(11) Where there is a relevant disposal which is exempted by section 8(3A)(*d*) or (*e*) of this Act, any such covenant as is mentioned in subsection (1) above shall cease to apply in relation to the property disposed of."

(8) In subsection (12) of that section after the words "Secretary of State" there shall be inserted the words "and 'relevant disposal' has the same meaning as in section 8 of this Act" and for the words "disposal falling within subsection (8) above" there shall be substituted the words "relevant disposal which is not exempted by section 8(3A) of this Act".

(9) Where any conveyance or grant executed in pursuance of Chapter I of Part I of the 1980 Act before the commencement date contains such a covenant as is mentioned in section 19(1) of that Act, then, as from that date, that covenant—

(*a*) shall be binding not only on the tenant and any successor in title of his but also on any person deriving title under him or any such successor; and

(*b*) shall have effect with such modifications as may be necessary to bring it into conformity with the amendments made by this section.

DEFINITIONS
"commencement date": s.66.

GENERAL NOTE
1980 Act
Under s.19 of the 1980 Act, landlords in rural areas, areas of natural beauty and national parks, have an option, subject to the consent of the Secretary of State, to include one of two types of restrictive covenant in a conveyance or grant: either they may limit the class of person to whom a relevant property can be resold, or thay may insert a pre-emption clause entitling the landlord to repurchase the property on a further disposal within 10 years. The purpose of the provision was to prevent purchase of such properties as "second homes", and the classes are defined to permit resale to those living or working in or around the areas in question.

Main Changes
The covenants operated with reference to the same classes of disposal as were subject to the repayment requirements of s.8 of the 1980 Act as unamended (see further notes to s.5 above) and the principal purpose of the present section is to amend s.19 in line with the amendments to s.8 of the 1980 Act effected by s.5 of this Act. The subsidiary purpose is to achieve the effect of rendering such covenants binding not only on a purchaser, but also on sublessees and mortgagees. The amendments are, as with s.5, effective in relation to conveyances and grants preceding the commencement of this Act.

Subs. (3)
The effect of the words "unless in relation to that or a previous such disposal" is that the landlord has only one opportunity to benefit from the pre-emption covenant, *i.e.* if offered the property back, and the landlord has refused or failed to accept within one month, the purchaser is not himself bound by the covenant on his own, later disposal.

Subs. (4)
This is (also) a technical amendment, providing a simpler definition of open market value than in the 1980 Act as unamended.

Subs. (5)
On a purchase under a pre-emption covenant, the price is to be reduced by any discount which the landlord is entitled to claim back, and the obligation to repay discount is thus discharged.

Subs. (7)
See notes to s.5 above.

Secretary of State's power to give directions as to covenants and conditions

9. After section 24 of the 1980 Act there shall be inserted the following sections—

"Secretary of State's power to give directions as to covenants and conditions

24A—(1) Where it appears to the Secretary of State that, if covenants or conditions of any kind were included in conveyances or grants of dwelling-houses of any description, the conveyances or grants would not conform with Parts I and II or, as the case may be, Parts I and III of Schedule 2 to this Act, he may direct landlords generally, landlords of a particular description or particular landlords not to include covenants or conditions of that kind in conveyances or grants of dwelling-houses of that description which are executed on or after a date specified in the direction.

(2) A direction given under this section may be varied or withdrawn by a subsequent direction so given.

(3) In this section and section 24B below any reference to conveyances or grants is a reference to conveyances or grants executed in pursuance of this Chapter.

Effect of directions on existing covenants and conditions

24B.—(1) If a direction under section 24A above so provides, the provisions of this section shall apply in relation to any covenant or condition which—

> (*a*) was included in a conveyance or grant executed before the date specified in the direction (in this section referred to as 'the specified date'); and
>
> (*b*) could not have been so included if the conveyance or grant had been executed on or after that date.

(2) The covenant or condition shall be discharged or (if the direction so provides) modified, as from the specified date, to such extent or in such manner as may be provided by the direction; and the discharge or modification shall be binding on all persons entitled or capable of becoming entitled to the benefit of the covenant or condition.

(3) The landlord by whom the conveyance or grant was executed shall within such period as may be specified in the direction—

> (*a*) serve on the person registered as the proprietor of the dwelling-house, and on any person registered as the proprietor of a charge affecting the dwelling-house, a written notice informing him of the discharge or modification; and
>
> (*b*) on behalf of the person registered as the proprietor of the dwelling-house, apply to the Chief Land Registrar (and pay the appropriate fee) for notice of the discharge or modification to be entered in the register;

and for the purposes of enabling the landlord to comply with the requirements of this subsection, the Chief Land Registrar shall (notwithstanding section 112 of the Land Registration Act 1925) allow any person authorised by the landlord to inspect and make copies of and extracts from any register or document which is in the custody of the Chief Land Registrar and relates to the dwelling-house.

(4) Notwithstanding anything in section 64 of the Land Registration Act 1925, notice of the discharge or modification may be entered in the register without the production of any land certificate outstanding in respect of the dwelling-house, but without prejudice to the power of the Chief Land Registrar to compel production of the certificate for the purposes mentioned in that section."

GENERAL NOTE

This is the first of three sections which introduce new sections to follow s.24 of the 1980 Act: in all, there are four such new sections (ss.24A-D) of which two are introduced by this section.

1980 Act

S.23 of the 1980 Act contains the powers of the Secretary of State to intervene by notice and "do all such things as appear to him necessary or expedient to enable secure tenants of the landlord . . . to which the notice relates to exercise the right to buy and the right to a mortgage . . ." (s.23(3)) "where it appears to [him] that tenants generally, or a tenant or tenants of a particular landlord, or tenants of a description of landlords have or may have difficulty in exercising the right to buy effectively and expeditiously . . ." s.23(1)).

The powers were considered by the Court of Appeal in *R.* v. *Secretary of State for the Environment, ex parte Norwich City Council* [1982] 1 All E.R. 737, 2 H.L.R. 1, C.A., where it was held that the powers should be used fairly, or fairly and reasonably, although the Court considered that the Secretary of State had complied with this requirement in that case.

The majority of the Court of Appeal held that the power of intervention was exercisable whenever it appeared to the Secretary of State that tenants had or might have difficulty in exercising the right to buy effectively or expeditiously, regardless of whether or not the landlord's behaviour was reasonable, provided the Secretary of State's own decision was one to which a reasonable man might come. In the exercise of the powers, the Secretary of State was entitled to consider the position of Norwich in relation to that of other authorities.

Notice of intervention must be in writing, but comes into force 72 hours after given: s.23(1). Save as the notice otherwise provides, no step taken by the landlord while it is in force, or before it was given, is to have any effect in relation to the exercise by a secure tenant of right to buy, or right to a mortgage: s.23(2). The Secretary of State, in exercise of his power to do what appears to him necessary or expedient to enable secure tenants to exercise these rights, is not bound to take the same steps as the landlord would have been bound to take: s.23(3).

S.24 of the 1980 Act enables the Secretary of State to make a "vesting order", to have the same effect as a conveyance or grant by the landlord, and includes provision for registration of title of the tenant as proprietor.

New s.24A

S.24A, added by this section, permits the Secretary of State to issue a direction, to landlords generally, landlords of a particular description, or to a particular landlord, which falls short of intervention. The provision permits the Secretary of State to specify covenants or conditions which are not to be included in conveyances or grants executed on or after a date stated in the direction. The power may be exercised when it appears that conveyances or grants would not conform with Sched. 2 of the 1980 Act (as amended; see further notes to s.7 above) were covenants or conditions of a particular kind to be included.

There is clearly validity in the proposition that "we have a clause which will put the Secretary of State in a position in which he will be interpreting legislation" (Mr Kaufman, Standing Committee B, October 27, 1983, col. 335). The government response was that 'the direction cannot be made unless the conveyance or grant is in breach of the 1980 Act' (Sir George Young, *ibid.* col. 337). This, however, ignores the breadth of the words "where it appears to the Secretary of State", which will of course be interpreted in line with the Norwich decision, *i.e.* if a covenant or condition could reasonably be considered to fall outside Sched. 2, an exercise of the power is unlikely to be challengeable, even although this is a lower test than "is in breach . . . ."

New s.24B

S.24B permits extension of a s.24A direction to include covenants or conditions which would have been prohibited by the s.24A direction had the conveyance or grant been executed after the date specified in the direction, but which were included in prior conveyances or grants. The direction can require discharge or modification of such covenants or conditions, to an extent or in a manner which it is to specify. The direction is also to state a time during which the landlord affected is to serve on (*a*) the registered proprietor of the property, and (*b*) any person registered as the proprietor of a charge affecting the property, notice of the discharge or modification, and during which the landlord is to apply to the Chief Land Registrar for notice of discharge or modification to be entered in the register.

In substance, therefore, the two new sections permit the Secretary of State to intervene in *terms* of conveyance or grant, without actual intervention in the sales programme or process, and to apply such intervention retrospectively.

Land Registration Act 1925, s.112
Under normal circumstances, inspection of, and copying from, the registers in the custody of the Chief Land Registrar, are accessible only to the registered proprietor of land or charge, persons authorised by such registered proprietor, court order and, otherwise, government departments and local authorities as authorised under the Land Registration Act 1925: *ibid.* s.112.

Land Registration Act 1925, s.64
Under normal circumstances, on every entry in the register of a disposition by the proprietor of registered land or charge, and on every registered transmission, and in every case other than as specifically mentioned in s.64 of the Land Registration Act 1925, where notice of any estate right or claim, or a restriction, is entered or placed on the register, the land certificate or charge certificate must be produced to the Chief Land Registrar: *ibid.*

Secretary of State's power to obtain information etc.

10. After section 24B of the 1980 Act there shall be inserted the following section—

"Secretary of State's power to obtain information etc.
24C.—(1) Where it appears to the Secretary of State necessary or expedient for the purpose of determining whether his powers under section 23, 24A or 24B above are exercisable, or for or in connection with the exercise of those powers, the Secretary of State may by notice in writing to a landlord require it—
  (*a*) at such time and at such place as may be specified in the notice, to produce any document; or
  (*b*) within such period as may be so specified or such longer period as the Secretary of State may allow, to furnish a copy of any document or supply any information;
and any officer of the landlord designated in the notice for that purpose or having custody or control of the document or in a position to give that information shall, without instructions from the landlord, take all reasonable steps to ensure that the notice is complied with.
  (2) Any reference in subsection (1) above to a landlord includes a reference to—
  (*a*) a landlord by whom a conveyance or grant was executed in pursuance of this Chapter; and
  (*b*) a body which has become a mortgagee in consequence of the exercise by a secure tenant of the right to a mortgage."

GENERAL NOTE
For an outline of the Secretary of State's existing powers of intervention, and of extensions wrought by the last section; see notes to s.9 above.

1980 Act
Under the existing powers of intervention, the Secretary of State "where it appears . . . necessary or expedient for the exercise of his powers under this section . . ." may serve written notice on the landlord requiring the production of documentation, or the supply of information (1980 Act s.24(5)). An officer, who is designated as such in the notice, or who has custody or control of documentation, or is in a position to provide the information, is bound to take all reasonable steps to ensure that the notice is complied with, regardless of instructions from the landlord (*ibid.*). The wording quoted at the beginning of this paragraph suggest that the powers described arise only *after* service of notice of intervention, *i.e.* as distinct from in order to find out whether or not to intervene (see Standing Committee B, October 27, 1983, col. 342).

New Section 24C

The new s.24C is broader: it clearly permits use of the power for the purpose of determining whether his powers under ss.23, 24A or 24B above are exercisable; it also permits specification of a time and place at which documentation is to be produced; it also permits the Secretary of State to require the production of copies, not merely original documentation; finally, it extends the jurisdiction as thus defined to mortgagees under the right to buy, which will include (*a*) the Housing Corporation on behalf of a housing association, or (*b*) a body which has taken over a local authority's mortgage. It would not seem, however, that a "private mortgagee" would have become a mortgagee in consequence of the exercise by a secure tenant of the right to a mortgage, for when a private mortgage is granted, the need to rely on the right to a mortgage is averted.

Secretary of State's power to give assistance

11. After section 24C of the 1980 Act there shall be inserted the following section—

"Secretary of State's power to give assistance

24D.—(1) Where, in relation to any proceedings or prospective proceedings to which this section applies, the actual or prospective party to the proceedings who has claimed to exercise or has exercised the right to buy, or is a successor in title of a person who has exercised that right, applies to the Secretary of State for assistance under this section, the Secretary of State may grant the application if he thinks fit to do so—

    (*a*) on the ground that the case raises a question of principle; or

    (*b*) on the ground that it is unreasonable having regard to the complexity of the case or to any other matter, to expect the applicant to deal with the case without any assistance under this section; or

    (*c*) by reason of any other special consideration.

(2) This section applies to any proceedings under this Chapter and any proceedings to determine any question arising under or in connection with this Chapter or any conveyance or grant executed in pursuance of this Chapter, other than proceedings to determine any question as to the value of a dwelling-house at the relevant time.

(3) Assistance by the Secretary of State under this section may include—

    (*a*) giving advice;

    (*b*) procuring or attempting to procure the settlement of the matter in dispute;

    (*c*) arranging for the giving of advice or assistance by a solicitor or counsel;

    (*d*) arranging for representation by a solicitor or counsel, including such assistance as is usually given by a solicitor or counsel in the steps preliminary or incidental to any proceedings, or in arriving at or giving effect to a compromise to avoid or bring to an end any proceedings;

    (*e*) any other form of assistance which the Secretary of State may consider appropriate,

but paragraph (*d*) above shall not affect the law and practice regulating the descriptions of persons who may appear in, conduct, defend, and address the court in, any proceedings.

(4) In so far as expenses are incurred by the Secretary of State in providing the applicant with assistance under this section, the recovery of those expenses (as taxed or assessed in such manner as may be prescribed by rules of court) shall constitute a first charge for the benefit of the Secretary of State—

   (*a*) on any costs which (whether by virtue of a judgment or order of a court or an agreement or otherwise) are payable to the applicant by any other person in respect of the matter in connection with which the assistance is given; and

   (*b*) so far as relates to any costs, on his rights under any compromise or settlement arrived at in connection with that matter to avoid or bring to an end any proceedings.

(5) A charge conferred by subsection (4) above is subject to any charge under the Legal Aid Act 1974 and to any provision of that Act for payment of any sum into the legal aid fund.

(6) Any expenses incurred by the Secretary of State in providing assistance under this section shall be paid out of money provided by Parliament; and any sums received by the Secretary of State by virtue of any charge conferred by subsection (4) above shall be paid into the Consolidated Fund.

(7) Any reference in this section to a solicitor includes a reference to the Treasury Solicitor."

GENERAL NOTE
For an outline of the Secretary of State's existing powers of intervention, and of extensions wrought by the last two sections; see notes to ss.9 and 10 above.

New s.24D
This third extension of the powers of the Secretary of State to intervene in exercise of the right to buy is not related to powers of the Secretary of State contained in the 1980 Act. S.24D was described as a right for the Secretary of State to grant "free and open-ended legal aid" (Mr Kaufman, Standing Committee B, November 1, 1983, col. 365) to individuals engaged in proceedings—actual or prospective—to determine any question arising under or in relation to the exercise of the right to buy (other than a question as to the value of the dwelling-house in issue).

The grant of this new form of legal aid is entirely in the discretion of the Secretary of State, save that the power is only exercisable by him if (i) the case raises a question of principle, or (ii) it is unreasonable to expect the applicant for assistance to deal with the case without this special class of assistance, having regard to the complexity of the case, or having regard to "any other matter", or (iii) on account of any other special consideration.

   "A number of matters could arise between a landlord and a tenant when the Secretary of State might intervene. For example, there might be a dispute over whether a dwelling was part of a sheltered scheme . . . There could be a dispute over whether a garage was land let together with the dwelling-house . . . There could be disputes about whether specific covenants were reasonable in the circumstances . . . There could be a dispute about the discount entitlement and about whether the dwelling was a house or a flat . . .

   In all such cases, the Secretary of State might take the view that the tenant had a strong case and he might consider that there was an important point of principle that could benefit from clarification by the courts. In each of those contexts, issues might be raised which a tenant could not reasonably be expected to tackle alone. We would not want to assist in every such case that came our way because that would be unrealistic. But those are the types of issues on which we might want to consider the case for assistance". (Sir George Young, Standing Committee B, November 1, 1983, col. 368).

The "aid" available is described in subs. (3) of the new section and includes advice, negotiations towards settlement, arranging for advice, assistance or representation by solicitor or counsel, or any other form of assistance which the Secretary of State considers appropriate. The assistance may include representation by the Treasury Solicitor, or may be by way of paying for private (legal) sector assistance.

Whereas under the Legal Aid Act 1974, legal aid is means-tested, there is no suggestion of means-testing aid under this section.

Finally, the Secretary of State's charge is subject to any Law Society charge under the 1974 Act, *i.e.* takes effect following a 1974 Act charge. It is presumably envisaged that this might arise where either a person has formerly been on legal aid, but subsequently secures Secretary of State assistance, or where the Secretary of State uses his powers to pay a legally-aided person's contribution.

Right to a shared ownership lease

Right to be granted a shared ownership lease

12.—(1) Where a secure tenant has claimed to exercise the right to buy and the conditions mentioned in subsection (2) below are satisfied, the tenant shall also have the right to be granted a shared ownership lease of the dwelling-house, that is to say a lease of the dwelling-house which—

(*a*) conforms with Schedule 3 to this Act; and

(*b*) subject to that, conforms with Parts I and III of Schedule 2 to the 1980 Act (terms of lease).

(2) The conditions referred to in subsection (1) above are—

(*a*) that the right to buy has been established and the tenant's notice under section 5(1) of the 1980 Act remains in force;

(*b*) that the tenant has claimed the right to a mortgage and the amount which the tenant is entitled, or is treated as entitled, to leave outstanding, or have advanced to him, on the security of the dwelling-house is less than the aggregate mentioned in section 9(1) of that Act; and

(*c*) that the tenant has, within the period of three months beginning with the service on him of the notice under section 12(4) of that Act or within that period as extended by section 16(5) of that Act, served a notice on the landlord claiming to be entitled to defer completion and has, within the same period, deposited the sum of £100 with the landlord.

DEFINITIONS

"dwelling-house": s.38 and 1980 Act s.3.

"right to buy": s.38 and 1980 Act s.1.

"secure tenant": s.38 and 1980 Act s.28.

"shared ownership lease": subs. (1).

GENERAL NOTE

This is the first of six sections introducing the "right to a shared ownership lease". (See also s.37 below for the transitional provisions. See also Sched. 11, in various paragraphs, applying provisions of the 1980 Act, including as amended and extended by this Act, to shared ownership. See *ibid.* para. 2, for rights under the Leasehold Reform Act 1967. See s.24, below, for voluntary shared ownership schemes.)

Shared ownership was described as "a new concept which I believe is not widely understood although I understand it is now proving quite popular, especially under the do-it-yourself shared ownership scheme. A recent parliamentary answer revealed that some 2,156 people had taken advantage of the scheme so far, quite apart from the shared ownership arrangements entered into by housing associations." (Mr John Fraser, Standing Committee B, November 1, 1983, col. 370.) (DIY shared ownership is a scheme under which the would-be purchaser finds the property to be the subject of a shared ownership lease.)

In outline, a shared ownership lease is one under which the tenant purchases a "tranche" or "slice" of a long lease, with the right to purchase successive tranches until the whole has been acquired. Pending acquisition of the whole, the tenant will pay a rent reduced according to the slice of the interest acquired by the tenant. There will additionally be a balance to pay where the landlord is also mortgagee of the portion acquired. The terms of the transaction are detailed in Sched. 3, and considered in the notes thereto. The following sections deal principally with qualifications to the exercise of the right, and with adaptation of the full right to buy procedure to the right to a shared ownership lease.

The right to a shared ownership lease arises only where (*a*) the tenant has claimed the right to buy (see 1980 Act Pt. 1, Chap. 1, as extensively amended by this Act; in particular, see 1980 Act s.5) *and* (*b*) the conditions set out in subs. (2) of this section are satisfied. The shared ownership lease is to conform (i) to Sched. 3, and, subject thereto, (ii) to Pts. I and III of Sched. 2 of the 1980 Act (again, as amended by this Act).

Subs. (2)

There are three conditions additional to that of having claimed the right to buy. The first is that the right to buy has been established, and the tenant's notice claiming it remains in force.

There is no statutory time limit on how long a notice will remain in force, but if the right to buy has been established, the landlord is obliged to fulfill the further stages of the procedure until the point is reached that the landlord is entitled (although not obliged) to serve notice to complete. The notice to complete procedure is as amended by s.6 above: see notes thereto. On non-compliance (deemed to include rent arrears of more than four weeks) with the (final) notice to complete, the initial notice claiming the right to buy is or may be deemed to have been withdrawn, which is the point which the present section clearly has in mind as "no longer in force" (along, presumably, with an express withdrawal of notice).

The second condition is that the tenant has claimed the right to a mortgage (see 1980 Act s.9). It follows that the scheme applies only to those who look to the public sector for the mortgage with which to exercise the right to buy, *i.e.* who do not obtain a mortgage on the private market (*cf.* Standing Committee B, November 1, 1983, col. 376).

The right to a mortgage is prima facie the right to leave outstanding (in the case of a local authority landlord) or have advanced (by the Housing Corporation, in the case of a housing association) the aggregate of three amounts: (*a*) purchase price; (*b*) costs properly chargeable by landlord or Corporation under s.21 of the 1980 Act as now amended by Sched. 11, para. 17, below) (currently £50; see S.I. 1980 No. 1390); and (*c*) costs discharged on behalf of the tenant by the landlord or the Corporation (*e.g.* survey or legal fees): 1980 Act s.9(1). (As to the latter costs; see also s.21 below.)

However, this 100 per cent. plus maximum is subject to the limit that it does not exceed the amount to be taken into account, in accordance with regulations under this section, as the tenant's available annual income multiplied by such factor as, under the regulations, is appropriate to it (1980 Act s.9(2)). Thus, as with any mortgage, there are two limits: the limit based on property, and the limit based on personality. Regulations have been made under this provision: see S.I. 1980 No. 1423.

If the amount available under s.9(2) is less than the 100 per cent. plus under s.9(1), the tenant acquires two rights. First, under the 1980 Act, s.16(4), the tenant acquires the right to defer completion for a period of two years from the notice claiming a right to buy (see notes to s.6 above—by June 1983 some 9,722 tenants had exercised this right, and of them 2,956 had subsequently proceeded to completion: Standing Committee B, November 3, 1983, col. 780).

Secondly, the tenant now acquires this right to a shared ownership lease. The right to a shared ownership lease, then, arises only when the full purchase price is not available from public funds, so that full ownership remains the preferred legislative priority, to the exclusion of shared ownership when funds are available.

The right to defer completion is exercisable within three months of service by the landlord (under s.12(4) of the 1980 Act) of its response to the tenant's claim to exercise the right to a mortgage (*ibid.* s.12(1)). That response informs the tenant of the right to defer completion (1980 Act s.12(5)) and of the effect of these shared ownership provisions (1980 Act s.12(5A) added by Sched. 11, para. 12 below).

At any time before service of a notice of completion, the tenant is entitled to seek a further decision on the claim to a mortgage, in which case the period during which the right to defer completion is exercisable is revived: 1980 Act s.16(8) (unless, of course, the new assessment deprives the tenant of the right altogether, because the s.9(1) 100 per cent. plus amount has become available; see 1980 Act s.16(4). In the same circumstances, the right to a shared ownership lease is lost; see s.13(4) below).

In order to exercise the right to defer completion, the tenant must not only claim it, but must also deposit with the landlord the sum of £100 (1980 Act s.16(4)). The third of the conditions contained in this subsection, then, on the fulfilment of which the tenant acquires the right to a shared ownership lease, is that the tenant has both claimed to defer completion, and deposited the sum of £100. (In the case of a deferred completion, the £100 will either be attributed to the purchase price on a later completion, or returned to the tenant on withdrawal—actual or deemed—from the transaction: 1980 Act s.16(7). If the tenant exercises this right to a shared ownership lease, the £100 is attributed to the tenant's initial contribution under its terms; see s.17(2) below.)

Notice claiming exercise of right

13.—(1) Where a secure tenant serves on the landlord a written notice claiming to exercise the right to be granted a shared ownership lease, the landlord shall (unless the notice is withdrawn) serve on the tenant within four weeks either—

(*a*) a written notice admitting the tenant's right; or

(*b*) a written notice denying the tenant's right and stating the reasons why, in the opinion of the landlord, the tenant does not have the right to be granted a shared ownership lease.

(2) A tenant's notice under subsection (1) above—

(*a*) shall state the initial share which he proposes to acquire; and

(*b*) may be withdrawn or varied at any time by notice in writing served on the landlord.

(3) On the service of a tenant's notice under subsection (1) above, any notice served by the landlord under subsection (2) or (6) of section 16 of the 1980 Act (notice requiring the tenant to complete the transaction in accordance with Chapter I of Part I of that Act) shall be deemed to have been withdrawn; and no notice shall be served by the landlord under the said subsection (2) or (6) whilst a tenant's notice under subsection (1) above remains in force.

(4) If, on the service by the tenant of a further notice under section 12(1) of the 1980 Act, the amount which he is entitled, or treated as entitled, to leave outstanding, or have advanced to him, on the security of the dwelling-house is equal to the aggregate mentioned in section 9(1) of that Act, the tenant shall not be entitled to exercise the right to be granted a shared ownership lease and any notice of his under subsection (1) above shall be deemed to have been withdrawn.

(5) Where a tenant's notice under subsection (1) above is withdrawn, or deemed to have been withdrawn, the tenant may, subject to subsection 16(6B) of the 1980 Act, complete the transaction in accordance with Chapter I of Part I of that Act.

DEFINITIONS

"initial share": Sched. 3, para 1.

"secure tenant": s.38 and 1980 Act s.28.

"shared ownership lease": s.12.

GENERAL NOTE

This section sets out the procedure to be followed on the exercise of the right to a shared ownership lease (see notes to s.12 above). It is the equivalent of s.5 of the 1980 Act in normal right to buy cases. The landlord has a four week period in which to admit or deny the right, in the latter case stating why it is of the opinion that the tenant does not have the right.

Subs. (2)

The notice claiming the right to a shared ownership lease must state the initial share which the tenant proposes to buy, although it may be withdrawn or varied at any time by notice in writing, in which latter case the landlord presumably enjoys a further four weeks in which to admit or deny notice as varied.

The initial share must be (*a*) not less than the minimum initial share, and (*b*) a multiple of the prescribed percentage: Sched. 3, para. 1. The minimum initial share is 50 per cent. or such other percentage as the Secretary of State may by order prescribe: *ibid*. para. 1(4). The prescribed percentage is 12.5 per cent. or as otherwise prescribed: *ibid*. para. 1(5). On the present figures, therefore, the tenant can seek to acquire 50 per cent., 62.5 per cent., 75 per cent. or 87.5 per cent. only.

Subs. (3)

If a tenant serves notice claiming the right to a shared ownership lease, a landlord's notice to complete under the 1980 Act s.16 (as amended by s.6 above; see notes thereto) whether a preliminary or a final notice to complete, is deemed to have been withdrawn, and no further such notice may be served so long as the notice claiming a shared ownership lease remains in force. If the landlord denies the tenant's right to a shared ownership lease, the notice to complete under the 1980 Act s.16 would still appear to be deemed to have been withdrawn and the landlord must therefore serve a new such notice, presumably contemporaneously with the notice denying the right to a shared ownership lease. If the landlord's denial is successfully challenged, the new notice to complete will be voided.

Subs. (4)

At any time before notice to complete, a tenant who has exercised the right to defer completion can serve a new notice claiming the right to a mortgage: 1980 Act s.16(8) and see notes to s.12 above. If the result of that application is to establish an entitlement to the full 1980 Act s.9(1) amount (100 per cent. plus) the right to defer completion is lost. This subsection makes similar provision in relation to the right to a shared ownership lease. Once the full amount is available from public funds, full ownership is to be acquired, in preference to and in exclusion of the right to shared ownership.

Subs. (5)

Once a notice claiming the right to a shared ownership lease either has actually been withdrawn, or is deemed to have been withdrawn (under subs. (4)) the tenant may proceed to full purchase.

Notice of initial contribution etc.

14.—(1) Where a secure tenant has claimed to exercise the right to be granted a shared ownership lease and that right has been established (whether by the landlord's admission or otherwise) the landlord shall, within eight weeks, serve on the tenant a written notice stating—

> (*a*) the amount which, in the opinion of the landlord, should be the amount of the consideration for the grant of the lease determined in accordance with paragraph 2(1) of Schedule 3 to this Act on the assumption that his initial share is as stated in the notice under section 13(1) above;
>
> (*b*) the effective discount on an acquisition of that share for that consideration determined in accordance with paragraph 6(3) of that Schedule;
>
> (*c*) the provisions which, in the opinion of the landlord, should be included in the lease; and
>
> (*d*) where the landlord is not a housing association, any variation in the provisions which, in the opinion of the landlord, should be contained in the deed by which the mortgage is to be effected.

(2) Where the landlord is a housing association, the landlord shall send a copy of the notice under subsection (1) above to the Housing Corporation; and the Housing Corporation shall, as soon as practicable after receiving that notice, serve on the tenant a written notice stating any variation in the provisions which, in the opinion of the Housing Corporation, should be contained in the deed by which the mortgage is to be effected.

DEFINITIONS

"initial share": Sched. 3, para. 1.
"secure tenant": s.38 and 1980 Act s.28.
"shared ownership lease": s.12.

GENERAL NOTE

This section takes the procedure for the grant of a shared ownership lease into the next stage (see first the notes to ss.12 and 13 above). It is the equivalent of a 1980 Act s.10 "offer notice" in relation to the full right to buy.

Once (and howsoever, *i.e.* including by legal proceedings) the right to a shared ownership lease has been established, the landlord has eight weeks to serve a notice stating: (*a*) how much it considers the tenant's payment is to be for a share of the proportion stated in the tenant's notice (see notes to s.10 above); (*b*) the amount of tenant's discount reflected in that payment; (*c*) what provisions are to be contained in the lease; and (*d*) what variations are to be contained in the provisions of the mortgage deed (in the case of a housing association, no such statement is to be included: instead, a copy of the notice is to be sent to the Housing Corporation, which, "as soon as practicable" must serve its own notice: subs. (2)).

The purchase price is initially as determined under Sched. 3, para. 2, and reflects both the same method of determination of value (1980 Act s.6) and the same level of discount (1980 Act s.7) as would apply on a full right to buy, scaled down to the tenant's initial share. The need to specify the discount separately is (*a*) so that the tenant can know that the correct amount has been allowed, and (*b*) so that the tenant can know what amount is vulnerable to repayment on early disposal—provision for recoupment of which is made in Sched. 3, para. 6 (see notes to Sched. 3).

The provisions which are to be included in the lease are to conform with Sched. 3 of this Act and Sched. 2, Pts. I and III of the 1980 Act; see s.12(1) above. The reference to a *variation* in the provisions which should be contained in the mortgage deed arises in the following way.

Under the 1980 Act, and in relation to the full right to buy, the terms of the mortgage deed are to conform with s.18 of that Act "unless otherwise agreed by the parties". The provisions to be contained in the mortgage are to be stated in the notice under the 1980 Act s.12(4), which responds to the tenant's claim to a mortgage. Such a notice will necessarily have been served prior to any claim to a shared ownership lease (see notes to s.12 above). Accordingly, the notice at this stage will be "varying" the provisions as earlier stated, to reflect the changed nature of the transaction.

The procedure does not require a new notice claiming the right to a mortgage, or therefore a new notice dealing with mortgage alone (*cf.* 1980 Act s.12). This equivalent of the 1980 Act s.10 offer notice accordingly subsumes the 1980 Act s.12 mortgage offer.

This does not mean that all shared ownership will necessarily be accompanied by an exercise of the right to a mortgage (*cf.* s.16(1) below "where a secure tenant exercises both the right to be granted a shared ownership lease and the right to a mortgage . . ."). It means, rather, that existing notices must be "adapted" to the new transaction. In practice, however, it is likely that the right to a mortgage will be extensively claimed under shared ownership, for the private building societies have not hitherto shown much enthusiasm for the various forms of shared ownership which have been advanced voluntarily, in particular through housing associations.

Change of landlord after notice claiming right

15. Where, after a secure tenant has given notice claiming to exercise the right to be granted a shared ownership lease, the interest of the landlord in the dwelling-house passes from the landlord to another body, all parties shall be in the same position as if the other body had become the landlord before the notice was given and had been given that notice and any further notice given by the tenant to the landlord and had taken all steps which the landlord had taken.

DEFINITIONS
"secure tenant": s.38 and 1980 Act s.28.
"shared ownership lease": s.12.

GENERAL NOTE
This section is substantively the same provision as applies to the full right to buy, following a notice claiming to exercise the right to buy or the right to a mortgage: 1980 Act s.14. A change of landlord will be an uncommon occurrence, because of the inhibitions on public sector disposals (other than under right to buy) without consent; see Housing Act 1957, ss.104 *et seq.* for local authority disposals, and Housing Act 1974, s.2 for housing association disposals. See also s.22 below). However, it could occur in the context of a transfer of stock between authorities, *e.g.* as has occurred with Greater London Council stock, and as continues to occur under the New Towns Act 1981.

The tenant will be treated as if the new landlord had been the landlord at the time of the notice claiming the right to a shared ownership lease, *i.e.* if the new landlord is one against which the right could have been exercised the tenant's position will be unchanged, while if the new landlord is one against which it could not have been exercised, the notice will be rendered nugatory.

Right to further advances

16.—(1) Where a secure tenant exercises both the right to be granted a shared ownership lease and the right to a mortgage, then, without prejudice to the provisions of section 18 of the 1980 Act, the deed by which the mortgage is effected shall, unless otherwise agreed between the parties, enable the tenant to require further sums to be advanced to him in the circumstances and subject to the limits stated in this section; and the right so conferred shall be exercisable, within three months of the tenant claiming to exercise his right to acquire an additional share, on the tenant serving written notice on the landlord or Housing Corporation.

(2) A notice under subsection (1) above may be withdrawn at any time by notice in writing served on the landlord or Housing Corporation.

(3) The amount which a tenant exercising the right to a further advance is entitled to have advanced to him is, subject to the limit imposed by this section, the amount of his additional contribution.

(4) The amount mentioned in subsection (3) above is subject to the limit that the aggregate of that amount and the amount for the time being secured by the mortgage does not exceed the amount to be taken into account, in accordance with regulations under this section, as the tenant's available annual income multiplied by such factor as, under the regulations, is appropriate to it.

(5) Where the right to a further advance belongs to more than one person the limit is that the aggregate of the amount mentioned in subsection (3) above and the amount for the time being secured by the mortgage does not exceed the aggregate of the amounts to be taken into account in accordance with the regulations as the available annual income of each of them, after multiplying each of those amounts by the factor appropriate to it under the regulations.

(6) The Secretary of State may by regulations make provision for calculating the amount which is to be taken into account under this section as a person's available annual income and for specifying a factor appropriate to it; and the regulations—

   (*a*) may provide for arriving at a person's available annual income by deducting from the sums taken into account as his annual income sums related to his needs and commitments, and may exclude sums from those to be taken into account as a person's annual income; and

   (*b*) may (without prejudice to the generality of subsection (10) below) specify different amounts and different factors for different circumstances.

(7) Where the amount which a tenant is entitled to have advanced to him is reduced by the limit imposed by this section, the landlord may, if it thinks fit and the tenant agrees, treat him as entitled to have advanced to him such amount exceeding that limit but not exceeding the amount mentioned in subsection (3) above as the landlord may determine.

(8) As soon as practicable after the service on it of a notice required by subsection (1) above the landlord or Housing Corporation shall serve on the tenant a written notice stating—

   (*a*) the amount which, in the opinion of the landlord or Housing Corporation, the tenant is entitled to have advanced to him on the assumption that the additional share is as stated in the tenant's notice under paragraph 3(1) of Schedule 3 to this Act;

   (*b*) if greater than that amount, the amount which, in the opinion of the landlord or Housing Corporation, the tenant would be entitled to have advanced to him if the additional share were such that his total share would be 100 per cent.;

(*c*) how that amount or those amounts have been arrived at; and

(*d*) the provisions which, in the opinion of the landlord or Housing Corporation, should be contained in the deed by which the further mortgage is effected.

(9) Any power to make regulations under this section shall be exercisable by statutory instrument which shall be subject to annulment in pursuance of a resolution of either House of Parliament.

(10) Regulations under this section may make different provision with respect to different cases or descriptions of case, including different provision for different areas.

DEFINITIONS
"additional contribution": Sched. 3, para. 4.
"secure tenant": s.38 and 1980 Act s.28.
"shared ownership lease": s.12.

GENERAL NOTE
This section applies where the tenant exercises the right to a mortgage in connection with a shared ownership lease (*cf.* notes to s.14 above). It contains the adaptations to shared ownership of the 1980 Act ss.9 (governing amount) and 18 (governing terms) in relation to the full right to buy.

Unless otherwise agreed by the parties, the mortgage deed is to contain provision enabling the tenant to obtain further advances, on three months' notice. The purpose is to fund the purchase of further tranches of equity. The price applicable to such further tranches is recalculated on notice of wish to make a further purchase; see notes to Sched. 3 below.

The tenant is entitled to further advances equal to the full amount of the additional contribution payable for further tranches of equity (see notes to Sched. 3 below) subject to the total amount thus secured not exceeding the tenant's "personal limit": *i.e.* the amount available having regard to income, in accordance with regulations to be made under this section (*cf.* 1980 Act s.9(2); see also notes to s.12 above). Provision is made (subs. (5)) equivalent to that applicable to a full purchase, for calculation of the personal limit when there is more than one person exercising the right (*cf.* 1980 Act s.9(3)).

The provisions of subss. (6) and (7) are similarly equivalent to the full purchase provisions (see 1980 Act s.9(4) and (5)) and (*a*) govern how the Secretary of State may determine personal limits, and (*b*) permit a *landlord*/mortgagee (not the Housing Corporation) to exceed the personal limits thus prescribed. The Housing Corporation already has adequate powers, under Housing Act 1974 s.9(2), to make their own decisions on this matter.

Subs. (8)
When notifying the tenant of its decision on the application for a further advance, the landlord or the Corporation must not only specify the amount the tenant is entitled to, but also: (*a*) how much the tenant would be entitled to if he was seeking to purchase the whole of the outstanding equity, if that would be a greater amount than the tenant is entitled to for the purchase of the further share specified in the request for a further advance; (*b*) how the amount or amounts have been arrived at; and (*c*) what provisions should be contained in the deed of further mortgage.

Completion

17.—(1) Where a secure tenant has claimed to exercise the right to be granted a shared ownership lease and that right has been established, then, as soon as all relevant matters have been agreed or determined, the landlord shall be bound, subject to the following provisions of this section, to make to the tenant a grant of a shared ownership lease of the dwelling-house for the appropriate term defined in sub-paragraph (2) of paragraph 11 of Schedule 2 to the 1980 Act (but subject to sub-paragraph (3) of that paragraph).

(2) Where the transaction is duly completed, the sum of £100 deposited by the tenant with the landlord shall be treated as having been paid towards the tenant's initial contribution.

(3) Subject to subsections (4) and (5) below, the landlord may at any time serve on the tenant a written notice—

(*a*) requiring him—

    (i) if all relevant matters have been agreed or determined, to complete the transaction within a period stated in the notice;

    (ii) if any relevant matters are outstanding, to serve on the landlord within that period a written notice to that effect specifying those matters; and

(*b*) informing the tenant of the effect of this subsection and of subsections (4), (5), (6) and (8) below;

and the period stated in a notice under this subsection shall be such period (not less than 56 days) as may be reasonable in the circumstances.

(4) A notice under subsection (3) above shall not be served at any time if, at that time—

(*a*) any requirement for the determination or re-determination of the value of the dwelling-house by the district valuer has not been complied with;

(*b*) any proceedings for the determination of any other relevant matter have not been disposed of; or

(*c*) any relevant matter stated to be outstanding in a written notice served on the landlord by the tenant has not been agreed in writing or determined.

(5) A notice under subsection (3) above shall not be served before the end of the period mentioned in section 16(3)(*c*) of the 1980 Act.

(6) If the tenant does not comply with a notice under subsection (3) above, the landlord may serve on him a further written notice—

(*a*) requiring him to complete the transaction within a period stated in the notice; and

(*b*) informing him of the effect of subsection (8) below;

and the period stated in a notice under this subsection shall be such period (not less than 56 days) as may be reasonable in the circumstances.

(7) At any time before the end of the period stated in a notice under subsection (6) above (or that period as extended under this subsection), the landlord may by written notice served on the tenant extend (or further extend) that period.

(8) If the tenant does not comply with a notice under subsection (6) above, the notice claiming to exercise the right to be granted a shared ownership lease and the notice claiming to exercise the right to buy shall be deemed to have been withdrawn at the end of the period stated in the notice under that subsection or, as the case may require, that period as extended under subsection (7) above.

(9) If the tenant has failed to pay rent or any other payment due from him as a tenant for a period of four weeks after it has been lawfully demanded from him, then, while the whole or part of it remains outstanding—

(*a*) the landlord shall not be bound to complete; and

(*b*) if a notice under subsection (6) above has been served on the tenant, the tenant shall be deemed not to comply with the notice.

(10) The duty imposed on the landlord by subsection (1) above shall be enforceable by injunction.

(11) On the grant of a shared ownership lease the secure tenancy of the dwelling-house shall come to an end and, if there is then a sub-tenancy, section 139 of the Law of Property Act 1925 shall apply as on a merger or surrender.

(12) In this section "relevant matters" means matters relating to the grant and to the amount to be left outstanding or advanced on the security of the dwelling-house.

DEFINITIONS
"secure tenant": s.38 and 1980 Act s.28.
"shared ownership lease": s.12.

GENERAL NOTE
With the additional qualification that non-compliance with a notice to complete leads to a deemed withdrawal of the notice claiming a right to a shared ownership lease *and* the notice claiming the right to buy (subs. (8)) this section reproduces s.16 of the 1980 Act. as amended by s.6 above, obliging a landlord to grant a lease, applying £100 deposit money towards the transaction (see notes to s.12 above), dealing with tenants in arrears, and other incidentals, and otherwise entitling the landlord to serve on the tenant preliminary and final notices to complete the transaction; see notes to s.6 above.

Other provisions with respect to disposals

Recovery of service charges

18.—(1) Subject to subsection (2) below, Schedule 4 to this Act shall apply in any case where—
(*a*) the requirements of subsection (3) below were satisfied with respect to a conveyance or grant of a dwelling-house which is not a flat within the meaning of Schedule 19 to the 1980 Act; and
(*b*) the conveyance or grant or, in the case of a conveyance which is an assignment of a lease, the lease enabled the vendor or lessor to recover from the purchaser or lessee a service charge, that is to say, an amount payable by the purchaser or lessee—
(i) which is payable, directly or indirectly, for services, repairs, maintenance or insurance or the vendor's or lessor's costs of management; and
(ii) the whole or part of which varies or may vary according to the relevant costs (within the meaning of Schedule 4 to this Act);
and in that Schedule expressions used in this section have the same meaning as in this section.
(2) Schedule 4 to this Act shall not apply to periods ending before the commencement date.
(3) The requirements of this subsection are satisfied with respect to a conveyance or grant if the vendor or lessor is one of the following bodies, namely—
(*a*) a local authority within the meaning of section 50 of the 1980 Act;
(*b*) a county council;
(*c*) the Commission for the New Towns;
(*d*) a development corporation;
(*e*) the Housing Corporation;
(*f*) a housing association falling within subsection (3)(*a*) of section 15 of the Rent Act 1977;
(*g*) an urban development corporation within the meaning of Part XVI of the Local Government, Planning and Land Act 1980; and
(*h*) the Development Board for Rural Wales.
(4) In this section and sections 19 and 20 below—
"conveyance" means a conveyance of the freehold or an assignment of a long lease;
"dwelling-house" includes a house within the meaning of the Housing Act 1957 (in this Part of this Act referred to as "the 1957 Act");
"grant" means a grant of a long lease;

"long lease" means a lease creating a long tenancy within the meaning of paragraph 1 of Schedule 3 to the 1980 Act.

DEFINITIONS
"commencement date": s.66.
"dwelling-house": s.38 and 1980 Act s.3.
"flat": 1980 Act Sched. 19, para. 16.
"house": s.38 and 1980 Act s.3.

GENERAL NOTE
This section and Sched. 4 concern service charges in respect of houses, *i.e.* as distinct from in respect of flats. Long leases of flats—including from public authorities—are within the service charge protection of Sched. 19 of the 1980 Act, replacing s.90–91A of the Housing Finance Act 1972. The principal impetus for this provision is the prospect of long leases of *houses* (*i.e.* not flats within the 1980 Act Sched. 19) (*cf.* s.1, above). In addition, a number of conveyances and grants of houses on estates, both under the right to buy and under voluntary sales programmes, have been subject to service charge provisions, and are accordingly included within this code of protection.

For this purpose, a flat is defined as a separate set of premises, whether or not on the same floor which: (*a*) forms part of a building; and (*b*) is divided horizontally from some other part of that building; and (*c*) is constructed or adapted for use for the purpose of a dwelling and is occupied wholly or mainly as a private dwelling (1980 Act Sched. 19, para. 16). The present section, then, applies to premises which are *not* flats.

A service charge is an amount payable—directly or indirectly—for services, repairs, maintenance, insurance, or the vendor's or lessor's costs of management, and the whole or part of which is or may be variable.

The section applies to disposals—freehold or long leasehold (subs. (4), and see 1980 Act Pt. 1, Chap. 1, and Sched. 3, para. 1) whether under right to buy or voluntary, and in the case of a lease whether by grant or assignment, by:

(*a*) a local authority (*i.e.* district council, London Borough Council, Greater London Council, Common Council of the City of London or the Council of the Isles of Scilly; see 1980 Act s.50(1)) of property under whatsoever powers held;

(*b*) a county council (*cf.* s.36 below);

(*c*) the Commission for the New Towns;

(*d*) a development corporation (meaning a development corporation established under, or as if under, the New Towns Act 1981; see 1980 Act s.50(1));

(*e*) the Housing Corporation;

(*f*) a registered housing association (see the Rent Act 1977, s.15(3)(*a*));

(*g*) an urban development corporation (see the Local Government, Planning and Land Act 1980); or

(*h*) the Development Board for Rural Wales (see the Development of Rural Wales Act 1976).

The extent and terms of the protection are described in the notes to Sched. 4 below, and are modelled on that available to long leaseholders of flats under the 1980 Act Sched. 19. The protection is not, however, available in respect of any period ending before the commencement date of this Act (subs. (2)).

Vesting of mortgaged dwelling-house in local authority etc.

19.—(1) Subject to subsection (2) below, Schedule 5 to this Act shall apply in any case where—

(*a*) the requirements of section 18(3) above were satisfied with respect to a conveyance or grant of a dwelling-house;

(*b*) the body by whom the conveyance or grant was executed (in that Schedule referred to as "the authority") is a mortgagee of the dwelling-house and as mortgagee has become entitled to exercise the power of sale conferred by section 101 of the Law of Property Act 1925 or by the mortgage deed; and

(*c*) the conveyance or grant contains a condition of the kind mentioned in section 104(6)(*b*) or (*c*) of the 1957 Act, a covenant imposing the limitation specified in section 19(4) of the 1980 Act or any other provision to the like effect and any period during which the provision has effect has not expired.

(2) Schedule 5 to this Act shall not apply where the conveyance or grant was executed before the passing of the 1980 Act.

(3) The vesting of a dwelling-house under Schedule 5 to this Act shall be treated as a relevant disposal for the purposes of section 104B of the 1957 Act or section 8 of the 1980 Act or any provision of the conveyance or grant to the like effect as the covenant required by section 104B(2) or section 8(1).

(4) Where any conveyance or grant executed before the commencement date contains both—

(a) the covenant required by section 104B(2) of the 1957 Act or section 8(1) of the 1980 Act or any other provision to the like effect; and

(b) a condition of the kind mentioned in section 104(6)(b) or (c) of the 1957 Act, a covenant imposing the limitation specified in section 19(4) of the 1980 Act or any other provision to the like effect,

the first mentioned covenant or provision shall have effect, as from that date, with such modifications as may be necessary to bring it into conformity with the provision made by subsections (1) and (3) above.

GENERAL NOTE

This section is concerned with the vesting of mortgaged property in the mortgagee. It applies to the same class of body as that to which the last section applies: see notes thereto.

When a mortgagee, on the default of the mortgagor, acquires power to sell property under the Law of Property Act 1925, s.101, the power is exercisable subject to a duty to obtain the best price that can be obtained for the property; see the Building Societies Act 1962, s.36(1); see also *Reliance Permanent Building Society* v. *Harwood-Stamper* [1944] Ch. 362. Such a sale must, in accordance with the duty of an ordinary fiduciary vendor, be at arm's length: *ibid.*

This proposition has caused something of a contradiction when the mortgagee has been a local or other public authority. Conveyances and grants by public authorities not uncommonly included a pre-emption clause. A pre-emption clause depresses value. If the mortgagor defaulted during the life of the pre-emption clause, what would the public authority/mortgagee's duty be?

New disposal provisions, and restrictions, were introduced by the 1980 Act; see s.91, introducing a new s.104 into the Housing Act 1957. In relation to disposals *preceding* the introduction of that new section, the dilemma posed in the last paragraph could be resolved by an application to the county court for leave to vest the property in the authority/mortgagee: 1980 Act s.112. Provision for compensation and accounting was made by 1980 Act s.113.

The present section introduces a similar power in relation to conveyances or grants executed on or after the passing of the 1980 Act (August 8, 1980) (subs. (2)). The details of how the power operates, and of compensation and accounting requirements, are now to be found in Sched. 5, below. The main principles are, however, the same, and permit the vesting of property in respect of which the body in question (a) is the mortgagee, and (b) has the power of sale, *i.e.* under s.101 of the Law of Property Act 1925, or under the deed.

The vesting can only occur, however, if the conveyance or grant contains *either* (i) a pre-emption clause, as defined in s.104(6)(b) of the 1957 Act (as substituted by s.91 of the 1980 Act) or as described in s.19(4) of the 1980 Act (as amended by s.9 above, *i.e.* property in national parks, areas of outstanding natural beauty and rural areas) or any other similar right of pre-emption, in each case the period for the exercise of which pre-emption entitlement not having expired, *or* (ii) a covenant prohibiting assignment or subletting (1957 Act s.104(6) (c)). It is, accordingly, applicable both to voluntary sales, and to right to buy sales.

Subs. (3)

A vesting operates as a disposal, for the purposes of repayment of a discount under a right to buy disposal (1980 Act s.8, as amended by s.5 above; see notes thereto) or under a voluntary disposal (see 1957 Act, s.104B, added by 1980 Act s.92, and as amended by Sched. 6 below) or under a similar right of recoupment of discount.

Subs. (4)
This subsection modifies existing (but not pre-1980 Act) covenants or provisions, to permit the amendments described above to take effect.

Local authority and Housing Corporation indemnities for certain mortgagees

20.—(1) Local authorities and the Housing Corporation may, with the approval of the Secretary of State, enter into agreements with recognised bodies making relevant advances on the security of dwelling-houses whereby, in the event of default by the mortgagor, and in circumstances and subject to conditions specified in the agreements, an authority or the Corporation binds itself to indemnify the recognised body in respect of—

(a) the whole or part of the mortgagor's outstanding indebtedness; and
(b) any loss or expense falling on the recognised body in consequence of the mortgagor's default.

(2) The agreement may also, where the mortgagor is made party to it, enable or require the authority or the Corporation in specified circumstances to take a transfer of the mortgage and assume rights and liabilities under it, the recognised body being then discharged in respect of them.

(3) The transfer may be made to take effect—

(a) on any terms provided for by the agreement (including terms involving substitution of a new mortgage agreement or modification of the existing one); and
(b) so that the authority or the Corporation are treated as acquiring (for and in relation to the purposes of the mortgage) the benefit and burden of all preceding acts, omissions and events.

(4) The Secretary of State may under subsection (1) above approve particular agreements or give notice that particular forms of agreement have his approval; and

(a) he may in either case make the approval subject to conditions;
(b) he shall, before giving notice that a particular form has his approval, consult such organisations representative of recognised bodies and local authorities as he thinks expedient.

(5) In this section—

"local authority" means a county or district council, the Greater London Council, a London borough council, the Common Council of the City of London or the Council of the Isles of Scilly;

"recognised body" means any body specified or of a class or description specified in an order made by statutory instrument by the Secretary of State with the consent of the Treasury;

"relevant advance" means an advance made to a person whose interest in the dwelling-house is or was acquired by virtue of a conveyance or grant with respect to which the requirements of section 18(3) above are or were satisfied.

(6) Before making an order under subsection (5) above varying or revoking an order previously made, the Secretary of State shall give an opportunity for representations to be made on behalf of any recognised body which, if the order were made, would cease to be such a body.

(7) Section 16(3) and (5) of the Restrictive Trade Practices Act 1976 (recommendations by services supply association to members) shall not apply to recommendations made to recognised bodies about the making of agreements under this section, provided that the recommendations are made with the approval of the Secretary of State, which may be withdrawn at any time on one month's notice.

General Note
Under the 1980 Act, s.111, local authorities and the Housing Corporation may enter into indemnity agreements with building societies within the Building Societies Act 1962 or the Building Societies Act (Northern Ireland) 1967. This section permits the Secretary of State to specify bodies or classes of body other than building societies, with which local authorities and the Housing Corporation may enter into similar such indemnities. Indemnities may, however, only be in respect of conveyances or grants by the same bodies to which the last two sections have applied (see notes to s.18 above). Transactions in question may be voluntary, or right to buy, sales.
"Our intention is to name as recognised bodies all the main mortgage lenders other than building societies, notably banks, insurance companies and friendly societies . . ." (Mr Gow, Standing Committee B, November 3, 1983, col. 486).

Local authority contributions towards certain mortgage costs

21.—(1) A local authority may contribute towards any costs incurred by any person in connection with any legal charge which secures, or any proposed legal charge which is intended to secure, a relevant advance made or proposed to be made to him by a body specified in subsection (2) below, but only to the extent that the contribution does not exceed such amount as may be specified in an order made by the Secretary of State.

(2) The bodies referred to in subsection (1) above are—

    (*a*) any recognised body; and

    (*b*) any building society within the meaning of the Building Societies Act 1962 or the Building Societies Act (Northern Ireland) 1967.

(3) An order under subsection (1) above shall be made by statutory instrument which shall be subject to annulment in pursuance of a resolution of either House of Parliament.

(4) In this section expressions used in section 20 above have the same meaning as in that section.

General Note
Local authorities may contribute towards, *i.e.* give grants towards, costs incurred in connection with mortgages on conveyances and grants by the bodies to which the last three sections have applied, whether the mortgage is granted by a building society or another "recognised body" (*cf.* notes to s.20). The Secretary of State may specify maximum amounts which may be so awarded. The power relates both to voluntary, and right to buy, disposals.
It was suggested that because the maximum which a local authority can charge a mortgagor is £50 (*cf.* Sched. 11, para. 17, below) while charges by private mortgagees could—and often would—be higher, some purchasers were deterred from going to the private sector and opted instead for the right to a mortgage from the authority (or Housing Corporation). This provision would give authorities a discretion, both in the case of an initial right to buy purchase, and in a case in which the mortgage was to be taken over by the private sector. (Standing Committee B, November 3, 1983, col. 488).

Consent to certain voluntary disposals

22.—(1) Except with the consent of the Secretary of State, a local authority shall not dispose of a dwelling-house to which this section applies otherwise than in pursuance of Chapter I of Part I of the 1980 Act or this Part of this Act.

(2) A dwelling-house is one to which this section applies if—

(*a*) it is let on a secure tenancy; or

(*b*) a lease of it has been granted in pursuance of Chapter I of Part I of the 1980 Act or this Part of this Act,

unless (in either case) it has been acquired or appropriated by the local authority for the purposes of Part V of the 1957 Act.

(3) A consent under this section may be given either generally to all local authorities or to any particular local authority or description of authority and either generally in relation to all dwelling-houses to which this section applies or in relation to any particular dwelling-house or description of dwelling-house to which this section applies.

(4) Any such consent may be given subject to such conditions as the Secretary of State sees fit to impose.

(5) Without prejudice to the generality of subsection (4) above, any such consent may be given subject to conditions as to the price, premium or rent to be obtained on a disposal of a dwelling-house to which this section applies, including conditions as to the amount by which, on a disposal of such a dwelling-house by way of sale or by the grant or assignment of a lease at a premium, the price or premium is to be, or may be, discounted by the local authority.

(6) Section 26(1) of the Town and Country Planning Act 1959 (power of local authorities etc. to dispose of land without consent) shall not apply to any disposal which requires a consent under this section.

(7) If—

(*a*) a local authority dispose of a dwelling-house to which this section applies; and

(*b*) the disposal is one which requires a consent under this section but is made without such a consent,

then, unless the disposal is to an individual (or to two or more individuals) and does not extend to any other dwelling-house to which this section applies, it shall be void and section 128(2) of the Local Government Act 1972 or, as the case may be, section 29 of the Town and Country Planning Act 1959 (protection of purchasers) shall not apply.

(8) For the purposes of this section the grant of an option to purchase the freehold of, or any other interest in, a dwelling-house to which this section applies is a disposal and any consent given under this section to such a disposal extends to any disposal made in pursuance of the option.

(9) In this section "local authority" has the same meaning as in section 20 above.

Definitions

"dwelling-house": s.38 and 1980 Act s.3.
"secure tenancy": s.38 and 1980 Act s.28.
"local authority": subs. (9) and s.20(5).

General Note

This section applies to disposals other than under the right to buy, of property which is let on a secure tenancy, or else is the subject of a long lease granted under the right to buy. It concerns, therefore, the creation or sale of other interests in such property, *e.g.* the creation of intervening interests. In either case, however, the section does *not* apply to the largest class of such properties, those where the property is held under Part V of the Housing Act 1957, *i.e.* housing stock held for general letting by district councils, London Borough Councils and the Greater London Council.

Part V stock disposals are governed, and restricted, by the Housing Act 1957, s.104. Non-Part V disposals are governed by somewhat less restrictive provisions, *e.g.* of the Local Government Act 1972, and the Town and Country Planning Act 1971. Even where consent is required under such other provisions, however, s.26 of the Town and Country Planning

Act 1959 permits disposal, *without consent*, at the best price, best consideration or best rent (as the case may be) that can reasonably be obtained . . ." (s.26(4)). (There is a similar power in s.123, Local Government Act 1972, but this cannot be used to empower an authority to act other than in accordance with, *inter alia*, the 1980 Act: *ibid.*, s.131.)

In such cases, therefore, disposals do not require the consent of the Secretary of State and there is, accordingly, the possibility of abuse by way of disposal by a landlord, to someone (a new landlord) not within right to buy, of non-Part V housing brought within right to buy (see s.36 below; *cf.* s.2 above). ("A local authority which is so minded is effectively in a position to frustrate a tenant's application to exercise his right to buy . . . by disposing of its interest in his home over his head to a third party who is not a right to buy landlord . . ." [Mr Gow, *Hansard*, H.C. Vol. 58, col. 611 (April 12, 1984].) The purpose of this section is to avoid such disposals, by removing the possibilities contained in the 1959 Act s.26.

The section applies to county councils, district councils, the Greater London Council, a London Borough Council, the Common Council of the City of London and the Council of the Isles of Scilly; see s.20 above. The section prohibits the disposal of a property of the class under consideration (non-Part V) (including the grant of an option to purchase the freehold or any other interest in the property; see subs. (8)) other than with the consent of the Secretary of State. Consent may be general or specific, and may be conditional, including as to price and discount.

Subs. (7)

Even where consent *is* needed, however, it would still normally be valid in favour of a purchaser, by reason of s.128(2) of the Local Government Act 1972, and s.29 of the Town and Country Planning Act 1959. These sections negate the common law rule that a disposal without a necessary consent is invalid (see *Rhyl UDC* v. *Rhyl Amusements Ltd.* [1959] 1 W.L.R. 465) and provide that a purchaser is not obliged ("concerned") to "see or enquire whether any such consent has been given . . ."

Subs. (7), accordingly, removes this protection, *unless* the sale is of one dwelling-house only, and to one or more individuals (*i.e.* not corporate bodies). It follows that ss.128 and 29 will still protect an individual purchaser of one dwelling, notwithstanding lack of consent. (For similar provisions; see also the 1980 Act ss.123 [amending the Housing Act 1974, s.2] and 137).

Covenants which must or may be imposed on certain voluntary disposals

23. Schedule 6 shall have effect for the purpose of making, in relation to section 104B (repayment of discount on early disposal) and section 104C (houses in National Parks and areas of outstanding natural beauty etc.) of the 1957 Act, provision corresponding to that made, in relation to sections 8 and 19 of the 1980 Act, by sections 5 and 8 above.

GENERAL NOTE

The amendments contained in s.5 above, to the 1980 Act, ss.8 (repayment of discount on early disposal) and 19 (dwelling-houses in National Parks, areas of natural beauty and rural areas) apply only to right to buy transactions. The amendments in Sched. 6 make corresponding provision in respect of voluntary sales.

Further advances in the case of certain voluntary disposals

24.—(1) Where—
  (*a*) a lease of a dwelling-house granted otherwise than in pursuance of this Part of this Act contains a provision to the like effect as that required by paragraph 3 of Schedule 3 to this Act; and
  (*b*) a body specified in section 18(3) above has, in the exercise of any of its powers, left outstanding or advanced any amount on the security of the dwelling-house,
that power shall include power to advance further amounts for the purpose of assisting the tenant to make payments in pursuance of that provision.
  (2) This section shall be deemed always to have had effect.

DEFINITIONS
    "dwelling-house": s.38 and 1980 Act s.3.

GENERAL NOTE
    This section applies to *voluntary* shared-ownership leases. It provides, for the avoidance of doubt, that power to lend on the *initial* "sale" includes power to advance monies with which to purchase subsequent tranches of equity, in the same way as a purchaser under a statutory shared-ownership lease can obtain further advances. The provision is deemed "always to have had effect".

Other rights of secure tenants

Grounds and orders for possession

25.—(1) In Part I of Schedule 4 to the 1980 Act (grounds on which court may order possession) after ground 5 there shall be inserted the following grounds—

"Ground 5A

The tenancy was assigned to the tenant, or to a predecessor in title of his who is a member of his family and is residing in the dwelling-house, by an assignment made by virtue of section 37A of this Act and a premium was paid either in connection with that assignment or the assignment which the tenant or predecessor himself made by virtue of that section.

In this paragraph 'premium' means any fine or other like sum and any other pecuniary consideration in addition to rent.

Ground 5B

The dwelling-house forms part of, or is within the curtilage of, a building to which sub-paragraph (2) of paragraph 1 of Part I of Schedule 1 to this Act applies and—

   (*a*) the dwelling-house was let to the tenant or a predecessor in title of his in consequence of the tenant or predecessor in title of his in consequence of the tenant or predecessor being in the employment of the landlord or of a body specified in sub-paragraph (3) of that paragraph; and

   (*b*) the tenant or any person residing in the dwelling-house has been guilty of conduct such that, having regard to the purpose for which the building is used, it would not be right for him to continue in occupation of the dwelling-house."

(2) In subsection (2) of section 34 of that Act (grounds and orders for possession) for the words "grounds 10 to 13" there shall be substituted the words "grounds 9A to 13" and in that Part of that Schedule after ground 9 there shall be inserted the following ground—

"Ground 9A

The dwelling-house either forms part of, or is within the curtilage of, a building to which sub-paragraph (2) of paragraph 1 of Part I of Schedule 1 to this Act applies or is situated in a cemetery and (in either case)—

   (*a*) the landlord reasonably requires the dwelling-house for occupation as a residence for some person engaged in the employment of the landlord or of a body specified in sub-paragraph (3) of that paragraph or with whom, conditional on housing being provided, a contract for such employment has been entered into; and

   (*b*) the dwelling-house was let to the tenant or to a predecessor in title of his in consequence of the tenant or predecessor being in the employment of the landlord or of a body so specified and the tenant or predecessor has ceased to be in that employment."

(3) After subsection (3) of that section there shall be inserted the following subsection—

"(3A) The matters to be taken into account by the court in determining whether it is reasonable to make an order on ground 13 shall include—

(*a*) the age of the tenant;

(*b*) the period during which the tenant has occupied the dwelling-house as his only or principal home; and

(*c*) any financial or other support given by the tenant to the previous tenant."

DEFINITIONS
"dwelling-house": s.38 and 1980 Act s.3.
"member of family": s.38 and 1980 Act s.50(3).

GENERAL NOTE
1980 Act
Orders for possession against secure tenants can only be made on specified grounds: 1980 Act s.34. Those grounds are set out in the 1980 Act Sched. 4. The first group of grounds requires proof of (*a*) the specified elements of the ground, and (*b*) that it is reasonable to make the order sought; the second group of grounds requires proof of (*a*) the specified elements of the ground, and (*b*) that suitable alternative accommodation will be available for the tenant when the order takes effect; the third group of grounds requires proof of (*a*) the specified elements of the ground, (*b*) that suitable alternative accommodation will be available for the tenant when the order takes effect, and (*c*) that it is reasonable to make the order sought.

Main Changes
This section contains four amendments to s.34 and Sched. 4 of the 1980 Act. The first cross-refers to the next section, which amends (and limits) assignment generally, but introduces a new right to assign, although only as between secure tenants, *i.e.* a right to exchange. This ground falls within the first class of grounds for possession (ground plus reasonableness.) The second amendment is a ground for possession against certain tied occupiers, which also falls within the first of these categories, while the third amendment is a further ground against the same tied occupiers, but within the third category (ground, plus, suitable alternative accommodation, plus reasonableness). The fourth amendment relates to Ground 13, which also falls within the third group, and which is commonly known as "underoccupation" (see further notes to subs. (3) below).

Subs. (1)
Under s.26, below, secure tenancies are generally incapable of assignment, save by virtue of an order under s.24 of the Matrimonial Causes Act 1973, and save to a potential successor: see the new s.37 of the 1980 Act added by s.26. However, a new 1980 Act s.37A, also added by s.26, below, *extends* the right to assign, as between secure tenants, *i.e.* by way of exchange.

The new Ground 5A is designed to prevent the charging of premiums on an "exchange assignment" under s.37A. It is offended if a premium has been paid "in connection with" either the assignment by which he (or predecessor) became the tenant, or an assignment which the tenant (or predecessor) "gave" in exchange. The ground is available whether the premium was paid by, or connected to an assignment entered into by, a predecessor in title of the present title, but only so long as the predecessor is (*a*) a member of the tenant's family, and (*b*) still living in the dwelling-house.

It would seem that the ground may arise whether tenant (or predecessor) paid or received the premium, although it must, of course, be reasonable to make the order sought.

Ground 5B refers back to s.2, above, and forward to s.36, below, and the class of tied occupant brought within *security* but excluded from the *right to buy* thereby; see notes thereto. It applies, however, only to property within the curtilage of a building, which may not include property in a cemetery (see the distinction observed in the new 1980 Act Schedule 1, Pt. 1, para. 1, substituted by s.2. See also Ground 9A, introduced by subs. (2);

see notes below). Note the requirement that the conduct of which the occupier is guilty must relate to the purpose for which the building is used.

Subs. (2)

This new ground for possession also relates back to s.2, excluding certain property subject to secure tenancies from the right to buy, and forward to s.36, extending to the tenants of county councils, and to certain tied occupiers, secure status (see notes thereto). An order for possession may be made, provided it is reasonable to do so and suitable alternative accommodation is to be made available, in relation to a dwelling-house which forms part of a "non-housing" building (see notes to s.2(1), above) or is in a cemetery (*cf.* Ground 5B, introduced by subs. (1) above).

The first element of the ground is that the landlord reasonably requires the property for someone in its employment, or the employment of one of the other bodies enjoying the benefit of the right to buy exclusion (see notes to s.2(1), above), or with whom there is a contract of employment conditional on housing being provided. This part of the ground is modelled on the Rent Act 1977, Sched. 15, Case 8, although note that, unlike under Case 8, the incoming occupier's employment need not be "whole-time".

The landlord's requirement must itself be reasonable (*cf. Kennealy* v. *Dunne* [1977] 1 Q.B. 837, C.A., under Rent Act 1977, Sched. 15, Case 11, where the ground refers only to the landlord "requiring"—*i.e.* not "reasonably requiring"— the property) which necessitates separate consideration from overall reasonableness (*R. F. Fuggle* v. *Gadsden* [1948] 2 K.B. 236, C.A.).

The second element of the ground is that the dwelling-house was let in consequence of employment with the landlord, or one of the specified classes of landlord employment with which disqualifies the occupier from exercise of the right to buy (see s.2 and notes thereto, above) and the tenant or predecessor has ceased to be in that employment.

Subs. (3)

Ground 13 applies when the secure tenant has become the tenant by "succession" under s.30 of the 1980 Act and is not the surviving spouse of the deceased tenant. Notice of intended proceedings (under the 1980 Act s.33) must be served no earlier than six, and no later than twelve, months after the death of the previous tenant. The principal element of the ground is that the accommodation afforded is more extensive than is reasonably required by the tenant.

This section adds, by way of amendment of the 1980 Act, s.34, three specific points to be taken into account when deciding the "reasonableness issue": the successor's age; the length of time he has occupied the premises as his only or principal home; and financial or other support which he has given to the deceased tenant. It is very hard indeed to see that any of these points would have been (unappealably) ignored by a court in any event and doubtless the point of embodying them in legislation is to underline their relative importance.

Assignments and other disposals of secure tenancies

26.—(1) For section 37 of the 1980 Act (effect of assignment or subletting etc.) there shall be substituted the following sections—

"Assignments

37.—(1) A tenancy to which subsection (2) below applies shall not be capable of being assigned, and if a tenancy to which subsection (3) below applies is assigned it ceases to be a secure tenancy, unless (in either case)—

(*a*) the assignment is made in pursuance of an order made under section 24 of the Matrimonial Causes Act 1973; or

(*b*) the assignment is made to a person in whom the tenancy would or might have vested by virtue of section 30 above had the tenant died immediately before the assignment, or in whom it would or might have so vested had the tenancy been a periodic tenancy; or

(*c*) the assignment is made by virtue of section 37A below.

(2) This subsection applies to any tenancy which—

(*a*) is a secure tenancy to which subsection (3) below does not apply; or

(*b*) would be such a tenancy if the condition described in section 28(3) above as the tenant condition were satisfied.

(3) This subsection applies to any secure tenancy which is for a term certain and was granted before 5th November 1982.

(4) Where—

(*a*) a tenancy ceases to be a secure tenancy by virtue of subsection (1) above; or

(*b*) a tenancy which would be a tenancy to which subsection (3) above applies if the condition described in section 28(3) above as the tenant condition were satisfied is assigned,

the tenancy cannot become a secure tenancy.

Assignments by way of exchange

37A.—(1) It is by virtue of this section a term of every secure tenancy that the tenant may, with the written consent of the landlord, assign the tenancy to a person to whom this subsection applies; and this subsection applies to any person who is the tenant under a secure tenancy and has the written consent of his landlord to assign the tenancy either to the first mentioned tenant or to another person to whom this subsection applies.

(2) The consent required by virtue of this section is not to be withheld except on one or more of the grounds set out in Schedule 4A to this Act and, if withheld otherwise than on one of those grounds, shall be treated as given.

(3) The landlord shall not be entitled to rely on any of the grounds set out in Schedule 4A to this Act unless, within 42 days of the tenant's application for the consent, the landlord has served on the tenant a notice specifying that ground and giving particulars of it.

(4) Where any rent lawfully due from the tenant has not been paid or any obligation of the tenancy has been broken or not performed, the consent required by virtue of this section may be given subject to a condition requiring the tenant to pay the outstanding rent, remedy the breach or perform the obligation.

(5) Except as provided by section (4) above, a consent required by this section cannot be given subject to a condition, and any condition imposed otherwise than as so provided shall be disregarded.

Other disposals

37B.—(1) If the tenant under a secure tenancy parts with the possession of the dwelling-house or sub-lets the whole of it (or sub-lets first part of it and then the remainder) the tenancy ceases to be a secure tenancy.

(2) Where, on the death of the tenant, a secure tenancy is vested or otherwise disposed of in the course of the administration of his estate, the tenancy ceases to be a secure tenancy unless—

(*a*) the vesting or other disposal is in pursuance of an order made under section 24 of the Matrimonial Causes Act 1973; or

(*b*) the vesting or other disposal is to a person in whom the tenancy would or might have vested by virtue of section 30 above had the tenancy been a periodic tenancy.

(3) Where—

(*a*) a tenancy ceases to be a secure tenancy by virtue of this section; or

(*b*) in the case of a tenancy which would be a secure tenancy if the condition described in section 28(3) above as the tenant condition were satisfied, the tenant parts with the possession of

the dwelling-house or sublets the whole of it (or sub-lets first
part of it and then the remainder),
the tenancy cannot become a secure tenancy."

(2) After Schedule 4 to the 1980 Act there shall be inserted, as Schedule 4A, the Schedule set out in Schedule 7 to this Act.

(3) Subject to subsection (4) below, section 37 of the 1980 Act as originally enacted shall be deemed never to have applied in relation to the assignment of secure tenancies.

(4) Nothing in subsection (3) above shall affect—

(*a*) in the case of a periodic tenancy, the operation of a notice to quit served on the tenant before the commencement date;

(*b*) in the case of a tenancy for a term certain, any proceedings for forfeiture in pursuance of a notice served on the tenant before that date.

DEFINITIONS
"commencement date": s.66.
"dwelling-house": s.38 and 1980 Act s.3.
"secure tenancy": s.38 and 1980 Act s.28.
"tenant condition": s.38 and 1980 Act s.28.

GENERAL NOTE
1980 Act
S.37 of the 1980 Act, for which this section substitutes three new sections, deals with the effect of (*a*) an assignment of a secure tenancy, (*b*) its transmission on death other than under the statutory succession provisions (see 1980 Act ss.30 and 31) and (*c*) subletting or parting with possession of the whole of a dwelling-house subject to a secure tenancy (as to subletting of part; see 1980 Act s.35). The statutory succession provisions concern only periodic tenancies (see 1980 Act s.30(1)). A fixed-term tenancy is left to devolve in accordance with usual principles, but subject to the provisions of s.37 of the 1980 Act as to whether or not, on such devolution, it retains the quality of security.

The displaced provisions were relatively straightforward. On assignment, a secure tenancy ceased to be secure *unless* the assignment was in pursuance of an order under s.24 of the Matrimonial Causes Act 1973 ("property transfer order") or to a person who would or might have succeeded, under the statutory succession provisions, had the tenant died immediately before the assignment. In effect, the provision permitted a pre-emptive assignment to a potential successor, *e.g.* if the tenant wished to prevent a dispute between one of two potential successors, or else permitting a tenant to assign to a potential successor, and then leave the premises, perhaps to retire to another town or even country (as in *Peabody Donation Fund* v. *Higgins* (1983) 10 H.L.R. 82, C.A.).

On devolution on death, the fixed-term tenancy ceased to be secure, again unless to a person who could have succeeded had the tenancy been periodic, or if its disposition was subject to a property transfer order. Security would be retained or lost, then, in the same circumstances as on an assignment.

As to subletting, or parting with possession of, the whole of the premises the subject of the secure tenancy (whether in one letting, or by letting in parts until the whole is let) the tenancy simply ceased to be secure.

Whether on account of assignment, devolution on death, or subletting or parting with possession of the whole, once security was lost for any of these reasons, the tenancy would not again become secure. If a secure tenancy ceased for a period of time to be secure, *e.g.* because of non-residence, and the assignment, etc., took place during a period when it was not secure, then security would similarly be finally lost.

It is the provisions governing assignment which have proved contentious. The 1980 Act did not permit or prohibit assignment: it merely dealt with the consequences. In the *Peabody* case, the tenancy agreement contained an absolute prohibition on assignment. The tenant, intending to retire to Ireland and wishing to permit his daughter to remain in their home, executed an assignment by deed. As such, it was an effective assignment, albeit one contrary to the terms of the tenancy.

The Court of Appeal held that s.37 of the 1980 Act applied to such an "illegal" assignment, and that as the daughter could have succeeded to the tenancy the tenancy remained secure. The daughter would, however, be vulnerable to an action for possession on the ground of breach of term of tenancy (requiring proof of reasonableness—1980, Sched. 4, Ground 1; see also notes to s.25 above).

In some cases, local authorities have "used" the assignment provisions as hitherto enacted, in order to diminish exercise of the right to buy. The use has been in this way. Two tenants wish to exchange with each other. They seek the permission of the authority, without which such an exchange could not take place. Under normal circumstances, new tenancies would have been granted, and since the 1980 Act, would have been secure. Instead, the authority would require the exchange to be by way of assignment. As the assignments would not be to potential successors, the tenancies would each cease to be secure. Both security of tenure, and right to buy would be lost. The new provisions go further than preventing such tactics: they introduce a positive "right to exchange".

Subs. (1)

New S.37: The new s.37 is concerned with assignment only. It prevents use of the technique described in the last paragraph, by deeming most secure tenancies to be incapable of assignment, other than (*a*) in the same circumstances described above and which applied under the former s.37, and (*b*) those under the "right to exchange"; see notes to s.37A, below.

Those not included are only fixed-term secure tenancies granted before November 5, 1982 and these continue to be subject to the old provision: the tenancy ceases to be secure unless the appropriate circumstances apply. It will now, however, be impossible for an authority to require "cross-assignments", in any other case, in the way described, for the reason that the secure tenancy is not *per se* susceptible of assignment (save as excepted).

The "lack of assignability" (again, save as excepted) applies also to what would be a secure tenancy, but for failure to fulfil the "tenant condition" of s.28(3) of the 1980 Act. It is this condition which requires that the tenant (or, if a joint tenancy, each of the tenants) is an individual (as distinct from corporate personality) and that the tenant (or, if a joint tenancy, at least one of the tenants) occupies the premises as an only or principal home. The new subs. (4) achieves the same effect, by "loss of security", where a pre-November 1982 term certain is involved.

New S.37A: The new s.37A introduces the "right to exchange" (see also notes to s.25, above, introducing a new ground for possession if a premium is charged in connection with its exercise).

The decision to introduce it "was taken in the light of the very patchy way in which landlords now allow their tenants to move homes. Some landlords are generous in their consideration of applications. They recognise the wider national sense behind rehousing people from outside their areas, despite their natural first duty towards their own rate-payers . . . Others are, to put it frankly, unhelpful, sometimes to the point of obstructiveness . . . I hope your Lordships all agree that the housing mobility of tenants...is to be encouraged . . . (Lord Bellwin, *Hansard* H.L. Vol. 448, col. 1268 (February 28, 1984)).

An exchange operates by way of an assignment, with written consent of the landlord, within s.37A(1). S.37A(1) applies to any other secure tenant—not necessarily of the same landlord—who has the written consent of his landlord to *the* or *an*- other secure tenant. The extension to "an" other is designed to permit three-way, or multiple, exchanges. Everyone involved must have permission to assign to another secure tenant, who himself has permission to assign to a secure tenant.

Consent is not to be witheld save on specified grounds. These are set out in a new 1980 Act Sched. 4A, and cover a range of circumstances. They are considered in the notes to Sched. 7, below. If withheld on any ground other than one of those specified, the consent is to be treated as given. Furthermore, the landlord can only rely on Sched. 4A grounds if it replies within 42 days' of application, specifying the ground and "giving particulars of it". It seems likely that this would be held to mean more than merely setting out the words of the Act, *i.e.* a landlord ought to apply the ground to the particular circumstances in issue.

In addition to the specified grounds of *objection*, however, the landlord is entitled to require payment of any rent arrears, or the remedying of any other breach of an obligation of the tenancy, as a *condition* of consent, and this entitlement is not limited by failure to reply within 42 days. No other conditions may be attached, and if such is specified it is to be disregarded.

The possibility of a conditional consent of this latter class—arrears or breach of obligation of tenancy—suggests that a failure by the landlord to reply within 42 days is *not* to be treated as the giving of consent (and the Act is silent on any "deemed consent" in this case; *cf.* 1980 Act s.35(3) and s.81(3) treating consent "unreasonably withheld" as given, a formulation that could have been easily applied here with minor adaptation; and *cf.* deemed consent if withholding is on any ground other than a specified ground, under this section).

If follows that if the landlord fails to reply at all, the tenant will need to take action, *e.g.* for an injunction or a declaration in the county court, under s.86 of the 1980 Act (see Sched.

11, para. 25) to compel a reply, and cannot simply proceed to assign in default. Such an assignment would be a non-assignment, by reason of the new s.37.

Note that on an exchange, an assign*ee* who is a successor (as defined in s.31 of the 1980 Act) remains a successor. In other words, the status of successor goes with the person of the tenant, rather than the tenancy, or the property, in question. Thus, if Tenant A, a successor, exchanges with Tenant B, a non-successor, Tenant A remains a successor in his new property, while Tenant B remains a non-successor in his. See Sched. 11, para. 23.

New S.37B: As for subletting, and disposition on death, the new s.37B is designed to restate the existing provisions, without reference to assignment, and with the substitution of the reference to the tenant condition in s.28(3) of the 1980 Act for an earlier, and somewhat more vague, formulation "at a time when a tenancy is not a secure tenancy..." (1980 Act s.37(3)(*b*)).

Subs. (3)

The former s.37 is deemed never to have been enacted (save as provided in subs. (4)). This is a surprisingly sweeping provision, presumably aimed at reinstating the security of those affected by "exchange-assignments" of the order described in the General Note, above. The new provisions will not apply in its place: contrast the wording of subs. (3) with, *e.g.* that of s.7(1), above ("shall have effect, and shall be deemed always to have had effect..."). It follows that all tenancies which have been thought to have ceased to be secure (other than those within subs. (4), below) have not done so, and remain secure (or regain security) with consequences (and, doubtless, arguments) across the range of rights of secure tenants.

Subs. (4)

Exempt from the "amnesty" and "reinstatement of security" described in the last paragraph are (*a*) those erstwhile insecure periodic tenancies in respect of which notices to quit have been served (n.b. not *expired*) before the commencement date, and (*b*) those fixed-term and equally insecure tenancies in respect of which a forfeiture notice has been served before the commencement date. Landlords have had, then, from publication of the provisions until commencement in which to opt for eviction, or reinstatement of security.

Rent not to increase on account of certain improvements

27. In section 39 of the 1980 Act (rent not to be increased on account of tenant's improvements) for paragraph (*b*) there shall be substituted the following paragraphs—

> "(*b*) if he has died and on his death the tenancy vested under section 30 above, at any time whilst the person in whom the tenancy so vested is a secure tenant of that dwelling-house; or
>
> (*c*) if he has assigned the tenancy and the assignment was made as mentioned in paragraph (*a*) or (*b*) of section 37(1) above, at any time whilst the assignee is a secure tenant of that dwelling-house; or
>
> (*d*) if the tenancy has been transferred to his spouse or former spouse by an order under paragraph 2 of Schedule 1 to the Matrimonial Homes Act 1983, at any time whilst the transferee is a secure tenant of that dwelling-house."

DEFINITIONS
"dwelling-house": s.38 and 1980 Act s.3.
"secure tenant": s.38 and 1980 Act s.28.

GENERAL NOTE
1980 Act

By s.39 of the 1980 Act the landlord under a secure tenancy is bound to disregard improvements carried out by the tenant when determining rent increases. This is, however, only so of the lawful improvements, *e.g.* under the 1980 Act ss.81 and 82, and only to the extent that the cost either actually was borne by the tenant or would have been so borne but for grant-aid under the Housing Act 1974, Part VII (see also the 1980 Act s.106). This protection was extended to the tenant's spouse, provided he or she succeeded to the secure tenancy on his or her death under the statutory succession provisions. (Note, incidentally, that it is only *improvements* which are disregarded: if a property is *repaired*, independently or ancillary to an improvement grant, the *repairs* will not be disregarded, but could well enhance the value of the property.)

Changes

The amendments extend the protection to three classes. First, it is extended to *anyone* who succeeds under the statutory succession provisions, *i.e.* not just a spouse. Second, it is extended to anyone to whom the tenancy is assigned or on whom it devolves, under the 1980 Act s.37(1)(*a*) or (*b*) (not, therefore including an "exchange-assignment"; see notes to s.26, above). Thirdly, it is extended to a spouse to whom the tenancy is transferred under the Matrimonial Homes Act 1983, *i.e.* not under s.24 of the Matrimonial Causes Act 1973, which is within s.37(1)(*a*), nor only—as before—on death. In each case, the change of tenant is, therefore, to another member of the family.

Note that the new tenant retains the protection so long as he or she remains the tenant, under *a* secure tenancy. Thus, if B succeeds to A's secure tenancy, but is subsequently granted a wholly new, secure tenancy, the rent still cannot be increased on account of the improvements.

Right to carry out repairs

28. After section 41 of the 1980 Act there shall be inserted the following section—

"Other rights of secure tenants

Right to carry out repairs

41A.—(1) The Secretary of State may by regulations make a scheme for entitling secure tenants, subject to and in accordance with the provisions of the scheme—

(*a*) to carry out to the dwelling-houses of which they are secure tenants repairs which their landlords are obliged by repairing covenants to carry out; and

(*b*) after carrying out the repairs, to recover from their landlords such sums as may be determined by or under the scheme.

(2) Regulations under this section may make such procedural, incidental, supplementary and transitional provision as may appear to the Secretary of State to be necessary or expedient.

(3) Without prejudice to the generality of subsection (2) above, regulations under this section—

(*a*) may provide for any question arising under the scheme to be referred to and determined by the county court; and

(*b*) may provide that where a secure tenant makes application under the scheme his landlord's obligation under the repairing covenant shall cease to apply for such period and to such extent as may be determined by or under the scheme.

(4) In this section 'repairing covenant', in relation to a dwelling-house, means a covenant (whether express or implied) obliging the landlord to keep in repair the dwelling-house or any part of the dwelling-house."

DEFINITIONS

"dwelling-house": s.38 and 1980 Act s.3.

"repairing covenant": s.38 and 1980 Act s.41A(4) (added by this section).

"secure tenant": s.38 and 1980 Act s.28.

GENERAL NOTE

This is the second of three new limbs of the "tenants charter" provisions of the 1980 Act. Pt. I, Chap. I of the 1980 Act gave secure tenants the right to buy, and the right to a mortgage. Pt. I, Chap. II gave them security of tenure (including rights of succession) and rights to published information about their terms of tenancy (1980 Act s.41), to be consulted on matters of housing management (1980 Act ss.42 and 43), and to information about allocation, transfer and exchange, and personal details about the tenant recorded by the authority (1980 Act s.44). Pt. III gave them the "right to improve" and s.106 of the 1980 Act added the possibility of improvement grants with which to do so. S.26 of this Act introduced the "right to exchange". The next section adds a right to information about heating charges.

This section is an enabling section, permitting the creation of a "right to repair". "There is general agreement that tenants on the whole suffer from an unsatisfactory repairs service from their landlords." (Standing Committee B, November 8, 1983, col. 523.)

The section applies to works within a landlord's repairing covenant, whether an express or implied covenant (subs. (4)). It accordingly applies to the provisions of s.32 of the Housing Act 1961, under which the landlord is responsible for repairs to the structure and exterior of a dwelling-house, and for specified utility installations (water, gas, electricity, for sanitation, and for heating, whether space or water; see *ibid.* s.32(1)).

The regulations may provide for the suspension of the landlord's obligations "for such period and to such extent as may be determined by or under the scheme" (subs. (3)(b)). The scheme can, however, apply only to covenants to repair the dwelling itself not, *e.g.* common parts (consider *Campden Hill Towers* v. *Gardner* [1977] Q.B. 823, 13 H.L.R. 64, C.A.). A roof of a top floor flat, while not in the possession of the top floor tenant, may yet fall within s.32, in an appropriate case and, consequently, may fall within a scheme: *Douglas-Scott* v. *Scorgie* (1984) 13 H.L.R. 97, C.A.

The essence of the section is to permit secure tenants to execute works for which the landlord is responsible, recouping the cost from the landlord. It recognises the considerable dissatisfaction that has been caused in many areas by delays in execution of repairs. The legislation is silent, however, on questions of "quality control", and ignores the legal and practical difficulties that may follow from negligent works (consider, for example, *Sleafer* v. *Lambeth Borough Council* [1960] 1 Q.B. 43, C.A.).

The point was not missed in Committee. "In respect of insurance cover, who will meet the difficulties that may arise if there are safety or health problems or if accidents occur? Who will cover the tenant? We need a clear exposition…about what precisely would happen in respect of insurance cover. I understand that insurance companies have certain worries in this respect". (Mr Heffer, Standing Committee B, November 10, 1983, cols. 560 *et seq.*)

The Secretary of State would appear to have power to incorporate provision for this class of issue, and other such issues, under subs. (2). (See also the description of the proposed scheme, which follows.)

On October 7, 1983, the Department of the Environment issued a letter inviting comment on *provisional* views on the scheme, by way of consultation. The *proposals* are based on the schemes of a number of authorities operating their own "right to repair" agreements, including that of Havering London Borough Council (see *Tenant Participation in the Repair and Maintenance of Council Houses*, published by Havering in December 1982). Other authorities mentioned as maintaining such schemes are the London Boroughs of Brent and Bromley, and the Northern Ireland Housing Executive (Standing Committee B, November 8, 1983, col. 518).

Considerable Committee debate was taken up by discussion not of the statutory provisions, but of the proposed scheme. The proposed scheme would exclude repairs costing the landlord less than £20, or more than £200, and repairs to the structure of blocks of flats and maisonettes (*cf.* observations above) and the exterior of individual flats and maisonettes.

The proposed scheme would start with a notice from tenant to landlord, in prescribed form, indicating how the tenant proposed to remedy the defect. Landlords would be required to respond within 21 days, either by withholding consent, granting consent or granting consent subject to reasonable conditions about nature and quality of workmanship. Reasons would have to be given for the withholding of consent, and these would be confined to a schedule: proposed repair unnecessary, not within scope of scheme, not suitable to remedy defect, landlord unable to gain access (after giving reasonable notice) to inspect defect. Additions might include the landlord's intention to do works itself, within 28 days, and repairs not reasonably necessary for the comfort of the tenant and will be included in a planned maintenance programme within one year.

When consent is granted, the landlord will have to state the amount which the landlord will pay on satisfactory completion of works. The landlord would specify a time (proposed as not less than 3 months) within which the tenant should claim, having carried out the works. The amount payable is proposed as not less than 75 per cent. of the cost to the landlord, with a discretion to pay more. Between grant of consent, and notification of completion of works (or withdrawal of application to repair) the landlord's repairing obligation in respect of the notified defect would be held in abeyance. The counter-notice would also advise the tenant of possible liability for damage or injury to person or property, and to consider the insurance position.

Payment would have to be made within 21 days of notification of agreement to pay, *i.e.* after the tenant notifies the landlord of the completion of the works and of the claim. If the payment is agreed, and the tenant is in arrears, the landlord could set the amount off against the debt. If the payment is withheld, on the grounds of unsatisfactory completion of works, the landlord would have to explain why the works were unsatisfactory, and give the tenant an opportunity either to finish the works properly or invite the landlord to do so. The latter would obviate the obligation to make any payment to the tenant.

If the landlord failed to comply with its obligations, *e.g.* to carry out a repair within a time specified in a counter-notice, or by failing to serve a counter-notice, the tenant would be able to carry out the repair and claim 100 per cent. of the cost to the landlord. The tenant's claim, however, would have to be submitted within 3 months of date of landlord's default. If the landlord did not specify its costs of doing the work, the tenant would be able to claim 100 per cent. of actual costs (within the specified limit, *i.e.* £20–£200). Disputes would be resolved in the county court.

Heating charges

29. After section 41A of the 1980 Act there shall be inserted the following section—

"**Heating charges**

41B.—(1) In this section—

'heating authority' means any of the following, namely a local authority, a development corporation, the Commission for the New Towns or the Development Board for Rural Wales, which—

(*a*) operates a generating station or other installation for producing heat; and

(*b*) supplies heat produced at that installation to any premises;

'heating charge' means an amount payable to a heating authority in respect of heat so produced and so supplied whether or not, in the case of heat supplied to premises let by the authority, it is payable as part of the rent;

'heating costs' means expenses incurred by a heating authority in operating a generating station or other installation for producing heat;

and a secure tenant is one to whom this section applies if a heating authority supplies heat produced at such an installation to the dwelling-house of which he is such a tenant.

(2) The Secretary of State may by regulations require heating authorities to adopt such methods for determining any heating charges payable by secure tenants to whom this section applies as will secure that the proportion of heating costs borne by each of those tenants is no greater than is reasonable.

(3) The Secretary of State may by regulations make provision for entitling secure tenants to whom this section applies, subject to and in accordance with the regulations, to require the heating authorities concerned—

(*a*) to furnish to them, in such form as may be prescribed by the regulations, such information as to heating charges and heating costs as may be so prescribed; and

(*b*) where any such information has been so furnished, to afford them reasonable facilities for inspecting the accounts, receipts and other documents supporting the information and for taking copies or extracts from them.

(4) Regulations under this section may make such procedural, incidental, supplementary and transitional provision as may appear to the Secretary of State to be necessary or expedient.

(5) Without prejudice to the generality of subsection (4) above, regulations under this section may provide for any question arising under the regulations to be referred to and determined by the county court.

(6) Any reference in this section to heat produced at an installation includes a reference to steam produced from, and air and water heated by, heat so produced."

DEFINITIONS
"development corporation": s.38 and 1980 Act s.50.
"dwelling-house": s.38 and 1980 Act s.3.
"heating authority": s.38 and 1980 s.41B (added by this section).
"heating charge": s.38 and 1980 Act s.41B (added by this section).
"heating costs": s.38 and 1980 Act s.41B (added by this section).
"local authority": s.38 and 1980 Act s.50.
"secure tenant": s.38 and 1980 Act s.28.

GENERAL NOTE
This third (*cf.* General Note to last section) new right for secure tenants meets a common complaint, of inadequate explanation for apparently high heating charges payable by tenants to their own authorities, under district, or "communal" (Mr Wyn Roberts, Standing Committee B, November 10, 1983, col. 610) heating schemes (which may be confined to a single estate, or may cover a wider geographical area). "We all agree that communal heating charges are a source of complaint by many tenant" (*ibid.*)

Whether or not payment is made as a part of the rent, a heating charge is a payment by a tenant of the authority's own property, to that authority, for heat both produced by them and supplied by them. The heating cost is the actual expenditure incurred in the operating of the generating station or other installation at which the heat is produced.

The Secretary of State may by regulation require heating authorities to adopt particular methods for determining heating charges, payable by secure tenants, in order to ensure that each tenant bears no greater proportion of the heating costs than is reasonable. Regulations may also provide for secure tenants to require the provision of information about heating charges and costs, in a prescribed form and to afford reasonable facilities for inspecting accounts, receipts and other documents supporting the information, and for taking copies or extracts from them.

In substance, this is a "service charge" protection, similar to that available (in private and public sectors) to leaseholders and other tenants of flats, and, now, some houses (*cf.* s.18 above).

Miscellaneous

Power to extend right to buy etc.

30.—(1) The Secretary of State may by order provide that, in cases falling within subsection (2) below, Part I of the 1980 Act and this Part of this Act shall have effect with such modifications as are specified in the order.

(2) The cases referred to in subsection (1) above are cases where there are in a dwelling-house let on a secure tenancy one or more interests to which this subsection applies; and this subsection applies to any interest which—

(a) is held by a body mentioned in section 18(3) above; and
(b) is immediately superior to the interest of the landlord or to another interest to which this subsection applies.

(3) An order under this section may make different provision with respect to different cases or descriptions of case and may contain such

consequential, supplementary or transitional provisions as appear to the Secretary of State to be necessary or expedient.

(4) The power to make an order under this section shall be exercisable by statutory instrument which shall be subject to annulment in pursuance of a resolution of either House of Parliament.

DEFINITIONS
   "dwelling-house": s.38 and 1980 Act s.3.
   "secure tenancy": s.38 and 1980 Act s.28.

GENERAL NOTE
   This section applies to property in respect of which there is a number of interests. The property must be let on a secure tenancy. In addition to the interest of the landlord, there must be an interest belonging to a local authority (meaning district council, London Borough Council, Greater London Council, Common Council of the City of London or the Council of the Isles of Scilly; see 1980 Act s.50) a county council, the Commission for the New Towns, a development corporation, the Housing Corporation, a registered housing association, an Urban Development Corporation or the Development Board for Rural Wales (see s.18(3) above).
   In relation to such a property, the Secretary of State may modify Pt. I of the 1980 Act (*i.e.* right to buy and security of tenure) and this Part of this Act. The purpose would seem to be to permit the Act to be amended so as to enable tenants to purchase freeholds, where on the face of the Act at present only a leasehold will be available, in cases where the superior interests belong to public landlords.

Dwelling-houses on public trust land

   31. Where a dwelling-house let on a secure tenancy is land held—
       (*a*) for the purposes of section 164 of the Public Health Act 1875 (pleasure grounds); or
       (*b*) in accordance with section 10 of the Open Spaces Act 1906 (duty of local authority to maintain open spaces and burial grounds),
then, for the purpose of Chapter I of Part I of the 1980 Act and this Part of this Act, the dwelling-house shall be deemed to be freed from any trust arising solely by virtue of its being land held in trust for enjoyment by the public in accordance with the said section 164 or, as the case may be, the said section 10.

DEFINITIONS
   "dwelling-house": s.38 and 1980 Act s.3.
   "secure tenancy": s.38 and 1980 Act s.28.

GENERAL NOTE
   The purpose of this section is to enable public trust land to be sold under the right to buy, as it has been extended by this Act, free from the trust; see also s.123 of the Local Government Act 1972, as amended by Sched. 23 of the Local Government, Planning and Land Act 1980.

Errors and omissions in notices

   32.—(1) A notice served by a tenant under Chapter I of Part I of the 1980 Act or this Part of this Act shall not be invalidated by any error in or omission from any particulars which are required by regulations under section 22 of that Act to be contained in the notice.
   (2) Where as a result of any such error or omission—

    (*a*) the landlord has mistakenly admitted or denied the right to buy in a notice under section 5(1) of the 1980 Act or the right to be granted a shared ownership lease in a notice under section 13(1) above; or

    (*b*) the landlord or the Housing Corporation has formed a mistaken opinion as to any matter required to be stated in a notice by any of the provisions specified in subsection (3) below and has stated that opinion in the notice,

the parties shall, as soon as practicable after they become aware of the mistake, take all such steps (whether by way of amending, withdrawing or re-serving any notice or extending any period or otherwise) as may be requisite for the purpose of securing that all parties are (as nearly as may be) in the same position as that in which they would have been if the mistake had not been made.

    (3) The said provisions are—

    (*a*) section 10(1)(*a*) of the 1980 Act (notice of purchase price);

    (*b*) section 12(4)(*a*) of that Act (notice of mortgage entitlement);

    (*c*) section 14(1)(*a*) above (notice of initial contribution);

    (*d*) section 16(8) above (notice of entitlement to further advance); and

    (*e*) paragraph 3(4)(*a*) of Schedule 3 to this Act (notice of additional contribution).

    (4) Subsection (2) above shall not apply in any case where the tenant has exercised the right to which the notice relates before the commencement date or before the parties become aware of the mistake.

DEFINITIONS
    "commencement date": s.66.
    "right to buy": s.38 and 1980 Act s.1.
    "shared ownership lease": s.12.

GENERAL NOTE
    An error in, or omission from, particulars required in connection with the exercise of right to buy, right to shared ownership lease, or right to mortgage, is not to invalidate the relevant notice. Instead, the parties are to take such steps as may be needed in order to put them all in the same position as if the mistake had not been made, or in a position as nearly the same as may be. This provision, however, not only does not apply to notices served prior to the commencement of this Act; it also does not apply to completed transactions (subs. (4)).

Housing association grant

    33.—(1) The Secretary of State may pay housing association grant under section 29 of the Housing Act 1974 (in this Part of this Act referred to as "the 1974 Act") to an association registered under section 13 of that Act in cases where, after a tenant has exercised or has claimed to exercise the right to buy or the right to be granted a shared ownership lease, the association carries out to the dwelling-house or to the building in which it is situated works of repair or improvement.

    (2) where in a case falling within subsection (1) above a housing association grant is made after the tenant has exercised the right to buy or the right to be granted a shared ownership lease, the Secretary of State may reduce the amount of the grant.

DEFINITIONS
    "dwelling-house": s.38 and 1980 Act s.3.
    "right to buy": s.38 and 1980 Act s.1.
    "shared ownership lease": s.12.

GENERAL NOTE
   This is the first of three sections governing the position of housing association tenants.
   A housing association grant (HAG) is the principal means of subsidising housing associations. HAG is only available for providing, improving or repairing "housing or residential accommodation" (Housing Act 1974, s.29(2)(*a*)–(*c*)) and ancillary land or buildings (*ibid.* s.29(2) ((*d*)–(*e*)). "Housing or residential accommodation" is defined (in *ibid.* s.29(2)) as "dwellings which are, or are to be, let or available for letting..." If "the right to buy is claimed or exercised while major repairs or improvement projects are underway . . . the association might make a loss on the sale if HAG is not paid in respect of those repairs." (*per* Lord Bellwin, *Hansard*, H.L. Vol. 449, col. 190 (March 6, 1984)).
   This section, accordingly, provides "a limited extension", (*ibid.*) to permit such payments, (subs. (1)) but also provides for grant *reduction* to take account of proceeds of sales completed before a grant is paid over (subs. (2)). The wording is not, therefore, considered to be wide enough to require *repayment* by an association of HAG already paid. That, however, is dealt with in s.30 of the Housing Act 1974, as amended by the next section.

Repayment of housing association grant

   34.—(1) In section 30(3) of the 1974 Act (repayment etc. of housing association grant in certain circumstances), after paragraph (*a*) there shall be inserted the following paragraph—

   "(*aa*) there has been paid to the association in respect of any land to which the grant relates an amount payable in pursuance of—

   (i) the covenant required by section 104B(2) of the Housing Act 1957 or section 8(1) of the Housing Act 1980 (covenant for repayment of discount) or any other provision to the like effect; or

   (ii) the provision required by paragraph 3, 6 or 7 of Schedule 3 to the Housing and Building Control Act 1984 (terms of shared ownership lease) or any other provision to the like effect;".

   (2) If, after a housing association grant has been made under section 29 of the 1974 Act to an association registered under section 13 of that Act—

   (*a*) there is such a disposal as is mentioned in paragraph (*a*) of subsection (3) of section 30 of that Act; or

   (*b*) there is made such a payment as is mentioned in paragraph (*aa*) of that subsection,

the association shall notify the Secretary of State of the disposal or payment and, if so required by written notice of the Secretary of State, shall furnish him with such particulars of and information relating to the disposal or payment as are specified in the notice.

   (3) Where a housing association grant has been so made, with Chief Land Registrar may furnish the Secretary of State with such particulars and information as he may reasonably require for the purpose of determining—

   (*a*) whether there has been such a disposal as is mentioned in paragraph (*a*) of subsection (3) of section 30 of the 1974 Act; or

   (*b*) whether there has been made such a payment as is mentioned in paragraph (*aa*) of that subsection.

   (4) The amendment made by subsection (1) above shall apply whether the payment was made before or after the commencement date.

DEFINITIONS
   "commencement date": s.66.

GENERAL NOTE

This is the second of three sections dealing with housing association tenants. See also General Note to ss.33, above, and 35 below.

In specified circumstances, the Secretary of State may require a housing association to repay Housing Association Grant (HAG) in whole or part. Those circumstances include the disposal of the property.

This section adds a new circumstance: the repayment of a discount, either on a right-to-buy sale (full or shared ownership) or following a voluntary sale.

Taken together with the provisions of subs. (2), the amendments mean that associations are now under a duty to notify the Secretary of State of post-grant-payment disposals, and repayments of discounts, and to provide him with such further particulars as he may by notice require, as a prelude to possible exercise of his powers to require repayment of HAG.

The repayment may be of part only: "Where dwelling-houses are sold at a discount or only a share in the dwelling is acquired, either under the right to buy or under the voluntary scheme, the capital receipt may occasionally be insufficient to meet a repayment of all the grant attributable to the dwelling. In such circumstances the Secretary of State will abate the recovery of grant to avoid the association making a loss." (Lord Bellwin, *Hansard*, H.L. Vol. 449, col. 191 (March 6, 1984)). This is true without the amendments in this section.

However, "a tenant may...decide to sell the house he has bought under the right to buy within the statutory period which requires him to repay a proportion of the discount. Or if he has a shared-ownership lease he may purchase an additional share or the whole of the rented portion of the dwelling. In either event there will be a further capital receipt for the housing association. There is currently no power to recover any outstanding balance of housing association grant in these circumstances. The new clause will provide it . . .." (*ibid.*)

Subs. (4)

Note that the amendment applies even in relation to HAG payments prior to the commencement date.

Provisions as respects certain tenants of charitable housing associations etc.

35.—(1) This section applies to any tenant of a publicly funded dwelling-house who, but for subsection (1) or (2)(*a*) of section 2 of the 1980 Act (exception for cases where landlord is a charitable housing association etc.), would have the right to buy; and a dwelling-house is publicly funded for the purposes of this section if housing association grant has been paid under section 29 of the 1974 Act in respect of a project which included—

(*a*) the acquisition of the dwelling-house;

(*b*) the acquisition of a building and the provision of the dwelling-house by means of the conversion of that building; or

(*c*) the acquisition of land and the construction of the dwelling-house on that land.

(2) The Secretary of State may pay housing association grant under section 29 of the 1974 Act to an association registered under section 13 of that Act in cases where the association first acquires a dwelling-house and then disposes of it at a discount to a tenant to whom this section applies.

(3) Where an association registered under section 13 of the 1974 Act contracts for the acquisition of a dwelling-house and, without taking the conveyance, grant or assignment, disposes of its interest to a tenant to whom this section applies, subsection (2) above and the following provisions, namely—

(*a*) section 122 of the 1980 Act and sections 104B(2) to (9) and 104C of the 1957 Act as applied by that section (disposals by housing associations);

(*b*) Part II of Schedule 1A to the 1980 Act (qualification and discount);

(*c*) section 2 of the 1974 Act (consent of Housing Corporation to disposals); and

(*d*) section 9(2) of that Act (loans by Housing Corporation), shall have effect as if the association first acquired the dwelling-house and then disposed of it to that tenant.

(4) Section 13 of the 1974 Act shall have effect as if the additional purposes or objects mentioned in subsection (3) of that section included the purpose or object of effecting transactions falling with subsection (2) above.

(5) In this section "dwelling-house" includes a house within the meaning of the 1957 Act.

DEFINITIONS

"dwelling-house": s.38 and 1980 Act s.3; see also subs. (5).
"right to buy": s.38 and 1980 Act s.1.

GENERAL NOTE

This is the third of the new sections dealing with housing association tenants: see ss.33 and 34 above. It is also the most contentious of this batch of new provisions. The history starts with the defeat of the government, in the previous Housing and Building Control Bill (which "fell" when Parliament was dissolved to enable the 1983 election to take place) in relation to a proposed extension of the right to buy to such tenants.

"This Bill does not contain a clause that would give the tenants of charitable housing associations the right to buy the home they live in, much as I myself, frankly, would have liked to have included it.

"Your Lordships will, however, be aware of the proposals for a new home ownership scheme for tenants of charitable housing associations . . . This scheme, in outline, would offer the chance of home ownership to tenants of charitable dwellings provided with housing association grant through a purchase on the open market with a discount similar to what they would have had under the right to buy. For every tenant who was able to take advantage of the scheme, a charitable dwelling would be vacated and become available for re-letting to a person or a family with accute housing needs in line with the objects of the charitable landlord..." (Lord Bellwin, *Hansard*, H.L. Vol. 447, col. 457 (Second Reading—January 30, 1984.))

Conceptually, the proposals contain a certain, if elusive, theoretical consistency. For many years now, private sector landlords have made substantial cash payments to persuade their tenants to go, either in order to convert and sell the vacated property, or to relet on an unprotected or unregulated letting. In recent years, such ex-tenants will commonly have used these payments in order to make up the deposit on a house-purchase. Housing associations are sometimes described as in the "quasi-public sector" (the phrase appears first to have been used in the Report of the Select Committee on Artisans' and Labourers' Dwellings [1881] in relation to Peabody). This "premium" may be described as one more of the many ways in which they straddle the sectors.

The new section was introduced on March 6, 1984. It is an enabling provision only, which will work by way of purchase by association, and resale to tenant, at the same price less discount. The details of the scheme are intended to be contained in the conditions for payment of HAG on the transaction. Much of the House of Lords' Committee debate was, however, taken up with these proposals (*cf.* s.28, above, where there was similar attention to a prospective scheme, and correspondingly little to the words of the Act itself).

The main features singled out for attention were:

"First, grant would normally be reserved to cases where the charitable landlord had refused to sell to the tenant the house in which he was living on terms equivalent to those that would be available under the right to buy" [*i.e.* voluntary sales]. "Second, the home selected by the tenant would be expected to fall within the value limits operated under the 'Do it yourself shared ownership' scheme. Those limits are £40,000 in Greater London, £35,000 in the home counties, and £30,000 elsewhere. Grant would be available on outright purchases, or on shared-ownership leases..." (Lord Bellwin, *Hansard*, H.L. Vol. 449, col. 193 (March 6, 1984)).

Lord Bellwin also explained that the calculation of discount will be governed by the tenant's existing property. No greater discount will be allowed than the tenant would be able to secure on that, although if the property purchased was cheaper than the tenanted property, the discount available would be of the same *percentage, i.e.* will produce a lower amount. Unlike under the right to buy, while discount will be on years of public tenancy, the right to join this scheme will only arise after a "reasonable period"—probably two years—*in the tenanted property.* Funds for the scheme will come from within the Housing Corporation's Approved Development Programme (as do funds for DIY shared ownership).

Subs. (1)

The provisions apply only to tenants of "publicly funded" dwellings who *would have* the right to buy, *but for* the 1980 Act s.2(1) or (2)(*a*), *i.e.* tenants of housing trusts and associations which are charities within the Charities Act 1960. "Publicly funded" is defined as the payment of HAG for acquisition of the tenanted property, or for acquisition of a building and provision of the tenanted property by conversion, or for acquisition of land and the construction of the tenanted property on it.

Subs. (2)

The circumstances in which HAG is normally available are outlined in the General Note to s.33, above. In the light of the extension contained in that section, this subsection is largely declaratory, *i.e.* s.29 of the Housing Act 1974, as amended, was probably wide enough without further amendment, although this subsection averts any argument on the point.

Subs. (3)

The scheme may work by way of exchange of contract by association, and immediate assignment of purchase entitlement to tenant, so that the association never takes a conveyance, grant or assignment in its own name. In such a case, the provisions of the last subsection will apply, *i.e.* HAG will remain available. Other provisions to apply are those requiring repayment of discount on an early disposal, Housing Corporation consent to disposal and Housing Corporation house-purchase lending powers, all in the same way as if the association had completed purchase before resale.

Meaning of "secure tenancy"

36.—(1) In section 28 of the 1980 Act (secure tenancies) paragraph (*d*) of subsection (2) and the word "or" immediately preceding that paragraph shall be omitted and after paragraph (*a*) of subsection (4) there shall be inserted the following paragraph—

"(*aa*) a county council;".

(2) In Schedule 3 to the 1980 Act (tenancies which are not secure tenancies) paragraph 3 shall be omitted and after paragraph 2 there shall be inserted the following paragraphs—

"2A. A tenancy is not a secure tenancy if the tenant is a member of a police force and the dwelling-house is provided for him free of rent and rates in pursuance of regulations made under section 33 of the Police Act 1964.

2B.—(1) A tenancy is not a secure tenancy if the tenant is an employee of a fire authority and—

   (*a*) his contract of employment requires him to live in close proximity to a particular fire station; and

   (*b*) the dwelling-house was let to him by the authority in consequence of that requirement.

(2) In this paragraph 'contract of employment' has the same meaning as in paragraph 2 above and 'fire authority' means a fire authority for the purposes of the Fire Services Acts 1947 to 1959.

2C.—(1) A tenancy is not a secure tenancy until the periods to be taken into account for the purposes of this paragraph amount in aggregate to more than three years if—

   (*a*) within the period of three years immediately preceding the grant the conditions mentioned in paragraph 2, 2A or 2B above have been satisfied with respect to a tenancy of the dwelling-house; and

   (*b*) before the grant of the tenancy the landlord notified the tenant in writing of the circumstances in which this exception applies and that in its opinion the proposed tenancy would fall within this exception.

(2) A period is to be taken into account for the purposes of this paragraph unless it is a period during which the conditions mentioned in paragraph 2, 2A or 2B above are satisfied with respect to the tenancy."

(3) In paragraph 6 of that Schedule after the words "the district or London borough", in the second and third places where they occur, there shall be inserted the words "or its surrounding area" and at the end of that paragraph there shall be added the words—

"In this paragraph 'surrounding area', in relation to a district or London borough, means the area which consists of each district or London borough that adjoins it."

(4) The paragraph inserted in Schedule 3 to the 1980 Act as paragraph 2C does not apply to a tenancy granted before the commencement date unless, immediately before that date, the interest of the landlord belongs to a county council.

(5) That paragraph and paragraphs 6 and 11 of that Schedule shall have effect in relation to a tenancy granted before the commencement date and in the case of which, immediately before that date, the interest of the landlord belongs to a county council as if for the words "before the grant of the tenancy" there were substituted the words "before the end of the period of three months beginning with the commencement of Part I of the 1984 Act".

DEFINITIONS
  "dwelling-house": s.38 and 1980 Act s.3.
  "secure tenancy": s.38 and 1980 Act s.28.

GENERAL NOTE
   This section extends to tenants of county councils, and to a number of tied occupiers, the status of secure tenancy—with the incident of right to buy (but subject to the additional circumstances in which the right to buy does not arise, tailored to the extensions contained in this section; see s.2, and notes thereto, above). The extension is also subject to exceptions (see notes to subsections below) and to new grounds for possession (see s.25, and notes thereto, above).
   Examples of the accommodation thus brought within security are: accommodation provided for police officers, "wardens and caretakers . . . and dwellings let on a short-term basis pending redevelopment . . ." (Mr Gow, *Hansard,* H.L. Vol. 51, col. 442 (December 21, 1983)). The latter seems an odd example, given the provisions of Sched. 3, para. 4 of the 1980 Act ("A tenancy is not a secure tenancy if the dwelling-house is on land which has been acquired for development . . . and . . . is used . . . pending development . . . as temporary housing accommodation . . .").
   However, some police and fire officers are taken back out of security, by the addition of new exceptions; see notes to subs. (2) below.
   In addition, the "mobility" exemption from security (1980 Act, Sched. 3, para. 6) has been amended.

Subs. (1)
   S.27(2) of the 1980 Act specifies the landlords whose tenants are secure. Hitherto, tenants of county councils have only been secure tenants if the county council provided the accommodation in question in the exercise of Local Government Act 1972 "reserve" housing powers (1980 Act s.27(2)(*d*)—repealed by this section). The addition of sub. (2)(*aa*) is the general extension (see General Note above) to tenants of all county councils, *i.e.* under whatsoever powers the accommodation is provided.

Subs. (2)
   New paras 2A-2C: Sched. 3 of the 1980 Act contains the list of lettings exempt from status as secure. Para. 3 dealt with certain service lettings, *i.e.* lettings of accommodation held for the purposes of functions under the Education Act 1944 and under those Acts specified in the Local Authority Social Services Act 1970, Sched. 1. It applied only to accommodation within the curtilage, or actually forming part, of buildings held for the same purposes (see further notes to s.2(1) above). The exemption is now repealed.

In its place are left the narrower provisions of Sched. 3., para. 2 of the 1980 Act. This exempts "premises occupied under contract of employment." The lettings concerned are those in relation to which the contract of employment requires the occupant to live in the dwelling in question "for the better performance of his duties", and to this extent resembles the common law test of service occupancy (as distinct from service tenancy). Unlike under the Rent Acts, secure status attaches under the Housing Act 1980 to licensees as well as tenants; see the 1980 Act s.48.

However, it is not necessary for there to be a coincidence of identity between landlord and employer (as is needed for common law service tenancy or occupany). Local authorities, development corporations, county councils, the Commission for the New Towns and the Development Corporation for Rural Wales, can provide accommodation within paragraph 2 for their own or each other's employees. "Tied accommodation", then, for the purposes of the 1980 Act, has a somewhat wider meaning than normal.

The addition of paras. 2A and 2B takes out of security a number of occupiers who would otherwise have been brought within it, *i.e.* police and fire officers.

Property occupied under para. 2, and the new paras. 2A–2B, may also be kept out of security for a period of three years, following such occupation, under the new para. 2C. (As Sched. 3, para. 3 is to be repealed, it might have been thought convenient so to number the new paragraph 2C. Perhaps this otherwise logical approach was not followed in order to avoid confusion between "old" and "new" para. 3 exempt lettings. *Sed quaere*.). Para. 2C operates by the grant of a tenancy or licence to a new occupier. The exemption only lasts for three years, so that the period of grace cannot be extended by the grant of, *e.g.* a six year lease. In either eventuality, written notice must be given not later than the grant (but *cf.* subs. (5) below).

The purpose of new para. 2C was explained in this way:

"The third exception that we are proposing is for dwellings normally reserved for occupation under contract of employment but exceptionally let otherwise on a short-term basis. Short term is defined as being for less than three years.

"Dwellings normally reserved for occupation by a warden or caretaker may exceptionally be let on a temporary basis to another person when the warden or caretaker has alternative accommodation conveniently situated. We do not want to discourage short-term lettings. [The] new clause...proposes that such tenancies should not be secure, provided that the tenant has been informed of his position prior to the commencement of his tenancy . . ." (Mr Gow, *Hansard*, H.L. Vol. 51, col. 444 (December 21, 1983)).

This new paragraph does not apply to a tenancy granted before the commencement date, unless by a county council, in which case the notice can be given within three months of commencement—as can any other notice required under Sched. 3, paras. 6 to 11 of the 1980 Act (see note to subs. (5) below).

Subs. (3)

Para. 6: Para. 6 Sched. 3 of the 1980 Act leaves out of security, for a period of one year, a tenancy granted to a person to meet his need for temporary accommodation while looking for permanent accommodation, in a district or London Borough in which he has a job or a job offer. It is a condition of the operation of the exemption that the tenant did not live in the same district or Borough immediately before the grant. The exemption requires notification before the grant that it is to apply.

The amendment extends the geographical area of the operation of the exemption. Residence must still not have been within the area of the district council or London Borough, but can still be in that of any adjoining district council or London Borough, but the need for accommodation, and the job, may be within either district council or London Borough, *or* an adjoining district or London Borough.

Subs. (5)

In relation to new para. 2C, and paras. 6 to 11 of Sched. 3 of the 1980 Act, which also include requirements of notice prior to grant of tenancy, notices may be given within three months of commencement, where a relevant or appropriate tenancy was granted by a county council before commencement, within three months of commencement.

Supplemental

Transitional provisions

37.—(1) This section applies where—

   (*a*) a secure tenant has claimed to exercise the right to buy, that right has been established and the tenant's notice under section 5(1) of the 1980 Act remains in force on the commencement date;

   (*b*) the tenant has claimed the right to a mortgage and the landlord or the Housing Corporation has, before the commencement date, served a notice on the tenant under section 12(4) of that Act; and

   (*c*) the amount which, in the opinion of the landlord or Housing Corporation, the tenant is entitled to leave outstanding, or to have advanced to him, on the security of the dwelling-house is less than the aggregate mentioned in section 9(1) of that Act.

(2) The landlord shall, within four weeks of the commencement date, serve on the tenant a notice in writing informing him to the effect of this Part of this Act so far as relating to the right to be granted a shared ownership lease; and that notice shall be accompanied by a form for use by the tenant in claiming in accordance with section 13(1) above, the right to be granted a shared ownership lease.

(3) Any notice served by the landlord under section 16(2) of the 1980 Act before the commencement date shall be deemed to have been withdrawn.

(4) No notice shall be served by the landlord under subsection (2) of section 16 of the 1980 Act earlier than, and a notice may be served by the tenant under subsection (4)(*c*) of that section at any time before, the expiration of the period of three months beginning with the service of the notice under subsection (2) above.

DEFINITIONS

"commencement date": s.66.

"right to buy": s.38 and 1980 Act s.1.

"secure tenant": s.38 and 1980 Act s.28.

"shared ownership lease": s.12.

GENERAL NOTE

This section is designed to "introduce" the right to be granted a shared ownership lease to those who would have qualified had this Act been in force at the time of service of a notice under s.12 of the 1980 Act (see notes to s.12 above) and whose notices claiming the right to buy remain in force at the date of commencement. Within four weeks of commencement, the landlord is bound to serve on such a tenant a notice informing him of the effect of Pt. 1 of this Act, together with a form on which to claim a shared ownership lease.

Subs. (3) deems as withdrawn any notice to complete under s.16(2) of the 1980 Act (as unamended), (see notes to s.6 above) served before the commencement date, and accordingly many tenants who have been served such notices in the past must now be considered as holding "live" claims for the purposes of this section.

Subs. (4)

Each such tenant has three months in which to respond to the "transitional" notice served under subs. (2), because no new (preliminary; see notes to s.6 above) notice to complete may be served during that period.

Interpretation of Part I

38.—(1) In this Part of this Act expressions used in Chapter I of Part I of the 1980 Act have the same meanings as in that Chapter.

(2) In this Part of this Act—

"the 1957 Act" means the Housing Act 1957;

"the 1974 Act" means the Housing Act 1974;

"the 1980 Act" means the Housing Act 1980;

"additional contribution" has the meaning given by paragraph 4(1) of Schedule 3 to this Act;

"additional share" shall be construed in accordance with paragraph 3 of that Schedule;

"the commencement date" means the date on which this Part of this Act comes into force;

"initial contribution" has the meaning given by paragraph 2(1) of Schedule 3 to this Act;

"initial share" shall be construed in accordance with paragraph 1 of that Schedule;

"shared ownership lease" has the meaning given by section 12(1) above;

"total share" has the meaning given by paragraph 3(9) of Schedule 3 to this Act.

PART II

SUPERVISION OF BUILDING WORK ETC. OTHERWISE THAN BY LOCAL AUTHORITIES

Supervision of plans and work by approved inspectors

Giving and acceptance of an initial notice

39.—(1) In any cases where—

(*a*) a notice in the prescribed form (in the enactments relating to building regulations referred to as an "initial notice") is given jointly to a local authority by a person intending to carry out work and a person who is an approved inspector in relation to that work;

(*b*) the initial notice is accompanied by such plans of the work as may be prescribed;

(*c*) the initial notice is accompanied by such evidence as may be prescribed that an approved scheme applies, or the prescribed insurance cover has been or will be provided, in relation to the work; and

(*d*) the initial notice is accepted by the local authority,

then, so long as the initial notice continues in force, the approved inspector by whom the notice was given shall undertake such functions as may be prescribed with respect to the inspection of plans of the work specified in the notice, the supervision of that work and the giving of certificates and other notices.

(2) A local authority to whom an initial notice is given—

(*a*) may not reject the notice except on prescribed grounds, and

(*b*) shall reject the notice if any of the prescribed grounds exists,

and in any cases where the work to which an initial notice relates is work of such a description that, if plans of it had been deposited with the local authority, the authority could, under any enactment, have imposed requirements as a condition of passing the plans, the local authority may impose the like requirements as a condition of accepting the initial notice.

(3) Unless, within the prescribed period, the local authority to whom an initial notice is given give notice of rejection, specifying the ground or grounds in question, to each of the persons by whom the initial notice was given, the authority shall be conclusively presumed to have accepted the

initial notice and to have done so without imposing any such requirements as are referred to in subsection (2) above.

(4) An initial notice shall come into force when it is accepted by the local authority, either by notice given within the prescribed period to each of the persons by whom it was given or by virtue of subsection (3) above and, subject to section 43(3) below, shall continue in force until—

(a) it is cancelled by a notice under section 44 below; or

(b) the occurrence of, or the expiry of a prescribed period of time beginning on the date of, such event as may be prescribed;

and building regulations may empower a local authority to extend (whether before or after its expiry) any such period of time as is referred to in paragraph (b) above.

(5) The form prescribed for an initial notice may be such as to require—

(a) either or both of the persons by whom the notice is to be given to furnish information relevant for the purposes of this Part of this Act, Part II or Part IV of the 1936 Act, Part II of the 1961 Act or any provision of building regulations; and

(b) the approved inspector by whom the notice is to be given to enter into undertakings with respect to his performance of any of the functions referred to in subsection (1) above.

(6) The Secretary of State may approve for the purposes of this section any scheme which appears to him to secure the provision of adequate insurance cover in relation to any work which is specified in an initial notice and is work to which the scheme applies.

(7) Building regulations may prescribe for the purposes of this section the insurance cover which is to be provided in relation to any work which is specified in an initial notice and is not work to which an approved scheme applies and may, in particular, prescribe the form and content of policies of insurance.

DEFINITIONS

the 1936 Act: s.51(1).
the 1961 Act: s.51(1).
approved inspector: ss.41(1) and 51(1).
carrying out of work: s.51(2).
initial notice: ss.39(1) and 51(1).
local authority: s.51 and s.76(2) of the Health and Safety at Work etc. Act 1974

GENERAL NOTE

Pt. II of this Act provides that an approved inspector may at the option of a person intending to carry out building work supervise the work instead of the local authority. This modifies to a considerable extent the statutory procedures to be followed to secure compliance with building regulations made by the Secretary of State for the Environment under ss.61 and 62 of the Public Health Act 1936, ss.4(2), 4(5) and 6(2) of the Public Health Act 1961, and ss.61(2) and 74(1)(c) of, and Sched. 5 of, the Health and Safety at Work etc. Act 1974.

Subs. (1)

Where an approved inspector and a developer have served a notice on the authority and the notice has been accepted the inspector has a statutory duty to undertake prescribed functions in connection with the supervision of the work. The notice must be in the prescribed form, accompanied by prescribed plans, and by prescribed evidence that either an approved insurance scheme applies to the work or prescribed insurance cover relating to the work has been or will be provided.

As to approved schemes and prescribed insurance, see subss. (6) and (7).

Subs. (2)

An authority may only reject an initial notice on prescribed grounds and must do so if such grounds exist. They may also impose requirements under any enactment which enables them to do so as a condition of passing plans deposited with them.

have imposed requirements as a condition: Under s.64 of the Public Health Act 1936, where plans deposited with an authority are defective or show that the proposed work would contravene any of the building regulations the authority (i) may reject the plans, or (ii) pass them subject to either or both of the following conditions, namely; (a) that such modifications as the authority may specify shall be made in the deposited plans, and (b) that such further plans as they may specify shall be deposited. An authority may only pass plans subject to this condition if the person by whom or on whose behalf they were deposited (a) has requested the authority to do so, or (b) has consented to their doing so.

Plans deposited with an authority must be refused by the authority in the following circumstances:

(1) if it is proposed to erect a building over a sewer, unless the authority, subject to any directions by the water authority, consider that consent can properly be given (s.25 of the Public Health Act 1936);

(2) if it is proposed to build on ground filled with offensive materials (s.54 *ibid.*);

(3) unless satisfactory provision is made for drainage (s.37 *ibid*), and sufficient provision is made for closet accommodation (s.43 *ibid.*), and satisfactory provision is made for water supply (s.137 *ibid.* as amended);

(4) if there is insufficient access for the removal of refuse (s.55 *ibid.*);

(5) in the case of public buildings, where satisfactory means of ingress and egress are not available (s.59 *ibid.*);

(6) in the case of plans for buildings other than residences, shops and offices, unless the authority are satisfied that the height of the chimneys is adequate (Clean Air Act 1956, s.10); and

(7) in the case of industrial buildings, unless the buildings will conform to the standards of insulation against loss of heat as prescribed by regulation.

An authority *may* reject plans for a house if they disclose (a) an absence of sufficient and suitable food storage accommodation (Public Health Act 1961, s.31), or (b) the lack of a bathroom with hot and cold water (Public Health Act 1961, s.33).

As to the obligation upon an authority to pass plans which are not defective or which do not show that the proposed work would contravene any of the building regulations; see *R. v. Cambridge Corporation, ex p. Cambridge Picture Playhouses* [1922] 1 K.B. 250.

As to the right of appeal against a local authority's rejection; see s.47.

Subs. (3)

If an authority has not rejected an initial notice within the prescribed period they are presumed to have accepted it.

As to the service of notices; see s.51(4) and s.285 of the Public Health Act 1936.

Subs. (4)

An initial notice comes into force when it is accepted by the local authority, and remains in force until either it is cancelled by another notice given by the approved inspector or the developer under s.44 or some prescribed event occurs or some prescribed period elapses after such an event. Local authorities may by the building regulations be empowered to extend such a period.

As to the service of notices; see s.51(4) and s.285 of the Public Health Act 1936.

Subs. (5)

The prescribed form for an initial notice may be such as to require (a) either or both of the persons giving it to furnish information relevant to this Act, the 1936 Act and the 1961 Act, and the building regulations, and (b) undertakings by the approved inspector in relation to his prescribed function. Most of the information needed in relation to the building regulations will be contained in the deposited plans and the notice required to be given under the regulations.

Effect of an initial notice

40.—(1) So long as an initial notice continues in force, the function of enforcing building regulations which is conferred on a local authority by section 4(3) of the 1961 Act shall not be exercisable in relation to the work specified in the notice and, accordingly—

(*a*) a local authority may not give a notice under section 65(1) of the 1936 Act (removal of alteration of work which contravenes building regulations) in relation to the work so specified; and (*b*) a local authority may not institute proceedings under section 4(6) of the 1961 Act for any contravention of building regulations which arises out of the carrying out of the work so specified.

(2) For the purposes of the enactments specified in subsection (3) below,—

(*a*) the giving of an initial notice accompanied by such plans as are referred to in section 39(1)(*b*) above shall be treated as the deposit of plans; and

(*b*) the plans accompanying an initial notice shall be treated as the deposited plans; and

(*c*) the acceptance or rejection of an initial notice shall be treated as the passing or, as the case may be, the rejection of plans; and

(*d*) the cancellation of an initial notice under section 44(5) below shall be treated as a declaration under section 66 of the 1936 Act that the deposit of plans is to be of no effect.

(3) The enactments referred to in subsection (2) above are—

(*a*) subsection (2) of section 65 of the 1936 Act (powers of local authority where work is executed without plans being deposited etc.);

(*b*) subsection (4) of that section (restriction of powers of local authority to act), in so far as it relates to a notice under subsection (2) thereof and to non-compliance with any such requirement as is referred to in that subsection;

(*c*) subsection (5) of that section (saving for right to obtain injunction for certain contraventions), in so far as it relates to a contravention of any enactment in the 1936 Act;

(*d*) section 14(6) of the Water Act 1973 (notice of proposal to erect or extend building over water authority's sewer); and

(*e*) sections 219 to 225 of the Highways Act 1980 (the advance payments code).

(4) For the purposes of section 13 of the Fire Precautions Act 1971 (exercise of fire authority's powers where provisions of building regulations as to means of escape apply)—

(*a*) the acceptance by a local authority of an initial notice relating to any work shall be treated as the deposit of plans of the work with the authority in accordance with building regulations; and

(*b*) The references in subsections (1)(ii) and (3)(*b*) of that section to matters or circumstances of which particulars are not or were not required by or under the building regulations to be supplied to the local authority in connection with the deposit of plans shall be construed as a reference to matters or circumstances of which particulars would not be or, as the case may be, would not have been required to be so supplied if plans were to be or had been deposited with the authority in accordance with building regulations.

DEFINITIONS
carrying out of work: s.51(2).
contravention: s.51(1).
initial notice: ss.39(1) and 51(1).
local authority: s.51 and s.76(2) of the Health and Safety at Work etc. Act 1974.

GENERAL NOTE
So long as an initial notice is in force the enforcement powers of the local authority are not to be exercised by the authority. For the purposes of ss.65(2), 65(4), and 65(5) of the 1936 Act; s.14(6) of the Water Act 1973; and ss.219 to 225 of the Highways Act 1980 (a) the giving of an initial notice is to be treated as the deposit of plans, (b) the plans accompanying the initial notice are to be treated as the deposited plans, (c) the acceptance or rejection of the notice is to be treated as the passing or rejection of deposited plans, and (d) the

cancellation of an initial notice under s.44(5) is to be treated as a declaration under s.66 of the 1936 Act that the deposit of plans is to be of no effect. There are parallel provisions in relation to fire precaution requirements.

Approved inspectors

41.—(1) In the enactments relating to building regulations "approved inspector" means a person who, in accordance with building regulations, is approved for the purposes of this Part of this Act—

(a) by the Secretary of State; or

(b) by a body (corporate or unincorporated) which, in accordance with the regulations, is designated by the Secretary of State for the purpose.

(2) Any such approval as is referred to in subsection (1) above may limit the description of work in relation to which the person concerned is an approved inspector.

(3) Any such designation as is referred to in subsection (1)(b) above may limit the cases in which and the terms on which the body designated may approve a person and, in particular, may provide that any approval given by the body shall be limited as mentioned in subsection (2) above.

(4) There shall be paid on an application for any such approval as is referred to in subsection (1) above—

(a) where the application is made to the Secretary of State, such fee as may be prescribed by building regulations;

(b) where the application is made to a body designated by him as mentioned in that subsection, such fee as that body may determine.

(5) Building regulations may—

(a) contain provision prescribing the period for which, subject to any provision made by virtue of paragraph (b) or (c) below, any such approval as is referred to in subsection (1) above shall continue in force;

(b) contain provision precluding the giving of, or requiring the withdrawal of, any such approval as is referred to in that subsection in such circumstances as may be prescribed by the regulations;

(c) contain provision authorising the withdrawal of any such approval or designation as is so referred to;

(d) provide for the maintenance by the Secretary of State of a list of bodies who are for the time being designated by him as mentioned in subsection (1) above and for the maintenance by the Secretary of State and by each designated body of a list of persons for the time being approved by him or them as mentioned in that subsection;

(e) make provision for the supply to local authorities of copies of any list of approved inspectors maintained by virtue of paragraph (d) above and for such copy lists to be made available for inspection; and

(f) make provision for the supply, on payment of a prescribed fee, of a certified copy of any entry in a list maintained by virtue of paragraph (d) above or in a copy list held by a local authority by virtue of paragraph (e) above.

(6) Unless the contrary is proved, in any proceedings (whether civil or criminal) a document which appears to the court to be a certified copy of an entry either in a list maintained as mentioned in subsection (5)(d) above or in a copy of such a list supplied as mentioned in subsection (5)(e) above—

(a) shall be presumed to be a true copy of an entry in the current list so maintained; and

(b) shall be evidence of the matters stated therein.

(7) In subsection (1) of section 62 of the 1974 Act (building regulations may require local authorities to undertake consultation in prescribed circumstances) after the words "local authorities" there shall be inserted the words "and approved inspectors".

(8) An approved inspector may make such charges in respect of the carrying out of functions referred to in section 39(1) above as may in any particular case be agreed between him and the person who intends to carry out the work in question or, as the case may be, by whom that work is being or has been carried out.

(9) Nothing in this Part of this Act prevents an approved inspector from arranging for plans or work to be inspected on his behalf by another person; but any such delegation—

(*a*) shall not extend to the giving of any certificate under section 42 or section 43 below; and

(*b*) shall not affect any liability, whether civil or criminal, of the approved inspector which arises out of functions conferred on him by this Part of this Act or by building regulations;

and, without prejudice to the generality of paragraph (*b*) above, an approved inspector shall be liable for negligence on the part of any person carrying out any inspection on his behalf in like manner as if it were negligence by a servant of his acting in the course of his employment.

DEFINITIONS
the enactments relating to building regulations: s.51(1).
local authority: s.51 and s.76(2) of the Health and Safety at Work etc. Act 1974.

GENERAL NOTE
This section provides for the approval of inspectors and related matters.

Subs. (1)
An approved inspector is a person approved either by the Secretary of State or by a body designated by him.

Subs. (2)
The approval of an inspector may be limited to particular kinds of work.

Subs. (3)
Building regulations may provide that the designation of an approving body may limit the kind of work for which the body can approve inspectors, and that the body may similarly limit their approval to particular kinds of work.

Subs. (4)
Fees are payable on an application for approval.

Subs. (5)
Building regulations may provide for the period of appointment, may preclude approval, or require the withdrawal of approval, in specified circumstances. They may provide for withdrawal of approval of an inspector or designation of a body, for the maintenance of lists of approved inspectors and designated bodies, for the supply of such lists to local authorities and their inspection by the public, and for the supply of a copy of an entry in such lists on payment of a prescribed fee.

Subs. (8)
The fee payable to an approved inspector is one agreed between the inspector and the developer.

Subs. (9)
An approved inspector may delegate work to another person, except the power to issue a certificate under s.42 (plans certificate) or s.43 (final certificate). Legal responsibility for the acts of the delegatee remains with the approved inspector.

An approved inspector by virtue of s.39 undertakes functions in relation to the inspection of plans, the suprevision of work and the giving of certificates and other notices. A failure on his part to discharge these functions or any of them properly may render the approved inspector liable for breach of contract (he undertakes work on payment of a fee) and/or liable for breach of statutory duty and/or liable in negligence.

The body of law concerning liability of authorities and officers of authorities for acts or omissions in regard to the carrying out of statutory functions under building regulations legislation has, it is submitted, relevance to the carrying out by approved inspectors of their functions under this Part of this Act.

In *Dutton* v. *Bognor Regis Urban District Council* [1972] 1 Q.B. 373 approval was given under the building by-laws in respect of a dwelling-house and it contained a footnote stating that all foundations were to be examined by the council's surveyor before being covered up. The council's building by-laws included detailed provisions as to foundations. At the end of 1959 the council's building inspector inspected the excavations for the foundations of the house and approved the works. In fact the works did not comply with the by-laws and ought not to have been approved, for a competent inspection would have revealed that the house was being built, in part, on insecure and made-up foundations. In 1960 the plaintiff bought the house as second owner. It deteriorated and a concrete slab on which a load-bearing wall had rested subsided away from the wall leaving it unsupported. *Held,* the council were liable. Cusack J. at first instance, said:

> "The purpose of the building by-laws, including the inspection of the site of the building in the course of erection, is the protection of the public. There is ample authority for saying that if a local authority exercises its statutory powers to the injury of a member of the public, the injured person may be entitled to sue: see for example *McClelland* v. *Manchester Corporation* [1912] 1 K.B. 118. In my view it must be in the contemplation of those who gave approval to building works that such approval will affect subsequent owners of the house. The council, through its building inspector, owed a duty to the plaintiff. The inspector was negligent. The council should therefore, on the facts as I find and the law as I believe it is, be found liable."

The decision was upheld by the Court of Appeal ([1972] 1 Q.B. 373). The Master of the Rolls said that the legislature had entrusted to the local authority a control so extensive over building work and the way in which it was done that it carried with it a duty to exercise that control properly and with reasonable care. So the authority, having a right of control over the building of a house, must take reasonable care to see that the by-laws are complied with. The inspectors must be diligent, visiting the work as occasion requires and carrying out their inspection with reasonable care.

But to whom, asked His Lordship, was that duty owed? Since *Hedley B. Byrne & Co. Ltd.* v. *Heller and Partners* [1964] A.C. 465 it is clear that the professional man who gives guidance to others owes a duty of care, not only to his client, but also to a another who he knows is relying on his skill to save him from harm. House foundations, the subject of the present appeal, are in a class by themselves. Once covered up they will not be seen again until the damage appears. The inspector must have known or ought to have known that. Applying Lord Atkin's test (the test of "Who is My Neighbour?" in *Donoghue* v. *Stevenson* [1932] 2 A.C. 562 at p. 580) the inspector should have had subsequent purchasers in mind when inspecting the foundations and ought to have realised that if he was negligent they might suffer damage. There was something in the defendant Counsel's contention that the duty should be limited to those immediately concerned and not to purchaser after purchaser down the line, but this could apply only where immediate inspection or opportunity of inspection, by a surveyor for a subsequent purchaser, might break the proximity.

Dutton v. *Bognor Regis Urban District Council* was considered and applied by the House of Lords in *Anns* v. *Merton London Borough Council* [1977] 2 W.L.R. 1024. In 1962 the appellant local council approved building plans for a block of flats, the construction of which was completed that year. In 1970 structural movements led to walls cracking and other damage; in 1972 the lessees commenced proceedings against, *inter alia,* the council, alleging negligence in failing to inspect the building walls properly or at all so as to ensure that the foundations were built to the appropriate depth as shown on the approved plans. Upon hearing the council's appeal concerning whether the actions were statute-barred, the House of Lords agreed further to consider whether the council were under a duty of care. It was held, *inter alia,* that where an inspection was made the duty was to take reasonable care, and that the standard of care had to be related to the duty to be performed, namely, to ensure compliance with by-laws.

Anns was applied in *Acrecrest* v. *Hattrell and Partners* [1982] 3 W.L.R. 1076. The plaintiff company employed the defendant builders and architects to build on their land a block of flats and garages. After completion cracks appeared caused by defective foundations. The defendants had prepared specifications providing for foundations three feet six inches deep but, at the plaintiff's request, revised that to three feet. The local authority building inspector instructed that in part of the site they were to be five feet deep and elsewhere three feet six inches deep or four feet deep. In fact the Building Regulations required five feet overall. The plaintiffs claimed damages for negligence and breach of contract against the defendant who joined the local authority as third parties to the action. The plaintiffs obtained judgment by consent against the defendant who proceeded to trial for contribution from the local authority. It was held that the local authority owed the plaintiffs a duty of care and apportioned their liability at 25 per cent. On appeal the Court of Appeal, dismissing the local authority's appeal, held that a building owner who had contracted the work to an independent contractor and who was not himself negligent was included in the class of persons to whom a local authority owed a duty to take reasonable care in inspection and approval of building works. Since the foundations were constructed in accordance with the requirements of the inspector there was a direct causal link between the negligence and the damage suffered by the plaintiff. An owner who employed a builder and architect did not thereby remove himself from the class of persons reasonably likely to be affected by the local authority's negligence or breach of statutory duty. Accordingly the local authority were liable as joint tortfeasors and the defendants were entitled to contribution from them.

If a local authority fails to take reasonable care in approving plans under the building regulations it may be liable in negligence; see *Dennis* v. *Charnwood Borough Council* [1982] 3 All E.R. 486.

In *Worlock* v. *Saws* [1981] E.G. 920 a builder with no previous experience built a bungalow, the foundations of which were defective. The authority's inspector failed to notice the defects and the bungalow suffered serious damage. On the question as to contribution to damages as between the builder and the local authority it was held that primary responsibility remained with the builder. In this case, however, as there was no architect, the supervisory role of the authority was of particular importance and the builder was held 60 per cent. to blame and the local authority 40 per cent.

In *Bluett* v. *Woodspring District Council* [1983] J.P.L. 242 it was held that a cause of action for negligent inspection had not accrued because although the inspection had been at fault the building was not such as to present imminent danger to the health and safety of those occupying it.

A cause of action accrues when physical damage occurs, not, as was at one time considered to be the case, when the damage could have been discovered with reasonable diligence; see *Pirelli General Cable Works Ltd.* v. *Oscar Faber and Partners* [1983] 1 All E.R. 61, in which certain dicta in *Sparham-Souter* v. *Town and Country Developments (Essex) Ltd.* [1976] Q.B. 858 at pp. 875, 880 and 881 were disapproved.

Plans certificates

42.—(1) Where an approved inspector—

   (*a*) has inspected plans of the work specified in an initial notice given by him, and

   (*b*) is satisfied that the plans neither are defective nor show that work carried out in accordance with them would contravene any provision of building regulations, and

   (*c*) has complied with any prescribed requirements as to consultation or otherwise,

he shall, if requested to do so by the person intending to carry out the work, give a certificate in the prescribed form (in the enactments relating to building regulations referred to as a "plans certificate") to the local authority and to that person.

(2) In any case where any question arises under subsection (1) above between an approved inspector and a person who proposes to carry out any work whether plans of the work are in conformity with building regulations, that person may refer the question to the Secretary of State for his determination; and an application for a reference under this subsection shall be accompanied by such fee as may be prescribed by building regulations.

(3) Building regulations may authorise the giving of an initial notice combined with a certificate under subsection (1) above and may prescribe

a single form for such a combined notice and certificate; and where such a prescribed form is used—

    (*a*) any reference in this Part of this Act to an initial notice or to a plans certificate shall be construed as including a reference to that form; but

    (*b*) should the form cease to be in force as an initial notice by virtue of subsection (4) of section 39 above, nothing in that subsection shall affect the continuing validity of the form as a plans certificate.

  (4) A plans certificate—

    (*a*) may relate either to the whole or to part only of the work specified in the initial notice concerned; and

    (*b*) shall not have effect unless it is accepted by the local authority to whom it is given.

  (5) A local authority to whom a plans certificate is given—

    (*a*) may not reject the certificate except on prescribed grounds; and

    (*b*) shall reject the certificate if any of the prescribed grounds exists.

  (6) Unless, within the prescribed period, the local authority to whom a plans certificate is given give notice of rejection, specifying the ground or grounds in question, to—

    (*a*) the approved inspector by whom the certificate was given, and

    (*b*) the other person to whom the approved inspector gave the certificate,

the authority shall be conclusively presumed to have accepted the certificate.

  (7) If it appears to a local authority by whom a plans certificate has been accepted that the work to which the certificate relates has not been commenced within the period of three years beginning on the date on which the certificate was accepted, the authority may rescind their acceptance of the certificate by notice, specifying the ground or grounds in question, given—

    (*a*) to the approved inspector by whom the certificate was given; and

    (*b*) to the person shown in the initial notice concerned as the person intending to carry out the work.

DEFINITIONS

  approved inspector: ss.41(1) and 51(1).
  carrying out of work: s.51(2).
  initial notice: ss.39(1) and 51(1).
  local authority: s.51 and s.76(2) of the Health and Safety at Work etc. Act 1974.

Subs. (1)

  Where an approved inspector has inspected plans and is satisfied that they show compliance with the building regulations, and has complied with any prescribed requirement as to consultation or otherwise, he must if the developer requests it give a certificate to the authority and the developer.

  As to the duty to consult with fire authorities; see ss.15, 16 and 17 of the Fire Precautions Act 1971.

Subs. (2)

  Where any question arises between an approved inspector and a developer as to whether plans comply with the building regulations, the developer may refer the question to the Secretary of State. (This subsection comes into operation on a date to be appointed by the Secretary of State; see s.66(2).)

Subs. (3)

  An initial notice may be combined with a plans certificate. Where an initial notice is cancelled (see s.44) the plans certificate remains valid.

Subs. (5)
A plans certificate may only be, and must be, rejected on prescribed grounds. As to an appeal against rejection; see s.47.

Subs. (6)
Failure to give notice of rejection within the prescribed time is deemed to be acceptance.

Subs. (7)
A plans certificate may be rescinded if work has not begun within three years of its acceptance by the authority. This provision is complementary to s.66 of the Public Health Act 1936.

Final certificates

43.—(1) Where an approved inspector is satisfied that any work specified in an initial notice given by him has been completed, he shall give—
    (*a*) to the local authority by whom the initial notice was accepted, and
    (*b*) to the person by whom the work was carried out,
such certificate with respect to the completion of the work and the discharge of his functions as may be prescribed (in the enactments relating to building regulations referred to as a "final certificate").
    (2) Subsections (4) to (6) of section 42 above shall have effect in relation to a final certificate as if any reference in those subsections to a plans certificate were a reference to a final certificate.
    (3) Where a final certificate has been given with respect to any of the work specified in an initial notice and that certificate has been accepted by the local authority concerned, the initial notice shall cease to apply to that work, but the provisions of section 40(1) above shall, by virtue of this subsection, continue to apply in relation to that work as if the initial notice continued in force in relation to it.

DEFINITIONS
    approved inspector: ss.41(1) and 51(1).
    carrying out of work: s.51(2).
    enactment: s.51(1).
    initial notice: ss.39(1) and 51(1).
    local authority: s.51 and s.76(2) of the Health and Safety at Work etc. Act 1974.

GENERAL NOTE
An approved inspector is required to give a certificate with respect to the completion of the work and the discharge of his prescribed functions. Upon acceptance by the authority the initial notice ceases to apply to that work, save that the authority's enforcement powers suspended on the acceptance of the initial notice under s.40(1) remain suspended. Those enforcement powers are contained in s.65(1) of the Public Health Act 1936 and s.4(6) of the Public Health Act 1961.

Cancellation of initial notice

44.—(1) If, at any time when an initial notice is in force—
    (*a*) the approved inspector becomes or expects to become unable to carry out (or to continue to carry out) his functions with respect to any of the work specified in the initial notice, or
    (*b*) the approved inspector is of the opinion that any of the work is being so carried out that he is unable adequately to carry out his functions with respect to it, or
    (*c*) the approved inspector is of the opinion that there is a contravention of any provision of building regulations with respect to any of that work and the circumstances are as mentioned in subsection (2) below,

the approved inspector shall cancel the initial notice by notice in the prescribed form given to the local authority concerned and to the person carrying out or intending to carry out the work.

(2) The circumstances referred to in subsection (1)(*c*) above are—

    (*a*) that the approved inspector has, in accordance with building regulations, given notice of the contravention to the person carrying out the work; and

    (*b*) that, within the prescribed period, that person has neither pulled down nor removed the work nor effected such alterations in it as may be necessary to make it comply with building regulations.

(3) If, at a time when an initial notice is in force, it appears to the person carrying out or intending to carry out the work specified in the notice that the approved inspector is no longer willing or able to carry out his functions with respect to any of that work, he shall cancel the initial notice by notice in the prescribed form given to the local authority concerned and, if it is practicable to do so, to the approved inspector.

(4) If any person fails without reasonable excuse to give to a local authority a notice which he is required to give by subsection (3) above he shall be liable on summary conviction to a fine not exceeding level 5 on the standard scale (as defined in section 75 of the Criminal Justice Act 1982).

(5) If, at a time when an initial notice is in force, it appears to the local authority by whom the initial notice was accepted that the work to which the initial notice relates has not been commenced within the period of three years beginning on the date on which the initial notice was accepted, the authority may cancel the initial notice by notice in the prescribed form given—

    (*a*) to the approved inspector by whom the initial notice was given; and

    (*b*) to the person shown in the initial notice as the person intending to carry out the work.

(6) A notice under subsection (1), (3) or (5) above shall have the effect of cancelling the initial notice to which it relates with effect from the day on which the notice is given.

<small>DEFINITIONS</small>
    approved inspector: ss.41(1) and 51(1).
    carrying out of work: s.51(2).
    contravention: s.51(1).
    initial notice: ss.39(1) and 51(1).
    local authority: s.51 and s.76(2) of the Health and Safety at Work etc. Act 1974.

<small>GENERAL NOTE</small>
    An approved inspector must serve notice on the local authority and developer, cancelling the initial notice, (a) when the inspector can no longer carry out his functions, (b) when the inspector considers that work is being carried out in a way which prevents him from carrying out his functions, (c) where the inspector considers that there is a contravention of the building regulations. The inspector will not proceed under (c) until he has given notice of a contravention to the developer, and the developer has not, within a prescribed period, altered the work to make it comply.

Subs. (5)
    Where it appears to the local authority that the work specified in an initial notice has not been commenced within three years of the acceptance of the notice the authority may cancel the notice. As to the service of notices; see s.51(4) and s.285 of the Public Health Act 1936.

Effect of initial notice ceasing to be in force

45.—(1) The provisions of this section apply where an initial notice ceases to be in force by virtue of paragraph (*a*) or paragraph (*b*) of subsection (4) of section 39 above.

(2) Building regulations may provide that, if—

    (*a*) a plans certificate was given before the day on which the initial notice ceased to be in force, and

    (*b*) that certificate was accepted by the local authority (before, on or after that day), and

    (*c*) before that day, that acceptance was not rescinded by a notice under section 42(7) above,

then, with respect to the work specified in the certificate, such of the functions of a local authority referred to in section 40(1) above as may be prescribed for the purposes of this subsection either shall not be exercisable or shall be exercisable only in prescribed circumstances.

(3) If, before the day on which the initial notice ceased to be in force, a final certificate was given in respect of part of the work specified in the initial notice and that certificate was accepted by the local authority (before, on or after that day), the fact that the initial notice has ceased to be in force shall not affect the continuing operation of section 43(3) above in relation to that part of the work.

(4) Notwithstanding anything in subsections (2) and (3) above, for the purpose of enabling the local authority to perform the functions referred to in section 40(1) above in relation to any part of the work not specified in a plans certificate or final certificate, as the case may be, building regulations may require the local authority to be provided with plans which relate not only to that part but also to the part to which the certificate in question relates.

(5) In any case where this section applies, the reference in subsection (4) of section 65 of the 1936 Act (twelve month time limit for giving certain notices) to the date of the completion of the work in question shall have effect, in relation to a notice under subsection (1) of that section, as if it were a reference to the date on which the initial notice ceased to be in force.

(6) Subject to any provision of building regulations made by virtue of subsection (2) above, if, before the initial notice ceased to be in force, an offence under section 4(6) of the 1961 Act (contravention of provisions of building regulations) was committed with respect to any of the work specified in that notice, summary proceedings for that offence may be commenced by the local authority at any time within six months beginning with the day on which the functions of the local authority referred to in section 40(1) above became exercisable with respect to the provision of building regulations to which the offence relates.

(7) The fact that an initial notice has ceased to be in force shall not affect the right to give a new initial notice relating to any of the work which was specified in the original notice and in respect of which no final certificate has been given and accepted; but where—

    (*a*) a plans certificate has been given in respect of any of that work, and

    (*b*) the conditions in paragraphs (*a*) to (*c*) of subsection (2) above are fulfilled with respect to that certificate, and

    (*c*) such a new initial notice is given and accepted,

section 42(1) above shall not apply in relation to so much of the work to which the new initial notice relates as is work specified in the plans certificate.

DEFINITIONS
final certificate: ss.43(1) and 51(1).
initial notice: ss.39(1) and 51(1).
local authority: s.51 and s.76(2) of the Health and Safety at Work etc. Act 1974.
plans certificate: ss.42(1) and (3) and 51(1) and (3).

GENERAL NOTE
By virtue of s.40(1) the suspension of the enforcement powers of a local authority continues only for so long as an initial notice is in force. An initial notice may cease to be in force in the circumstances described in s.39(4). This section imposes certain limitations on the local authority's powers in respect of work to which plans certificates or final certificates were given while the initial notice was still in force.

Subs. (2)
Provision may be made by regulation to deal with the situation where a plans certificate was given before the day on which the initial notice ceased to be in force, and was accepted. Some or all of the local authority's functions referred to in s.40(1) shall not be exercisable or shall be exercisable only in prescribed circumstances. These functions are concerned with enforcement.

Subs. (3)
If a final certificate in respect of part of the work was given before the day on which the initial notice ceased to be in force, and was accepted, s.43(3) continues to operate in respect of that part of the work.

Subs. (4)
Building regulations may require local authorities to be given plans of work which has been the subject of a certificate. This is to enable an authority to carry out enforcement functions regarding work not in the certificate.

Subs. (5)
Under s.65 of the Public Health Act 1936, if any work to which building regulations are applicable contravenes any of the building regulations, the authority may by notice require the owner to pull down or alter the work. But no such notice may be served after the expiration of twelve months from the date of completion of the work. In the circumstances in which this section applies the period of twelve months will run from the date on which the initial notice ceased to have effect.

Subs. (6)
Under s.4(6) of the Public Health Act 1961 an authority may institute a prosecution in the Magistrates' Court for an offence of contravening the building regulations. Pursuant to s.127 of the Magistrates Courts Act 1980 proceedings may be commenced within six months of the offence being committed. In the circumstances to which this section applies the period of six months will run from the date on which the local authority's powers became exercisable.

Supervision of their own work by public bodies

Giving, acceptance and effect of public body's notice

46.—(1) This section applies where a body (corporate or unincorporated) which acts under any enactment for public purposes and not for its own profit and is, or is of a description which is, approved by the Secretary of State in accordance with building regulations (in this Part of this Act referred to as a "public body")—

(*a*) intends to carry out in relation to a building belonging to it work to which the substantive requirements of building regulations apply; and

(*b*) considers that the work can be adequately supervised by its own servants or agents; and

(*c*) gives to the local authority in whose district the work is to be carried out notice in the prescribed form (in the enactments relating to building regulations referred to as a "public body's notice") together with such plans of the work as may be prescribed.

(2) A public body's notice shall be of no effect unless it is accepted by the local authority to whom it is given; and that local authority—3

(*a*) may not reject the notice except on prescribed grounds, and

(*b*) shall reject the notice if any of the prescribed grounds exists, and in any case where the work to which the public body's notice relates is work of such a description that, if plans of it had been deposited with the local authority, the authority could, under any enactment, have imposed requirements as a condition of passing the plans, the local authority may impose the like requirements as a condition of accepting the public body's notice.

(3) Unless, within the prescribed period, the local authority to whom a public body's notice is given give notice of rejection, specifying the ground or grounds in question, the authority shall be conclusively presumed to have accepted the public body's notice and to have done so without imposing any such requirements as are referred to in subsection (2) above.

(4) Section 40 above shall have effect for the purposes of this section—

(*a*) with the substitution of a reference to a public body's notice for any reference to an initial notice; and

(*b*) with the substitution, in subsection (2)(*a*), of a reference to subsection (1)(*c*) of this section for the reference to section 39(1)(*b*).

(5) The form prescribed for a public body's notice may be such as to require the public body by whom it is to be given—

(*a*) to furnish information relevant for the purposes of this Part of this Act, Part II or Part IV of the 1936 Act, Part II of the 1961 Act or any provision of building regulations; and

(*b*) to enter into undertakings with respect to consultation and other matters.

(6) Where a public body's notice is given and accepted by the local authority to whom it is given, the provisions of Schedule 8 to this Act shall have effect, being provisions which correspond, as near as may be, to those made by the preceding provisions of this Part of this Act for the case where an initial notice is given and accepted.

DEFINITIONS

the 1936 Act: s.51(1).
the 1961 Act: s.51(1).
building: see General Note.
carrying out of work: s.51(2).
enactment: s.51(1).
local authority: s.51 and s.76(2) of the Health and Safety at Work etc. Act 1974.

GENERAL NOTE

This section together with Sched. 8 provides that public bodies approved by the Secretary of State may supervise the work they carry out on their own buildings. By virtue of s.51(4) the definition of "building" for this purpose is that contained in s.74(1) of the Health and Safety at Work etc. Act 1974. The text of s.74 appears in the notes to subs. (4) of s.51, below.

A public body may serve a notice similar to an initial notice under s.39, accompanied by prescribed plans. The procedure in relation to a public body's notice is similar to the procedure in relation to an initial notice. The appropriate modifications are contained in Sched. 8.

Subs. (2)

See note to subs. 2 of s.39 as to statutory grounds of rejection of application for approval under building regulations and as to conditions which may be attached to the passing of plans.

Subs. (3)

As to the right of appeal in case of rejection, see s.47.

Supplemental

Appeals

47.—(1) A person aggrieved by the local authority's rejection of—

(a) an initial notice or a public body's notice, or

(b) a plans certificate, a final certificate, a public body's plans certificate or a public body's final certificate,

may appeal to a magistrates' court acting for the petty sessions area in which is situated land on which will be or has been carried out any work to which the notice or certificate relates.

(2) On an appeal under this section the court shall—

(a) if they determine that the notice or certificate was properly rejected, confirm the rejection; and

(b) in any other case, give a direction to the local authority to accept the notice or certificate.

(3) The procedure on appeal to a magistrates' court under this section shall be by way of complaint for an order and the Magistrates' Courts Act 1980 shall apply to the proceedings.

DEFINITIONS

carrying out of work: s.51(2).
final certificate: ss.43(1) and 51(1).
initial notice: ss.39(1) and 51(1).
local authority: s.51 and s.76(2) of the Health and Safety at Work etc. Act 1974.
plans certificate: ss.42(1) and (3) and 51(1) and (3).
public body's final certificate: s.51(1) and Sched. 8, para. 3.
public body's plans certificate: ss.51(1) and Sched. 8, para. 2.

GENERAL NOTE

This section gives a right of appeal to the magistrates' court against a local authority's rejection of an initial notice, a plans certificate or a final certificate given by an approved inspector or public body. The court may confirm the rejection or give a direction to the authority to accept the notice or certificate.

By virtue of s.51(4), the provisions of s.300 of the Public Health Act 1936 apply to appeals under this section. The time for bringing an appeal is 21 days from the date on which the council's rejection was served on the person desiring to appeal. The document notifying the council's rejection must state the right of appeal and the time within which an appeal may be brought.

Subs. (3)

As to the issue of a summons on complaint, see s.51 of the Magistrates' Courts Act 1980.

Register of notices and certificates

48.—(1) Every local authority shall keep, in such manner as may be prescribed, a register containing such information as may be prescribed with respect to initial notices, public body's notices and certificates given to them, including information as to whether such notices or certificates have been accepted or rejected.

(2) The information which may be prescribed under subsection (1) above with respect to an initial notice includes information with respect to the insurance cover provided with respect to the work in which the initial notice relates.

(3) The reference in subsection (1) above to certificates is a reference to plans certificates, final certificates, public body's plans certificates, public body's final certificates and certificates given under section 64(2C) of the 1936 Act (which provision is set out in section 56 below).

(4) Every register kept under this section shall be available for inspection by the public at all reasonable hours.

DEFINITIONS
final certificate: ss.43(1) and 51(1).
initial notice: ss.39(1) and 51(1).
local authority: s.51 and s. 76(2) of the Health and Safety at Work etc. Act 1974.
plans certificate: ss.42(1) and (3) and 51(1) and (3).
public body's notice: ss.46(1) and 51(1).
public body's final certificate: s.51(1) and Sched. 8, para. 3.
public body's plans certificate: ss.51(1) and Sched. 8, para. 2.

GENERAL NOTE
This section requires local authorities to keep registers of notices and certificates, indicating whether they were accepted or rejected, to be available for public inspection at all reasonable hours.

Subs. (1)
certificates: see subs. (3).

Subs. (2)
insurance cover: see s.39(1)(*c*).

Offences

49.—(1) If any person—
   (*a*) gives a notice or certificate which purports to comply with the requirements of this Part of this Act or, as the case may be, of section 64(2C) of the 1936 Act and which contains a statement which he knows to be false or misleading in a material particular, or
   (*b*) recklessly gives a notice or certificate which purports to comply with those requirements and which contains a statement which is false or misleading in a material particular,
he shall be guilty of an offence.
   (2) A person guilty of an offence under subsection (1) above shall be liable—
   (*a*) on summary conviction, to a fine not exceeding the statutory maximum (as defined in section 74 of the Criminal Justice Act 1982) or imprisonment for a term not exceeding six months or both; and
   (*b*) on conviction on indictment, to a fine or imprisonment for a term not exceeding two years or both.
   (3) Where an approved inspector or person approved for the purposes of section 64(2C) of the 1936 Act is convicted of an offence under this section, the court by or before which he is convicted shall, within one month of the date of conviction, forward a certificate of the conviction to the person by whom the approval was given.

DEFINITIONS
the 1936 Act: s.51(1).
approved inspector: ss.41(1) and 51(1).

GENERAL NOTE
It is an offence (a) to give a notice or certificate which the person giving it knows to contain a false or misleading statement or (b) to give a notice or certificate recklessly where it contains a false or misleading statement.

Subs. (1)
false or misleading in a material particular: In *R.* v. *Kylsant (Lord)* [1932] 1 K.B. 442 it was held that a written statement may be false within the meaning of the Larceny Act 1861, s.84, not only because of what it stated by also because of what it withheld, omitted or implied.

recklessly: See *R.* v. *Lawrence* [1981] 1 All E.R. 974, where Lord Diplock said, at p.982, that recklessness on the part of the doer of an act presupposes that there is something in the circumstances that would have drawn the attention of an ordinary purdent individual to the possibility that his act was capable of causing the kind of serious harmful consequences that the section that created the offence was intended to prevent, and that the risk of those harmful consequences occurring was not so slight that an ordinary prudent individual would feel justified in treating them as negligible. It is only when this is so that the doer of the act is acting *recklessly* if, before doing the act, he either fails to give any thought to the possibility of there being any such risk, or having recognised that there was such a risk, he nevertheless goes on to do it. See also *R.* v. *Caldwell* [1981] 1 All E.R. 964, at p.966, and *Derry* v. *Peek* (1889) 14 App. Cas. 337, *R.* v. *Grunwald* [1963] 1 Q.B. 965, and *Shawnigan Ltd.* v. *Vokins & Co. Ltd.* [1961] 3 All E.R. 396.

Information, reports and returns

50. Where an initial notice or a public body's notice has continued in force for any period, the local authority by whom it was accepted may require the approved inspector or public body by whom it was given to furnish them with any information which—

(*a*) they would have obtained themselves if during that period their function of enforcing building regulations had continued to be exercisable in relation to the work specified in the notice; and

(*b*) they require for the purpose of performing their duty under section 230 of the Local Government Act 1972 (reports and returns);

and that section shall have effect as if during that period that function had continued to be so exercisable.

DEFINITIONS
approved inspector: ss.41(1) and 51(1).
initial notice: ss.39(1) and 51(1).
local authority: ss.51 and 76(2) of the Health and Safety at Work etc. Act 1974.
public body's notice: ss.46(1) and 51(1).

GENERAL NOTE
enforcing building regulations: See notes to s.45(5) and (6).
s.230 of the Local Government Act 1972: Under this provision the Secretary of State may call for reports, returns and other information.

Interpretation of Part II

51.—(1) In this Part of this Act—
"the 1936 Act" means the Public Health Act 1936;
"the 1961 Act" means the Public Health Act 1961;
"the 1974 Act" means the Health and Safety at Work etc. Act 1974;
"approved inspector" has the meaning assigned to it by section 41(1) above;
"contravention", in relation to any provision of building regulations, includes a failure to comply with that provision;
"enactment" includes any enactment contained in a local Act;
"the enactments relating to building regulations" means this Part of this Act and the enactments referred to in section 76(1) of the 1974 Act;
"final certificate" has the meaning assigned to it by section 43(1) above;
"initial notice" has the meaning assigned to it by section 39(1) above;
"plans certificate" has the meaning assigned to it by section 42(1) above;
"public body" and "public body's notice" have the meaning assigned to them by section 46(1) above;
"public body's final certificate" has the meaning assigned to it by paragraph 3 of Schedule 8 to this Act; and

"public body's plans certificate" has the meaning assigned to it by paragraph 2 of that Schedule.

(2) Any reference in this Part of this Act to the carrying out of work includes a reference to the making of a material change of use, as defined by and for the purposes of building regulations.

(3) Any reference in this Part of this Act to an initial notice given by an approved inspector is a reference to a notice given by him jointly with another person as mentioned in section 39(1)(*a*) above.

(4) Sections 74 and 76 of the 1974 Act (construction and interpretation) shall have effect as if the preceding provisions of this Part of this Act (other than subsection (1) above) were included in Part III of the 1974 Act.

GENERAL NOTE
Subs. (1)
   the enactments relating to building regulations: S.76(1) is reproduced under the notes to subs. (4).

Subs. (4)
   S.74 of the Health and Safety at Work etc. Act 1974 is reproduced below.
   74.—(1) For the purposes of any enactment to which this subsection applies—
      (*a*) "building" means any permanent or temporary building and, unless the context otherwise requires, includes any other structure or erection of whatever kind or nature (whether permanent or temporary), and in this paragraph, "structure or erection" shall include a vehicle, vessel, hovercraft, aircraft or other movable object of any kind in such circumstances as may be prescribed (being circumstances which in the opinion of the Secretary of State justify treating it for those purposes as a building);
      (*b*) unless the context otherwise requires, any reference to a building includes a reference to part of a building, and any reference to the provision of services, fittings and equipment in or in connection with buildings, or to services, fittings and equipment so provided, includes a reference to the affixing of things to buildings or, as the case may be, to things so affixed; and
      (*c*) references to the construction or erection of a building shall include references to—
         (i) the carrying out of such operations (whether for the reconstruction of a building, the roofing over of an open space between walls or buildings, or otherwise) as may be designated in building regulations as operations falling to be treated for those purposes as the construction or erection of a building, and
         (ii) the conversion of a movable object into what is by virtue of paragraph (*a*) above a building,
      and "construct" and "erect" shall be construed accordingly.
   (2) The preceding subsection applies to sections 61 to 71 of the 1936 Act and to any other enactment (whether or not contained in the 1936 Act or this Act) which relates to building regulations or mentions "buildings" or "a building" in a context from which it appears that those expressions are there intended to have the same meaning as in the said sections 61 to 71.
   (3) Unless the context otherwise requires, references in this Act or any other enactment (whether passed before or after this Act) to building regulations shall, in any particular case in relation to which any requirement of building regulations is for the time being dispensed with, waived, relaxed or modified by virtue of section 6 of the 1961 Act, section 66 of this Act or any other enactment, be construed as references to building regulations as they apply in that case.
   S.74 provides for the first time a comprehensive definition of "building" for the purposes of the building regulations and certain related enactments. The regulations can only apply to "buildings" as defined. The term was not defined by the Public Health Acts 1936 and 1961 or by the Building Regulations 1972 themselves. There are many decisions as to what is and what is not a building under other legislation: see *South Shields Corporation* v. *Wilson Bros.* (1901) 65 J.P. 294 (wooden shed intended for use as a stable); *Richardson* v. *Brown*

(1885) 49 J.P. 661 (wooden structure on wheels used as a butcher's shop and connected to the main gas supply); *Stevens* v. *Gourley* (1859) 7 C.B.(N.S.) 99 (a house built without foundations); *Venner* v. *McDonnell* [1897] 1 Q.B. 421 (movable seating at an exhibition); *Moran & Son* v. *Marsland* [1909] 1 K.B. 774 (covered storage reservoirs); *Schweder* v. *Worthing Gas Light & Coke Co.* [1912] 1 Ch. 83 (underground vault); *Regent's Canal & Dock Co.* v. *L.C.C.* [1912] 1 Ch. 583 (canal and retaining walls); *Morrison* v. *Commissioners of Inland Revenue* [1915] 1 K.B. 716 and *Att.-Gen. and Great Yarmouth Port Commissioners* v. *Harrison* (1920) 85 J.P. 54 (walls and fences); *Gery* v. *Black Lion Brewery Co.* (1891) 55 J.P. 711 (sunken boiler); *Mackenzie* v. *Abbott* (1926) 24 L.G.R. 44 (petrol pump); *Newell* v. *Ormskirk Urban District Council* (1907) 71 J.P. 119 (portable wooden theatre); *Super Sites* v. *Keen* [1938] 2 All E.R. 471 (advertisement hoarding); *Portsmouth Corpn.* v. *Thomas* (1959) 178 E.G. 273 (back wall). The new definition is extremely wide, and s.74(1)(*a*) enables the Secretary of State to apply the building regulations to movable objects in circumstances in which, in his opinion, it is justifiable to treat such a movable object as a building.

S.76 of the Health and Safety at Work etc. Act 1974 is reproduced below.

76.—(1) The following provisions, namely—
   (*a*) so much of Part II of the 1936 Act as relates to building regulations;
   (*b*) so much of Part II of the 1961 Act as relates to building regulations; and
   (*c*) this Part, except section 75 and Schedule 7;
shall be construed as one; and Part XII of the 1936 Act shall have effect as if the provisions mentioned in paragraph (*b*) and (*c*) above (as well as those mentioned in paragraph (*a*)) were contained in Part II of that Act.

(2) For the purposes of the provisions mentioned in subsection (1)(*a*) to (*c*) above—
   (*a*) "local authority" means a district council, the Greater London Council, a London borough council, the Sub-Treasurer of the Inner Temple or the Under-Treasurer of the Middle Temple, and includes the Council of the Isles of Scilly; and
   (*b*) the definitions of "local authority" in section 1(2) of the 1936 Act and section 2(3) of the 1961 Act shall not apply;
and in section 1(1) of the 1961 Act (Part II of that Act to be construed as one with Part II of the 1936 Act), after the words "Part II of this Act" there shall be inserted the words ", except so much of it as relates to building regulations,".

(3) In this Part—
   "the 1936 Act" means the Public Health Act 1936;
   "the 1961 Act" means the Public Health Act 1961;
   "the substantive requirements of building regulations" means the requirements of building regulations with respect to the design and construction of buildings and the provision of services, fittings and equipment in or in connection with buildings (including requirements imposed by virtue of section 65(1) or (2)(*a*) or (*b*)), as distinct from procedural requirements.

(4) In this Part, in sections 61 to 71 of the 1936 Act and in sections 4 to 8 of the 1961 Act "prescribed" means prescribed by building regulations.

PART III

MISCELLANEOUS AMENDMENTS RELATING TO BUILDING WORK

Exemptions and relaxations for public bodies

Exemption of local authorities etc. from procedural requirements of building regulations

52.—(1) Building regulations may exempt—
   (*a*) a local authority,
   (*b*) a county council, and
   (*c*) any other body which acts under any enactment for public purposes and not for its own profit and is prescribed for the purpose of this section by building regulations,

from compliance with any requirements of those regulations which are not substantive requirements.

(2) A local authority, county council or other body which is exempted as mentioned in subsection (1) above is in subsection (3) below referred to as an "exempt body".

(3) Without prejudice to the obligation of an exempt body to comply with substantive requirements of building regulations, the function of enforcing building regulations which is conferred on local authorities by section 4(3) of the 1961 Act shall not be exercisable in relation to work carried out by an exempt body and, accordingly—

(*a*) nothing in subsections (1) to (4) of section 65 of the 1936 Act (powers to require removal or alteration of certain work) shall apply in relation to work so carried out; and

(*b*) a local authority may not institute proceedings under section 4(6) of the 1961 Act for any contravention of building regulations by an exempt body.

(4) In this section "substantive requirements of building regulations" has the meaning assigned to it by section 76(3) of the 1974 Act.

DEFINITION
local authority: s.62(1).

GENERAL NOTE
Building regulations may exempt certain public bodies from compliance with the procedural requirements of the regulations. There must be compliance with substantive requirements.

Subs. (1)
  substantive requirements: See subs. (4).

Subs. (3)
  As to enforcement powers of authorities; see note to s.45(5) and (6).

Subs. (4)
  S.76(3) of the Health and Safety at Work etc. Act 1974 provides as follows
  "the substantive requirements of building regulations" means the requirements of building regulations with respect to the design and construction of buildings and the provision of services, fittings and equipment in or in connection with buildings (including requirements imposed by virtue of section 65(1) or (2)(*a*) or (*b*)), as distinct from procedural requirements.

Power of certain public bodies to relax requirements of building regulations for their own works

53.—(1) After subsection (2) of section 6 of the 1961 Act there shall be inserted the following subsections:

"(2A) If—

(*a*) building regulations so provide as regards any requirement contained in the regulations, and

(*b*) a public body considers that the operation of any such requirement would be unreasonable in relation to any particular work carried out or proposed to be carried out by or on behalf of the public body,

the public body may give a direction dispensing with or relaxing that requirement.

(2B) In subsection (2A) above "public body" means—

(*a*) a local authority;

(*b*) a county council; and

(*c*) any other body which is prescribed for the purposes of section 52 of the Housing and Building Control Act 1984."

(2) In subsection (1) of section 8 of the 1961 Act (opportunity for representations about proposals to relax building regulations) after the words "local authority", in the first and second places where they occur, there shall be inserted the words "or other body", for the words "application is" there shall be substituted the words "direction is proposed to be" and for the words "before publication of the notice" there shall be substituted the words "where the direction is proposed to be made on an application".

(3) In subsections (2) and (5) of that section after the words "local authority", in each place where they occur, there shall be inserted the words "or other body" and in subsection (3) of that section for the words "application is" there shall be substituted the words "direction is proposed to be".

(4) In section 15(1) of the Fire Precautions Act 1971 (consultation with fire authority prior to exercise by local authority of powers under section 6 of the 1961 Act) after the words "local authority", in the first place where they occur, there shall be inserted the words "or a public body, as defined in section 6(2B) of that Act, proposes to exercise the power conferred on it by section 6(2A) of that Act" and after the words "local authority", in the second place where they occur, there shall be inserted the words "or other body".

DEFINITION
  local authority: s.62(1).

GENERAL NOTE
  Under s.6 of the Public Health Act 1961 the Secretary of State may relax a requirement of the building regulations in respect of a particular case where he considers that requirement to be unreasonable. By virtue of subs. (2) this power may be exercised by local authorities if the building regulations so provide. This section makes amendments to the 1961 Act so as to empower certain public bodies to relax prescribed building regulations for their own work.

Subs. (2) and (3)
  These subsections amend s.8 of the 1961 Act (which requires advertisement of proposals to relax building regulations) so as to bring public bodies under the duty to advertise where it is proposed to relax the operation of any building regulation requirement.

Subs. (4)
  A public body is required to consult the fire authority on any proposal to relax a regulation concerned with structural fire precautions.

Approved documents giving practical guidance

Approval of documents for purposes of building regulations

54.—(1) For the purpose of providing practical guidance with respect to the requirements of any provision of building regulations, the Secretary of State or a body designated by him for the purposes of this section may—

  (*a*) approve and issue any document (whether or not prepared by him or by the body concerned), or

  (*b*) approve any document issued or proposed to be issued otherwise than by him or by the body concerned,

if in the opinion of the Secretary of State or, as the case may be, the body concerned the document is suitable for that purpose.

(2) References in this section and section 55 below to a document include references to any part of a document; and accordingly, in relation to a document of which part only is approved, any reference in the

following provisions of this section or in section 55 below to the approved document is a reference only to the part of it which is approved.

(3) An approval given under subsection (1) above shall take effect in accordance with a notice which is issued by the Secretary of State or, as the case may be, the body giving the approval and which—

(*a*) identifies the approved document in question;

(*b*) states the date on which the approval of it is to take effect; and

(*c*) specifies the provisions of building regulations for the purposes of which the document is approved.

(4) The Secretary of State or, as the case may be, the body which gave the approval may—

(*a*) from time to time approve and issue a revision of the whole or any part of an approved document issued by him or it for the purposes of this section; and

(*b*) approve any revision or proposed revision of the whole or any part of any approved document;

and subsection (3) above shall, with the necessary modifications, apply in relation to an approval which is given under this subsection to a revision as it applied in relation to an approval which is given under subsection (1) above to a document.

(5) The Secretary of State or, as the case may be, the body which gave the approval may withdraw his or its approval of a document under this section; and such a withdrawal of approval shall take effect in accordance with a notice which is issued by the Secretary of State or body concerned and which—

(*a*) identifies the approved document in question; and

(*b*) states the date on which the approval of it is to cease to have effect.

(6) References in subsections (4) and (5) above and in section 55 below to an approved document are references to that document as it has effect for the time being, having regard to any revision of the whole or any part of it which has been approved under subsection (4) above.

(7) Where a body ceases to be a body designated by the Secretary of State for the purposes of this section, subsections (4) and (5) above shall have effect as if any approval given by that body had been given by the Secretary of State.

(8) The power to designate a body for the purposes of this section shall be exercisable by order made by statutory instrument which shall be subject to annulment in pursuance of a resolution of either House of Parliament.

GENERAL NOTE

The Secretary of State may approve and issue any document which in his opinion gives suitable practical guidance with respect to the building regulations. The document may come from him, or from a body designated by him for the purpose, or from any other source.

As to compliance or non-compliance with approved documents; see s.55.

Subs. (1)

document: See subs. (2).

Subss. (4) and (5)

As to an approved document; see subs. (6).

Compliance or non-compliance with approved documents

55.—(1) A failure on the part of any person to comply with an approved document shall not of itself render him liable to any civil or criminal proceedings; but if, in any proceedings whether civil or criminal, it is alleged that any person has at any time contravened a provision of building regulations—

(*a*) a failure to comply with a document which at that time was approved for the purposes of that provision may be relied upon as tending to establish liability; and

(*b*) proof of compliance with such a document may be relied on as tending to negative liability.

(2) In any proceedings, whether civil or criminal,—

(*a*) a document purporting to be a notice issued as mentioned in section 54(3) above shall be taken to be such a notice unless the contrary is proved; and

(*b*) a document which appears to the court to be the approved document to which such a notice refers shall be taken to be that approved document unless the contrary is proved.

GENERAL NOTE
This section indicates the relevance of documents approved for the purposes of s.54 in criminal and civil proceedings. Criminal proceedings may be taken by the local authority under s.4(6) of the Public Health Act 1961. Offences against the building regulations can be committed even though work on the buildings concerned is not yet complete; see *Sunley Homes Ltd.* v. *Borg* [1970] 1 Q.B. 115. Under s.65 of the Public Health Act 1936 an authority may by notice require an owner to pull down or alter work which contravenes any of the building regulations. An action founded in the tort of negligence may lie against a builder; see the cases referred to under the notes to s.41.

Certification and reports

Certificates of compliance with building regulations

56.—(1) In section 64 of the 1936 Act (passing or rejection of plans etc.) immediately before subsection (3) (appeals to magistrates' courts) there shall be inserted the following subsection—

"(2C) Where the deposited plans are accompanied by—

(*a*) a certificate given by a person approved for the purposes of this subsection to the effect that the proposed work, if carried out in accordance with the deposited plans, will comply with such provisions of the regulations prescribed for the purposes of this subsection as may be specified in the certificate, and

(*b*) such evidence as may be prescribed that an approved scheme applies, or the prescribed insurance cover has been or will be provided, in relation to the certificate,

the local authority may not except in prescribed circumstances reject the plans on the ground that they are defective with respect to any provisions of the regulations which are so specified or that they show that the proposed work would contravene any of those provisions."

(2) For subsection (3) of section 64 of the 1936 Act there shall be substituted the following subsection—

"(3) In any case where a question arises under this section between a local authority and a person who proposes to carry out any work—

(*a*) whether plans of the proposed work are in conformity with building regulations; or

(*b*) whether the local authority are prohibited from rejecting plans of the proposed work by virtue of subsection (2C) above,

that person may refer the question to the Secretary of State for his determination; and an application for a reference under this subsection shall be accompanied by such fee as may be prescribed by building regulations."

(3) After that subsection there shall be inserted the following subsection—

"(3A) Where deposited plans accompanied by such a certificate and such evidence as are mentioned in subsection (2C) above are passed by the local authority, or notice of the rejection of deposited plans so accompanied is not given within the prescribed period from the deposit of the plans, the authority may not institute proceedings under section 4(6) of the 1961 Act for any contravention of building regulations which—

    (*a*) arises out of the carrying out of the proposed work in accordance with the plans; and

    (*b*) is a contravention of any of the provisions of the regulations specified in the certificate."

(4) Building regulations may make provision for the approval of persons for the purposes of subsection (2C) of section 64 of the 1936 Act—

    (*a*) by the Secretary of State; or

    (*b*) by a body (corporate or unincorporated) which, in accordance with the regulations, is designated by the Secretary of State for the purpose;

and any such approval may limit the description of work, or the provisions of the regulations, in relation to which the person concerned is so approved.

(5) Any such designation as is referred to in paragraph (*b*) of subsection (4) above may limit the cases in which and the terms on which the body designated may approve a person and, in particular, may provide that any approval given by the body shall be limited as mentioned in that subsection.

(6) There shall be paid on an application for any such approval as is referred to in subsection (4) above—

    (*a*) where the application is made to the Secretary of State, such fee as may be prescribed by building regulations;

    (*b*) where the application is made to a body designated by him as mentioned in that subsection, such fee as that body may determine.

(7) The Secretary of State may approve for the purposes of subsection (2C) of section 64 of the 1936 Act any scheme which appears to him to secure the provision of adequate insurance cover in relation to any certificate which is given under paragraph (*a*) of that subsection and is a certificate to which the scheme applies.

(8) Building regulations may prescribe for the purposes of subsection (2C) of section 64 of the 1936 Act the insurance cover which is to be provided in relation to any certificate which is given under paragraph (*a*) of that subsection and is not a certificate to which an approved scheme applies and may, in particular, prescribe the form and content of policies of insurance.

(9) Building regulations may—

    (*a*) contain provision prescribing the period for which, subject to any provision made by virtue of paragraph (*b*) or (*c*) below, any such approval as is referred to in subsection (4) above shall continue in force;

    (*b*) contain provision precluding the giving of, or requiring the withdrawal of, any such approval as is referred to in that subsection in such circumstances as may be prescribed by the regulations;

    (*c*) contain provision authorising the withdrawal of any such approval or designation as is so referred to;

    (*d*) provide for the maintenance by the Secretary of State of a list of bodies who are for the time being designated by him as mentioned in subsection (4) above and for the maintenance by the Secretary of State and by each designated body of a list of persons for the time being approved by him or them as mentioned in that subsection;

    (*e*) make provision for the supply to local authorities of copies of any list of approved persons maintained by virtue of paragraph (*d*) above and for such copy lists to be made available for inspection; and

(*f*) make provision for the supply, on payment of a prescribed fee, of a certified copy of any entry in a list maintained by virtue of paragraph (*d*) above or in a copy list held by a local authority by virtue of paragraph (*e*) above.

(10) Unless the contrary is proved, in any proceedings (whether civil or criminal) a document which appears to the court to be a certified copy of an entry either in a list maintained as mentioned in subsection (9)(*d*) above or in a copy of such a list supplied as mentioned in subsection (9)(*e*) above—

(*a*) shall be presumed to be a true copy of an entry in the current list so maintained; and

(*b*) shall be evidence of the matters stated therein.

DEFINITIONS
local authority: s.62.

GENERAL NOTE
Subs. (1)
Where deposited plans are accompanied by a certificate from an approved person that the proposed work, if carried out in accordance with those plans, will comply with prescribed provisions of the building regulations and that prescribed evidence that an approved insurance scheme applies or that prescribed insurance cover has or will be provided, the authority may not reject the plans, except in prescribed circumstances, on the grounds that they are defective in respect of, or show that the work would contravene, the regulation specified in the certificate.
As to insurance; see s.39(1)(*c*).

Subs. (2)
The amendment substitutes the Secretary of State for the Magistrates' Court.

Subs. (3)
An authority may not prosecute under s.4(6) of the 1961 Act for a contravention of any provision of the regulations specified in the certificate where the work is carried out in accordance with the deposited plans.

Subs. (4)
Provision may be made in the building regulations for the approval of persons for the purposes of issuing certificates of compliance.

Subs. (5)
This provision is in line with the provision in s.41(3).

Subss. (7) and (8)
These provisions correspond to those appearing in s.39(6) and (7).

Subs. (9)
These provisions correspond to those contained in s.41(5).

Subs. (10)
This provision corresponds with the provision in s.41(6).

Methods of challenging section 65 notices

57.—(1) After section 65 of the 1936 Act there shall be inserted the sections set out in Schedule 9 to this Act.

(2) Section 67 of the 1936 Act (joint applications to the Secretary of State for determination of certain questions relating to building regula-

tions) shall cease to have effect except as respects applications referred to the Secretary of State before this subsection comes into force.

GENERAL NOTE
Subs. (1)
   See notes to Sched. 9.

Miscellaneous

Charges by local authorities for performing functions relating to building regulations

58. Building regulations may authorise local authorities, subject to and in accordance with the regulations, to fix by means of schemes and to recover such charges for or in connection with the performance of functions of theirs relating to building regulations as they may determine in accordance with principles prescribed by the regulations.

DEFINITION
   local authority: s.62(1).

Amendments of enactments relating to building regulations

59.—(1) In section 9(3) of the 1961 Act (consultation with Building Regulations Advisory Committee and other bodies before making building regulations) after the word "regulations", in the first place where it occurs, there shall be inserted the words "containing substantive requirements as defined in section 76(3) of the Health and Safety at Work etc. Act 1974".
   (2) The following provisions of the 1974 Act, namely—
       (*a*) subsection (5) of section 61 (which provides for the repeal of section 71 of the 1936 Act but has not been brought into force); and
       (*b*) subsections (6) and (7) of section 63 (which make provision consequential on that repeal),
shall cease to have effect.
   (3) In Schedule 6 to the 1974 Act (amendments of enactments relating to building regulations) paragraphs 1, 2, 5(*a*), 5(*d*), 6 and 7 (most of which are not yet in operation and none of which is yet fully in operation) shall be deemed not to have been enacted, and accordingly (and having regard to section 53(1) above)—
       (*a*) subsection (4) of section 64 of the 1936 Act and section 6 of the 1961 Act shall have effect as set out in Schedule 10 to this Act, and
       (*b*) section 65 of the 1936 Act and sections 7 and 8 of the 1961 Act shall continue to have effect (for all purposes) without regard to any provision of the said Schedule 6.

GENERAL NOTE
Subs. (1)
   Statutory consultation on proposals to make building regulations is limited to substantive, as opposed to procedural, requirements.

Subs. (2)
   The effect of the amendment is to keep s.71 of the 1936 Act in force. S.71 exempts certain buildings from the building regulations; namely, buildings required for the purposes of any school or other educational establishment erected or to be erected according to plans approved by the Secretary of State, and any buildings belonging to statutory undertakers and held or used by them for the purposes of their undertaking.

Subs. (3)
   The provisions in Sched. 6 to the 1974 Act, amending previous legislation, are repealed. Insofar as they have been brought into operation at all, they were operative only for the purpose of making regulations. No such regulations have been made.

Amendments of enactments relating to sanitation and buildings

60.—(1) Part XII of the 1936 Act (enforcement and other general provisions) shall have effect as if so much of Part II of the 1961 Act (sanitation and buildings) as does not relate to buildings regulations were contained in Part II of the 1936 Act.

(2) In the following provisions, namely—

(*a*) so much of Part II of the 1936 Act (sanitation and buildings) as does not relate to building regulations;

(*b*) sections 137 and 138 of that Act (certain buildings to be supplied with water); and

(*c*) so much of Part II of the 1961 Act as does not relate to building regulations,

expressions which are defined by subsection (1) of section 82 of the 1974 Act shall have the meanings given by that subsection.

GENERAL NOTE

This section is concerned with the application of definitions to the provisions named.

"As the House will be aware, the existing law relating to buildings and building regulations is spread in an untidy fashion over a number of statutes. The Law Commission is currently working on a Bill to consolidate those enactments and the present Bill into a single building Bill, which it is hoped will be introduced later this Session. I am sure that the House will welcome this proposal, which, some may say, is long overdue.

One of the problems of the existing maze of legislation is that marginally different definitions and procedural provisions apply to different parts of the enactments. The new clause . . . will ensure that the set of definitions given in the Health and Safety at Work etc. Act 1974 applies to all parts of these enactments." (Mr Roberts, *Hansard*, H.C. Vol. 58, col. 625 (April 12, 1984)).

Repeal of the Building Control Act 1966

61.—(1) The Building Control Act 1966 (which regulates building and constructional work) shall cease to have effect.

(2) In consequence of subsection (1) above, the enactments mentioned in Part I of Schedule 12 to this Act are hereby repealed to the extent specified in the third column of that Schedule.

Interpretation of Part III

62.—(1) In this Part of this Act—

"the 1936 Act" means the Public Health Act 1936;

"the 1961 Act" means the Public Health Act 1961;

"the 1974 Act" means the Health and Safety at Work etc. Act 1974;

"contravention", in relation to any provision of building regulations, includes a failure to comply with that provision;

"local authority" has the meaning assigned to it by subsection (2)(*a*) of section 76 of the 1974 Act.

(2) Any reference in this Part of this Act to the carrying out of work includes a reference to the making of a material change of use, as defined by and for the purposes of building regulations.

GENERAL NOTE

Subs. (1)

local authority: see note to s.51(4).

PART IV

MISCELLANEOUS AND GENERAL

Financial provisions

63.—(1) There shall be paid out of money provided by Parliament the administrative expenses of the Secretary of State under this Act and any increase attributable to this Act in the sums so payable under any other enactment.

(2) There shall be paid out of or into the Consolidated Fund or the National Loans Fund any increase attributable to this Act in the sums so payable under any other enactment.

Minor and consequential amendments

64. The enactments mentioned in Schedule 11 to this Act shall have effect subject to the amendments there specified (being minor amendments and amendments consequential on the preceding provisions of this Act).

Repeals

65. The enactments mentioned in Part II of Schedule 12 to this Act are hereby repealed to the extent specified in the third column of that Schedule.

Short title, commencement and extent

66.—(1) This Act may be cited as the Housing and Building Control Act 1984.

(2) The following provisions of this Act namely—

    (*a*) sections 42(2), 56(2), 57(2) and 58;

    (*b*) so far as relating to the amendments of section 69 of the Health and Safety at Work etc. Act 1974, section 64 and Schedule 11; and

    (*c*) so far as relating to the repeals of section 67 of the Public Health Act 1936 and section 62(3) of the said Act of 1974, section 65 and Part II of Schedule 12,

shall come into force on such day as the Secretary of State may by order made by statutory instrument appoint; and different days may be so appointed for different provisions or for different purposes.

(3) Except as provided by subsection (2) above, this Act shall come into force at the end of the period of two months beginning with the day on which this Act is passed.

(4) This Act does not extend to Scotland or Northern Ireland.

SCHEDULES

Section 1.   SCHEDULE 1

EXTENSION OF RIGHT TO BUY TO CERTAIN CASES WHERE LANDLORD DOES NOT OWN FREEHOLD

1. In section 1(8) (right to acquire freehold or long lease) and section 10(1)(*a*) (notice of purchase price and right to a mortgage) of the 1980 Act for the words "long lease" there shall be substituted the word "lease".

2. In section 6(4)(*a*) of the 1980 Act (assumptions on the grant of a lease) for the words from "for 125 years" onwards there shall be substituted the words "with vacant possession for the appropriate term defined in sub-paragraph (2) of paragraph 11 of Schedule 2 to this Act (but subject to sub-paragraph (3) of that paragraph)".

3. In section 14 of the 1980 Act (change of landlord after notice claiming right to buy or right to a mortgage) for the words "the freehold of" there shall be substituted the words "the interest of the landlord in".

4. In section 16(1) of the 1980 Act (completion) for paragraphs (*a*) and (*b*) there shall be substituted the following paragraphs—

"(*a*) if the dwelling-house is a house and the landlord owns the freehold, a grant of the dwelling-house for an estate in fee simple absolute; and

(*b*) if the landlord does not own the freehold or (whether or not the landlord owns it) the dwelling-house is a flat, a grant of a lease of the dwelling-house for the appropriate term defined in sub-paragraph (2) of paragraph 11 of Schedule 2 to this Act (but subject to sub-paragraph (3) of that paragraph);".

5. At the end of section 17 of the 1980 Act (conveyance of freehold and grant of lease) there shall be inserted the words "and other matters".

6. Section 18 of the 1980 Act (right to a mortgage—terms of mortgage deed) shall be renumbered as subsection (1) of that section, in that provision as so renumbered the words from "but the Secretary of State" onwards shall be omitted and after that provision as so renumbered there shall be inserted the following subsections—

"(2) Where the mortgagor's interest in the dwelling-house is leasehold and the term of the lease is less than 25 years, subsection (1)(*b*) above shall have effect as if the reference to 25 years were a reference to the term of the lease.

(3) The Secretary of State may by order prescribe additional terms to be contained in any deed by which a mortgage is effected in pursuance of this Chapter or vary the provisions of subsections (1)(*a*) and (*b*) and (2) above, but only in relation to deeds executed after the order comes into force."

7. In subsection (3) of section 20 of the 1980 Act (registration of title) for the words "subsection (2)" there shall be substituted the words "subsection (1)(*b*)" and for subsections (1) and (2) of that section there shall be substituted the following subsections—

"(1) Where the landlord's title to the dwelling-house is not registered—

(*a*) section 123 of the Land Registration Act 1925 (compulsory registration of title) shall apply in relation to the conveyance of the freehold or the grant of a lease in pursuance of this Chapter whether or not the dwelling-house is in an area in which an Order in Council under section 120 of that Act is for the time being in force and, in the case of a lease, whether or not the lease is granted for a term of not less than 40 years;

(*b*) the landlord shall give the tenant a certificate stating that the landlord is entitled to convey the freehold or make the grant subject only to such incumbrances, rights and interests as are stated in the conveyance or grant or summarised in the certificate; and

(*c*) section 8 of that Act (application for registration of leasehold land) shall apply in relation to a lease granted in pursuance of this Chapter notwithstanding that it is a lease for a term of which not more than 21 years are unexpired.

(1A) Where the landlord's interest in the dwelling-house is a lease, a certificate under subsection (1)(*b*) above shall also state particulars of that lease and, with respect to each superior title, the following particulars, namely—

(*a*) where it is registered, the title number;

(*b*) where it is not registered, whether it was investigated in the usual way on the grant of the landlord's lease.

(2) Where the landlord's title to the dwelling-house is registered, section 22 of the said Act of 1925 (registration of dispositions of leaseholds) shall apply in relation to a lease granted in pursuance of this Chapter notwithstanding that it is granted for a term not exceeding 21 years."

8. In section 24 of the 1980 Act (vesting orders)—

(*a*) in subsection (3) after the word "If" there shall be inserted the words "the landlord's title to" and the word "land" shall be omitted;

(*b*) in subsection (4) after the words "an absolute title" there shall be inserted the words "or, as the case may require, a good leasehold title"; and

(*c*) in subsection (5) after the word "Where" there shall be inserted the words "the landlord's title to" and the word "land" shall be omitted.

9. After paragraph 5 of Part I of Schedule 1 to the 1980 Act (circumstances in which right to buy does not arise) there shall be inserted the following paragraph—

"6.—(1) The dwelling-house is held by the landlord on a tenancy from the Crown.

(2) This paragraph does not apply if either—

(*a*) the landlord is entitled to grant a lease in pursuance of this Chapter without the concurrence of the appropriate authority (disregarding for this purpose paragraph 19A of Schedule 2 to this Act); or

 (*b*) the appropriate authority notifies the landlord that as regards any Crown interest affected the authority will give its consent to the granting of such a lease.

(3) For the purposes of this paragraph 'tenancy from the Crown' means a tenancy of land in which there is a Crown interest superior to the tenancy and 'Crown interest' and 'appropriate authority' in relation to a Crown interest mean respectively—

 (*a*) an interest comprised in the Crown Estate, and the Crown Estate Commissioners or other government department having the management of the land in question;

 (*b*) an interest belonging to Her Majesty in right of the Duchy of Lancaster, and the Chancellor of the Duchy;

 (*c*) an interest belonging to the Duchy of Cornwall, and such person as the Duke of Cornwall or the possessor for the time being of the Duchy appoints;

 (*d*) any other interest belonging to a government department or held on behalf of Her Majesty for the purposes of a government department, and that department."

10.—(1) For paragraph 11 of Schedule 2 to the 1980 Act (terms of leases) there shall be substituted—

"11.—(1) A lease shall be for the appropriate term defined in sub-paragraph (2) below (but subject to sub-paragraph (3) below) and at a rent not exceeding £10 per annum, and the following provisions shall have effect with respect to the other terms of the lease.

(2) If at the time the grant is made the landlord's interest in the dwelling-house is not less than a lease for a term of which more than 125 years and five days are then unexpired the appropriate term is a term of not less than 125 years; in any other case it is a term expiring five days before the term of the landlord's lease of the dwelling-house (or, as the case may require, five days before the first date on which the term of any lease under which the landlord holds any part of the dwelling-house is to expire).

(3) If the dwelling-house is a flat contained in a building which also contains one or more other flats and the landlord has, since the passing of this Act, granted a lease of one or more of them for the appropriate term, the lease of the dwelling-house may be for a term expiring at the end of the term for which the other lease (or one of the other leases) was granted."

(2) In paragraph 12 (common use of premises and facilities) after the word "Where" there shall be inserted the words "the dwelling-house is a flat and".

(3) In paragraph 13 of that Schedule (covenants by landlord)—

 (*a*) sub-paragraph (1) shall be renumbered as sub-paragraph (1A) of that paragraph;

 (*b*) at the beginning of that provision as so renumbered there shall be inserted the words "Subject to paragraph 13A(3) below";

 (*c*) immediately before that provision as so renumbered there shall be inserted the following sub-paragraph—

  "(1) This paragraph applies where the dwelling-house is a flat."; and

 (*d*) in sub-paragraph (2) for the words "sub-paragraph (1)(*a*)" there shall be substituted the words "sub-paragraph (1A)(*a*)".

(4) After paragraph 13 of that Schedule there shall be inserted the following paragraph—

"13A.—(1) This paragraph applies where the landlord's interest in the dwelling-house is leasehold.

(2) There shall be implied, by virtue of this Schedule, a covenant by the landlord to pay the rent reserved by the landlord's lease and, except in so far as they fall to be discharged by the tenant, to discharge its obligations under the covenants contained in that lease.

(3) A covenant implied by virtue of paragraph 13(1A) above shall not impose on the landlord any obligations which the landlord is not entitled to discharge under the provisions of the landlord's lease or a superior lease.

(4) Where the landlord's lease or a superior lease or any agreement collateral to the landlord's lease or a superior lease contains a covenant by any person imposing obligations which, but for sub-paragraph (3) above, would be imposed by a covenant implied by virtue of paragraph 13(1A) above, there shall be implied by virtue of this Schedule, a covenant by the landlord to use its best endeavours to secure that that person's obligations under the first mentioned covenant are discharged."

(5) In paragraph 14 of that Schedule (covenant by tenant) for the words from "to keep" onwards there shall be substituted the following paragraphs—

"(*a*) where the dwelling-house is a house, to keep the dwelling-house in good repair (including decorative repair);

(*b*) where the dwelling-house is a flat, to keep the interior of the dwelling-house in such repair."

(6) Paragraph 15 of that Schedule (avoidance of certain agreements) shall be renumbered as sub-paragraph (1) of that paragraph, in that provision as so renumbered paragraph (*b*) and the words "and paragraph 16 below" shall be omitted and after that provision as so renumbered there shall be inserted the following sub-paragraph—

"(2) Where the dwelling-house is a flat, any provision of the lease or of any agreement collateral to it shall be void in so far as it purports—

(*a*) to enable the landlord to recover from the tenant any part of any costs incurred by the landlord in discharging or insuring against any obligations imposed by a covenant implied by virtue of paragraph 13(1A)(*a*) or (*b*) above; or

(*b*) to enable any person to recover from the tenant any part of any costs incurred, whether by him or by any other person, in discharging or insuring against any obligations to the like effect as obligations which, but for paragraph 13A(3) above, would be imposed by a covenant so implied;

but subject to paragraph 16 below."

11.—(1) For the heading of Part IV of Schedule 2 to the 1980 Act (charges on freehold) there shall be substituted the heading "CHARGES AND OTHER MATTERS".

(2) In paragraph 18 of that Schedule for the words "the freehold", where first occurring, there shall be substituted the words "the interest of the landlord".

(3) After paragraph 19 of that Schedule there shall be inserted the following paragraph—

"19A. Any provision of a lease held by the landlord or a superior landlord, or of any agreement (whenever made) shall be void in so far as it would otherwise—

(*a*) prohibit or restrict the grant of a lease in pursuance of the right to buy or the subsequent disposal (whether by way of assignment, sub-lease or otherwise) of a lease so granted; or

(*b*) authorise any forfeiture or impose on the landlord or superior landlord any penalty or disability in the event of a lease being granted in pursuance of the right to buy or of a subsequent disposal of a lease so granted."

12. After sub-paragraph (2) of paragraph 1 of Schedule 3 to the 1980 Act (tenancies which are not secure tenancies) there shall be inserted the following sub-paragraph—

"(2A) For the purposes of this paragraph a tenancy granted in pursuance of Chapter I of Part I of this Act is a long tenancy notwithstanding that it is granted for a term not exceeding 21 years."

GENERAL NOTE

This Schedule effects the amendments to the 1980 Act which reflect the extension of the right to buy to cases where the landlord does not own the freehold, but has a sufficient interest to grant a lease; see notes s.1. "It is unsatisfactory to have such complicated referential legislation without a Keeling schedule. (Mr Fraser, Standing Committee B, col. 78, July 14, 1983.).

"A Keeling schedule . . . is aimed at assisting the comprehension of Members of amendments to complex legislation. I am very much in favour of anything that makes it easier for hon. Members to understand legislation. This Bill is relatively simple compared with others. We are basically amending the 1980 Act, so only two documents are needed to understand it." (Sir George Young, Standing Committee B, July 19, 1983). A Keeling schedule appears as Sched. 10 of this Act.

The complaint of the lack of a Keeling schedule was raised again in the House of Lords; see *Hansard*, H.L. vol. 450, col. 1389 (March 22, 1984). Lord Bellwin, for the government, confessed that—even though "in five years . . . I have dealt with about 25 Bills, so I am not rising to my feet as a beginner" (*ibid.*, col. 1379)—he had "never heard of the Keeling schedules. . ." (*ibid*, col. 1391) again even though the Act (and as it then was the Bill) contains one.

Para. 1: All leases under the right to buy provisions prior to the amendments brought about by this Act would have been "long" leases, *i.e.* leases for 125 years (or a lesser period if the right was exercised by a second or subsequent tenant in a block of flats, in which case the lease could be coterminous with the first or earlier leases. Parliament in 1980 left to their successors the problems which might arise in 2084, when the coterminous provision might have resulted in leases of less than 21 years).

Under the new provisions, leases of *houses* can be for less than 21 years—21 years *less* 5 days (see the 1980 Act, s.2(3), as amended by s.1(3) above) dated from the "relevant time"; *i.e.* date of the notice claiming the right to buy (1980 Act, s.3(5)) and therefore also *less* the time taken for the exercise to be carried through. In the event, the present amendment merely alters a reference from "long lease" to "lease".

Para. 2: S.6(4) of the 1980 Act defines the purchase price for a lease; this amendment is also a consequence of the variation from a 125 years norm; see notes to para. 1 above.

Para. 3: Again, this is a "consequential amendment, reflecting the inclusion of landlords who do not own the freehold.

Para. 4: S.16(1) of the 1980 Act contains the landlord's "duty to complete" (see also notes to s.6 above). This paragraph is a further consequential amendment, reflecting the prospect of leases of houses of which the landlord does not own the freehold.

Para. 5: This cross-refers to the amendments in para. 11 of this Schedule; see below.

Para. 6: S.18 of the 1980 Act deals with the terms of a mortgage deed. Unless otherwise agreed between the parties, it provides for repayment in equal instalments of principal and interest, over a period of 25 years (unless the mortgagor requires a shorter period, or the mortgagee agrees a longer period). The deed may contain other terms agreed by the parties or as determined by the county court as "reasonably required" by either.

Under the provision as unamended, the Secretary of State has the power to prescribe additional terms, or vary either repayment requirements or the length of the mortgage term. This power is "moved" to the new subs. (3), and extended to include the variation of the new subs. (2). Subs. (2) is otherwise consequential, reflecting the prospect of relatively short leases.

Para. 7: Under s.20 of the 1980 Act on the exercise of the right to buy, the title is to be registered, whether or not the land is in an area of compulsory registration under s.120, Land Registration Act 1925 (*ibid.*, s.123). Compulsory registration does not normally apply to leases of less than 40 years (*ibid.*) but as a result of the present amendments will apply to such leases granted under the right to buy. There are similar amendments to ss.8 and 22 of the 1925 Act to permit the registration (otherwise not permitted) of leases of 21 years or less. Certificates are to be in a form, and signed by an officer of the landlord (or other person), as may be approved by the Chief Land Registrar: s.20(3) of the 1980 Act, as amended by this paragraph.

Para. 8: These are all consequential amendments, applicable to the possibility of "vesting orders" made by the Secretary of State in the exercise of his powers of intervention under the Act (see further, notes to s.9 above).

Para. 9: This is an important and substantive provision. Exempt from the general extension of the right to buy to cases where the landlord does not own the freehold are cases where the interest superior to that of the landlord is the Crown. However, the exemption does not apply (and therefore the right to a lease *is* available) if *either* (i) (without the benefit of Sched. 2 of the 1980 Act, para. 19A, added by para. 11, below) under the terms of the lease the landlord would be entitled to grant the sub-lease claimed by the tenant without the permission of the Crown, *or* (ii) the Crown consents to the grant of the sub-lease, through the offices of the specified bodies.

Para. 10: The presumption in favour of a lease of 125 years not only remains, but is extended to houses. The provision for coterminous leases is retained, but only, of course, in relation to flats. The innovatory element of the amendment is that sub-leases are to be for five days less than the landlord's lease.

Where the landlord holds more than one lease in respect of a property, *i.e.* on different parts, then the sub-lease is to expire five days before the earliest expiry date of any of the landlord's leases. (For example: The landlord takes a lease on one flat in house subdivided into two flats. Subsequently, the same landlord takes a lease for the same length of the other flat. The lease of the first flat will expire before the lease of the second. The landlord then removes the subdivision and sublets the whole house to a secure tenant. The tenant has the right to a sub-lease expiring five days before landlord's *first* lease.)

No *minimum* period is prescribed in this paragraph, but the right to buy (including a sub-lease) does not arise unless the landlord has a lease of at least 21 years in respect of a house, and 50 years in respect of a flat, as at the date of service of the notice claiming the right: see s.1(3) above, amending the 1980 Act, s.2(3); see also s.3(3) of the 1980 Act; see further notes to para. 1 above.

Under the unamended 1980 Act, leases were only applicable in the case of flats, and Sched. 2, para. 12 of the 1980 Act required the inclusion in leases of rights to the same use of facilities and services, in common with other occupants of a block, as the tenant enjoyed before purchase. The amendment to para. 12 ensures that this provision remains applicable *only* in the case of flats, and is not extended to leases of houses.

Sched. 2, para. 13 of the 1980 Act governs repairing obligations in blocks of flats. The current amendments are (as the last amendment) designed to confine its applicability to flats, and not leases of houses. The new para. 13A deals with additional covenants in sub-leases governing landlord's obligations, and is applicable both to flats and houses. Where the superior landlord retains the repairing obligations which under the 1980 Act, Sched. 2, para. 13, are placed under the right to buy on the tenant's landlord (mesne tenant) the mesne tenant is placed under an obligation to use its best endeavours to ensure that the superior landlord complies with those duties.

Sched. 2, para. 14 of the 1980 Act governs the (limited) tenant's obligations which, in relation to a flat, are unchanged (interior in good repair—including decorative repair) but in relation to a house will now include the structure and exterior.

Sched. 2, para. 15 of the 1980 Act voids any term of a lease (a) prohibiting or restricting, wholly or in part, an assignment or sub-letting, (b) imposing on the tenant any part of the landlord's costs in discharging (or insuring against) its major repairing obligations in flats, and (c) introducing a forfeiture or penalty clause against a tenant who relies on his rights under the Schedule. However, the assignment/sub-letting provision is to be read subject to s.19 of the 1980 Act (dwellings in National Parks, rural areas and areas of natural beauty; see notes to s.8 above) and there are exceptions to the prohibition against passing on landlord's repairing cost.

Those exceptions are contained in Sched. 2, para. 16 of the 1980 Act and cover a "reasonable part" of the cost of: (i) works *not* amounting to the making good of structural defects (even though within the landlord's major repairing obligations); (ii) works which *do* amount to the making good of structural defects within a defined class; and (iii) insurance costs related to either of these two heads. These three classes of cost may legitimately be passed on to the tenant, normally under a service charge provision.

A tenant can be made to pay in respect of structural defects (see the 1980 Act Sched. 2, para. 15 as amended by Sched. 11 below, and para. 17 as amended by s.7, above; see further the notes thereto) if *either* the landlord's "offer notice" under the 1980 Act s.10 informed the tenant of the defect's existence, and provided an estimate of what the tenant's share of the costs would be, *or* the landlord did not become aware of the defect's existence until ten years after grant of lease.

The present amendments reflect the applicability of the repairing part of these provisions to flats alone, rather than leases of houses, and are intended to prevent their circumvention by charges from the superior landlord being passed on to the tenant.

Para. 11: This is a private sector intervention. This amendment voids any provision in the mesne tenant/landlord's lease which would otherwise prevent or limit the grant of a sub-lease under the right to buy, or interfere with the terms of such a sub-lease by limiting the sub-tenant's further rights of disposal (by assignment or subleasing) or penalise the mesne tenant/landlord for granting a sub-lease under the right to buy or for a subsequent disposal of such a sub-lease.

Para. 12: A lease granted under the right to buy provisions is not to be treated as a secure tenancy, even if not qualifying as a long tenancy, *i.e.* exceeding 21 years, under Sched. 3, para. 1 of the 1980 Act.

Section 3.   SCHEDULE 2

SCHEDULE INSERTED AFTER SCHEDULE 1 TO 1980 ACT

SCHEDULE 1A

QUALIFICATION AND DISCOUNT

PART I

DETERMINATION OF RELEVANT PERIOD FOR THE PURPOSES OF
SECTIONS 1(3) AND 7(1)

1. The period to be taken into account for the purposes of section 1(3) of this Act and the period which under section 7(1) of this Act is to be taken into account for the purposes of

discount shall be the period qualifying, or the aggregate of the periods qualifying, under the following provisions of this Part of this Schedule.

2.—(1) A period qualifies under this paragraph if it is a period during which, before the relevant time—

(*a*) the secure tenant;

(*b*) the secure tenant's spouse; or

(*c*) the secure tenant's deceased spouse,

was a public sector tenant or the spouse of a public sector tenant.

(2) A period shall not qualify by virtue of sub-paragraph (1)(*a*), (*b*) or (*c*) above as a period during which the person there mentioned was the spouse of a public sector tenant unless during that period that person occupied as his only or principal home the dwelling-house of which his spouse was such a tenant.

(3) A period shall not qualify by virtue of sub-paragraph (1)(*b*) above unless the secure tenant and his spouse were living together at the relevant time.

(4) A period shall not qualify by virtue of sub-paragraph (1)(*c*) above unless the secure tenant and his deceased spouse were living together at the time of the death.

(5) For the purposes of this paragraph a person who, as a joint tenant under a public sector tenancy, occupied a dwelling-house as his only or principal home shall be treated as the public sector tenant under that tenancy.

3.—(1) A period qualifies under this paragraph if it is a period during which, before the relevant time—

(*a*) the secure tenant;

(*b*) the secure tenant's spouse; or

(*c*) the secure tenant's deceased spouse,

was an armed forces occupier or the spouse of an armed forces occupier.

(2) A period shall not qualify by virtue of sub-paragraph (1)(*a*), (*b*) or (*c*) above as a period during which the person there mentioned was the spouse of an armed forces occupier unless during that period that person occupied the accommodation of which his spouse was such an occupier.

(3) A period shall not qualify by virtue of sub-paragraph (1)(*b*) above unless the secure tenant and his spouse were living together at the relevant time.

(4) A period shall not qualify by virtue of sub-paragraph (1)(*c*) above unless the secure tenant and his deceased spouse were living together at the time of the death.

4.—(1) This paragraph applies where the public sector tenant of a dwelling-house died or otherwise ceased to be a public sector tenant of the dwelling-house, and thereupon a child of his who occupied the dwelling-house as his only or principal home (in this paragraph referred to as "the new tenant") became the public sector tenant of the dwelling-house (whether under the same or under another public sector tenancy).

(2) A period during which the new tenant, since reaching the age of sixteen, occupied as his only or principal home a dwelling-house of which a parent of his was the public sector tenant or one of joint tenants under a public sector tenancy, being either—

(*a*) the period at the end of which he became the public sector tenant; or

(*b*) a period ending not earlier than two years before another period falling within this sub-paragraph,

shall be regarded for the purposes of paragraph 2 above as a period during which he was a public sector tenant.

(3) For the purposes of this paragraph two persons shall be treated as parent and child if they would be so treated under paragraphs (*a*) and (*b*) of section 50(3) of this Act.

Part II

Reduction of Discount in Certain Circumstances

5. There shall be deducted from the discount an amount equal to any previous discount qualifying, or the aggregate of any previous discounts qualifying, under paragraph 6 below.

6.—(1) A previous discount qualifies under this paragraph if it was given—

(*a*) to the person or one of the persons exercising the right to buy;

(*b*) to the spouse of that person or one of those persons; or

(*c*) to the deceased spouse of that person or one of those persons.

(2) A previous discount shall not qualify by virtue of sub-paragraph (1)(*b*) above unless the person concerned and his spouse were living together at the relevant time.

(3) A previous discount shall not qualify by virtue of sub-paragraph (1)(*c*) above unless the person concerned and his deceased spouse were living together at the time of the death.

7.—(1) Where the whole or any part of a previous discount has been recovered by the person by whom it was given (whether by the receipt of a payment determined by reference to the discount or by a reduction so determined of any consideration given by that person or in any other way), so much of the discount as has been so recovered shall be disregarded for the purposes of paragraph 6 above.

(2) Any reference in this paragraph to the person by whom a previous discount was given includes a reference to any successor in title of his.

8. Where a previous discount was given to two or more persons jointly, paragraphs 6 and 7 above shall be construed as if each of those persons had been given an equal proportion of that discount.

PART III

SUPPLEMENTAL

9.—(1) For the purposes of this Schedule, a tenancy which is not a long tenancy and under which a dwelling-house is let as a separate dwelling is a public sector tenancy at any time when the conditions described below as the landlord condition and the tenant condition are satisfied.

(2) The landlord condition is that the interest of the landlord belongs to—

    (a) a local authority within the meaning of section 50(1) of this Act, a county council, a district council within the meaning of the Local Government Act (Northern Ireland) 1972 or, in Scotland, a regional, district or islands council, a joint board or joint committee of such a council or the common good of such a council or any trust under its control;

    (b) the Housing Corporation;

    (c) the Scottish Special Housing Association;

    (d) the Northern Ireland Housing Executive;

    (e) a development corporation established by an order made or having effect as if made under the New Towns Act 1981 or the New Towns (Scotland) Act 1968 or an urban development corporation within the meaning of Part XVI of the Local Government Planning and Land Act 1980)

    (f) the Commission for the New Towns;

    (g) the Development Board for Rural Wales;

    (h) a housing association which falls within paragraph (a) of subsection (3) of section 15 of the 1977 Act but does not fall within paragraph (d) of that subsection;

    (i) a housing association which falls within paragraph (e) of section 10(2) of the Tenants' Rights, Etc. (Scotland) Act 1980 but is not a registered society within the meaning of section 11 of that Act;

    (j) a registered housing association within the meaning of Chapter II of Part II of the Housing (Northern Ireland) Order 1983;

    (k) a housing co-operative within the meaning of Schedule 20 to this Act or section 5 of the Housing Rents and Subsidies (Scotland) Act 1975; or

    (l) any predecessor of any person falling within the foregoing paragraphs;

or that, in such circumstances as may be prescribed for the purposes of this sub-paragraph by order of the Secretary of State, the interest of the landlord belongs to a person who is so prescribed.

(3) The tenant condition is that the tenant is an individual and occupies the dwelling-house as his only or principal home or, where the tenancy is a joint tenancy, each of the joint tenants is an individual and at least one of them occupies the dwelling-house as his only or principal home.

(4) References in this paragraph to a public sector tenancy or a public sector tenant are, in relation to any time before the commencement of Part I of the 1984 Act, references to a tenancy which would have been a public sector tenancy if that Part had then been in force or to a person who would have then been a public sector tenant; and for the purpose of determining whether a person would have been a public sector tenant and his tenancy a public sector tenancy, a housing association shall be deemed to have been registered under Part II of the 1974 Act, or Chapter II of Part VII of the Housing (Northern Ireland) Order 1981, if it is or was so registered at any later time.

(5) Where a person who is not the tenant of a dwelling-house has a licence (whether or not granted for a consideration) to occupy the dwelling-house and the circumstances are such that, if the licence were a tenancy, it would be a public sector tenancy, then, subject to sub-paragraph (6) below, this Schedule applies to the licence as it applies to a public

sector tenancy and, as so applying, has effect as if expressions appropriate to a licence were substituted for "landlord", "tenant", "public sector tenant", "tenancy" and "public sector tenancy".

(6) Sub-paragraph (5) above does not apply to a licence which was granted as a temporary expedient to a person who entered a dwelling-house or any other land as a trespasser (whether or not before another licence to occupy that or another dwelling-house had been granted to him).

10.—(1) In this Schedule—

"armed forces occupier" means a person who occupies accommodation provided for him as a member of the regular armed forces of the Crown;

"conveyance" means a conveyance of the freehold or an assignment of a long lease;

"dwelling-house" includes a house within the meaning of the 1957 Act;

"grant" means a grant of a long lease;

"long lease" means a lease creating a long tenancy within the meaning of paragraph 1 of Schedule 3 to this Act or a tenancy falling within paragraph 1 of Schedule 2 to the Housing (Northern Ireland) Order 1983;

"previous discount" means a discount which was given, before the relevant time, on a conveyance or grant with respect to which the requirements of sub-paragraph (2) below were satisfied;

"public sector tenant" means a tenant under a public sector tenancy;

"regular armed forces of the Crown" has the same meaning as in section 1 of the House of Commons Disqualification Act 1975;

"relevant time" has the meaning given by section 3(5) of this Act.

(2) The requirements of this sub-paragraph are satisfied with respect to a conveyance or grant of a dwelling-house if the vendor or lessor is—

(*a*) a person falling within paragraph 9(2) above; or

(*b*) in such circumstances as may be prescribed for the purposes of this sub-paragraph by order of the Secretary of State, a person who is so prescribed.

GENERAL NOTE

This Schedule introduces a new 1980 Sched. 1A in three parts. Pt. I (a) harmonises periods of qualification to buy with periods of qualification for discount, (b) adds to the periods of qualification as thus harmonised, and (c) gives to children of secure tenants an absolute right to buy in place of a former discretionary inclusion; see notes to s.3 above. Pt. II alters the basis for calculation of discount for previous purchasers; see notes to s.3 above. Pt. III is supplemental.

Part I

The key to the extensions is to be found in the concept of the "public sector tenancy", as defined in para. 9. Broadly, it is time spent as a public sector tenant which serves as qualifying time, either for the purposes of right to buy or for discount.

Para. 1: The periods identified in the following paragraphs are to be added together to constitute entitlement, either to buy or to discount.

Para. 2: The first period to be taken into account is a period in which (a) the secure tenant, or (b) his or her spouse, or (c) his or her deceased spouse, was (i) a public sector tenant, or (ii) the spouse of a public sector tenant. The period ceases at the date of service of the notice claiming the right to buy ("the relevant time": 1980 Act s.3(5)).

However, certain periods apparently qualifying are excluded. The first is that time spent by the tenant, tenant's spouse or tenant's deceased spouse as the spouse of a public sector tenant does not qualify unless during that time he or she was occupying the property as his or her only or principal home: para. 2(2).

Thus, if ex-H was a public sector tenant of property A, and the parties separated, and W is the secure tenant now seeking to establish the right to buy at property B, or count a period for discount, she will only be able to count the time she spent in property A as her only or principal home. If, therefore, on separation, *she* left the former home,' she also abandoned the acquisition of a further period at property A. If ex-H left, however, then even though he remained the secure tenant of property A, and was not living with her, she can continue to acquire more time.

Reliance may only be placed on a period of public sector tenancy of a spouse, if the secure tenant and spouse are living together at the time the right to buy is claimed: para. 2(3). Similarly, reliance may only be placed on a period of public sector tenancy of a deceased spouse, if the secure tenant and deceased spouse were living together at the time of death: para. 2(4). However, occupation as a joint public sector tenant counts as occupation as a sole public sector tenant, provided the property in question was occupied as an only or principal home: para. 2(5).

Para. 3: Additional to the period or periods to be taken into account under the last paragraph is a period or periods prior to the service of the notice claiming the right to buy, during which the secure tenant or his or her spouse or deceased spouse occupied armed forces accommodation: para. 3(1). Such periods may only be added, however, if both (then) spouses occupied the armed forces accommodation: para. 3(2). Further, the time of a spouse or deceased spouse can only be added if the secure tenant was living with the spouse at the time of the right to buy claim, or at the time of death: para. 3(3), (4).

Para. 4: The child of a public sector tenant, who becomes a secure tenant (whether or not because of statutory succession; see notes to s.26 above introducing a new 1980 Act s.37, under the provisions of which a secure tenant may assign to a child who could have qualified under the statutory succession provisions had the tenant died—and whether or not under the same tenancy) will be able to count time spent in the property, provided such time was occupation as an only or principal home.

Only time from the age of 16 is to be taken into account. Furthermore, the time to be taken into account must be immediately before the date when the new tenant took over, or a period ending not more than two years before that date. There will have to be *some* period (of at least one year) immediately before taking over, because there could otherwise be no succession (see 1980 Act s.30) and if there is no capacity for succession there is no right to take an assignment (and remain secure); see notes to s.26 above. The alternative limb, therefore, permits the addition of a continuous period (of however long) ending within the prior two years.

Part II

Para. 5: See notes to s.3 above. The new principle governing discount for second-time purchasers is to deduct actual discounts previously allowed, rather than excluding periods of time prior to the previous purchase. All qualifying previous discounts are to be deducted.

Para. 6: A previous discount qualifies if it was given to the purchaser, or one of the purchasers, or the spouse of the purchaser or one of the purchasers, or the deceased spouse of the purchaser or one of the purchasers. However, a previous discount given to a spouse is not to count unless the purchaser (or one of the purchasers) and the spouse were living together at the date of the notice claiming the right to buy (*i.e.* the relevant time; see 1980 Act s.3(5)). Similarly, unless the purchaser (or one of the purchasers) and deceased spouse were living together at the time of death, the deceased spouse's previous discount is not to count.

Para. 7: If the previous discount was the subject of a repayment under the 1980 Act s.8 (see also s.5 above) it is to be reduced by the amount of the repayment.

Para. 8: If a previous discount was given to joint purchasers, only one or less than all of whom is or are now the subject of reduced discount, the previous discount is to be treated as having been allowed in equal proportions.

Part III

Para. 9: This defines the "public sector tenant" who, when he acquires a secure tenancy, will be able to claim time for the purposes of qualification to buy, and to discount. Long tenancies within the 1980 Act, Sched. 3, para. 1 are excluded. Tenants of housing associations qualify if the association is, or becomes, registered (not including co-operative and co-ownership societies within s.74 of the Industrial and Provident Societies Act 1965 (see Rent Act 1977, s.15(3)(*d*)), including housing *management* co-operatives). The Secretary of State has the power to prescribe further landlords for the purposes of this provision.

The definition set out in this paragraph proceeds through the key elements of the definition of secure tenancy itself, and leans heavily on the 1980 Act in this respect, although, of course, expanding where necessary. A public sector tenancy is one "let as a separate dwelling" (see the 1980 Act s.28(1)). The tenant condition is the same as in s.28(3) of the 1980 Act. The extension to licensees mirrors s.48(1) of the 1980 Act and the exclusion of sometime squatters corresponds to s.48(2) of that Act.

Section 12.   SCHEDULE 3

TERMS OF A SHARED OWNERSHIP LEASE

Tenant's initial share

1.—(1) Subject to sub-paragraph (2) below, the tenant's initial share in the dwelling-house shall be as stated in his notice under section 13(1) of this Act.

(2) The tenant's initial share in the dwelling-house shall be a multiple of the prescribed percentage and shall not be less than the minimum initial share.

(3) The lease shall state the tenant's initial share in the dwelling-house.

(4) In this paragraph "minimum initial share" means 50 per cent. or such other percentage as the Secretary of State may by order prescribe.

(5) In this paragraph and paragraph 3 below "the prescribed percentage" means 12.5 per cent. or such other percentage as the Secretary of State may by order prescribe.

Tenant's initial contribution

2.—(1) The consideration for the grant of the lease (in this Part of this Act referred to as the tenant's initial contribution) shall be determined by the formula—

$$C = \frac{S(V - D)}{100}$$

where—

C = the tenant's initial contribution;

S = the tenant's initial share expressed as a percentage;

V = the amount agreed between the parties or determined by the district valuer as the amount which, under this paragraph, is to be taken as the value of the dwelling-house at the relevant time;

D = the discount which, if the tenant were exercising the right to buy, would be applicable under section 7 of the 1980 Act.

(2) The value of the dwelling-house at the relevant time shall be taken to be the price which, at that time, it would realise if sold on the open market by a willing vendor—

(*a*) where the dwelling-house is a house and the landlord owns the freehold, on the assumptions stated in subsection (3) of section 6 of the 1980 Act;

(*b*) where the landlord does not own the freehold or (whether or not the landlord owns it) the dwelling-house is a flat, on the assumptions stated in subsection (4) of that section,

and (in either case) disregarding any improvements made by any of the persons specified in subsection (5) of that section and any failure by any of those persons to keep the dwelling-house in good internal repair.

Additional shares

3.—(1) The lease shall contain provision enabling the tenant to acquire additional shares in the dwelling-house; and the right so conferred shall be exercisable at any time during the term of the lease on the tenant serving written notice on the landlord.

(2) Subject to sub-paragraph (3) below, an additional share shall be as stated in the tenant's notice under sub-paragraph (1) above.

(3) An additional share shall be the prescribed percentage or a multiple of the prescribed percentage.

(4) Where the tenant claims to exercise the right to acquire an additional share, the landlord shall, as soon as practicable, serve on the tenant a written notice stating—

(*a*) the amount which, in the opinion of the landlord, should be the amount of the consideration for that share determined in accordance with paragraph 4(1) below on the assumption that the share is as stated in the notice under sub-paragraph (1) above; and

(*b*) the effective discount on an acquisition of that share for that consideration determined in accordance with paragraph 6(3) below.

(5) Where the dwelling-house is a house and the landlord owns the freehold, the lease shall also provide that, on his acquiring an additional share such that his total share will be 100 per cent., the tenant shall be entitled to require the freehold to be conveyed either to himself or to such other person as he may direct; and the right so conferred shall be exercisable at any time during the term of the lease on the tenant serving written notice on the landlord.

(6) As soon as practicable after such a right as is mentioned in sub-paragraph (5) above has become exercisable, the landlord shall serve on the tenant a written notice—

(*a*) informing the tenant of the right; and

(*b*) stating the provisions which, in the opinion of the landlord, should be contained in the conveyance.

(7) A conveyance executed in pursuance of such a right as is mentioned in sub-paragraph (5) above—

(*a*) shall conform with Parts I and II of Schedule 2 to the 1980 Act (terms of conveyance);

(*b*) shall preserve the effect of the covenant required by paragraph 6(1) below; and

(*c*) where the lease contains any such covenant as is mentioned in section 19(1) of the 1980 Act, shall preserve the effect of that covenant.

(8) A notice required by this paragraph may be withdrawn at any time by notice in writing served on the landlord.

(9) Any reference in this Part of this Act to a tenant's total share is a reference to his initial share plus any additional share or shares in the dwelling-house acquired by him.

Additional contributions

4.—(1) The consideration for an additional share (in this Part of this Act referred to as an additional contribution) shall be determined by the formula—

$$C = \frac{S(V - D)}{100}$$

where—

C = the additional contribution;

S = the additional share expressed as a percentage;

V = the amount agreed between the parties or determined by the district valuer as the amount which, under this paragraph, is to be taken as the value of the dwelling-house at the time when the notice under paragraph 3(1) above is served;

D = the discount which, on the assumptions stated in sub-paragraph (2) below, would be applicable under section 7 of the 1980 Act.

(2) The said assumptions are that—

(*a*) the shared ownership lease had not been granted and the secure tenancy had not come to an end; and

(*b*) the tenant was exercising the right to buy and his notice under paragraph 3(1) above were a notice under section 5(1) of the 1980 Act.

(3) The value of the dwelling-house at the time when the notice under paragraph 3(1) above is served shall be taken to be the price which, at that time, the interest of the tenant would realise if sold on the open market by a willing vendor on the assumption that any mortgages of that interest and any liability under the covenants required by paragraphs 6(1) and 7(1) below would be discharged by the vendor and disregarding—

(*a*) any interests in or rights over the dwelling-house created by the tenant;

(*b*) any improvements made by the tenant or any of the other persons specified in section 6(5) of the 1980 Act; and

(*c*) any failure by the tenant or any of those persons—

   (i) where the dwelling-house is a house, to keep the dwelling-house in good repair (including decorative repair);

   (ii) where the dwelling-house is a flat, to keep the interior of the dwelling-house in such repair.

Rent

5.—(1) The lease shall provide that, for any period for which the tenant's total share is less than 100 per cent., the rent payable under the lease shall be determined by the formula—

$$R = \frac{F(100 - S)}{100}$$

where—

R = the rent payable;

F = the amount determined by the landlord as the rent which would be payable for that period if the shared ownership lease had not been granted and the secure tenancy had not come to an end, but excluding any element attributable to rates or to services provided by the landlord;

S = the tenant's total share expressed as a percentage.

(2) The lease shall also provide that, for any such period, if the Secretary of State by order so provides—

(*a*) the rent payable under the lease as so determined; or

(*b*) any amount payable by the tenant under the lease which is payable, directly or indirectly, for repairs, maintenance or insurance,

shall be adjusted in such manner as may be provided by the order.

(3) The lease shall provide that, for any period for which the tenant's total share is 100 per cent., the rent payable under the lease shall be £10 per annum.

(4) In making a determination under sub-paragraph (1) above, the landlord shall take into account all matters which appear to it to be relevant including, in particular, where comparable dwelling-houses in the locality are let on secure tenancies, the rents payable under those tenancies.

(5) The Secretary of State may by order under sub-paragraph (2) above provide for such adjustment as he considers appropriate having regard to the differing responsibilities for repairs, maintenance and insurance of a tenant under a shared ownership lease and a secure tenant.

(6) In this paragraph "rates" includes charges for services performed, facilities provided or rights made available by a water authority.

Repayment of discount on early disposal

6.—(1) The lease shall contain a covenant binding on the tenant and his successors in title to pay to the landlord on demand the amount specified in sub-paragraph (2) below if, within a period of five years commencing with the acquisition by the tenant of his initial share or the acquisition by him of an additional share, there is a relevant disposal which is not exempted by sub-paragraph (5) below; but if there is more than one such disposal, then only on the first of them.

(2) The amount payable under the covenant is the aggregate of the following amounts, namely—

(*a*) an amount equal to the effective discount (if any) to which the tenant was entitled on the acquisition of his initial share; and

(*b*) for each additional share acquired by the tenant, an amount equal to the effective discount (if any) to which the tenant was entitled on the acquisition of that share,

but reduced, in each case, by 20 per cent. of the discount for each complete year that elapses after the acquisition and before the disposal.

(3) The effective discount to which the tenant was entitled on the acquisition of his initial share or an additional share shall be determined by the formula—

$$E = \frac{S \times D}{100}$$

where—

E = the effective discount;

S = the tenant's initial share or, as the case may be, the additional share expressed (in either case) as a percentage;

D = the discount which was applicable by virtue of paragraph 2(1) or, as the case may be, paragraph 4(1) above.

(4) A disposal is a relevant disposal for the purposes of this paragraph and paragraphs 7 to 9 below if it is—

(*a*) an assignment of the lease; or

(*b*) the grant of a lease or sub-lease for a term of more than twenty-one years otherwise than at a rack rent,

whether the disposal is of the whole or part of the dwelling-house; and for the purposes of paragraph (*b*) above it shall be assumed that any option to renew or extend a lease or sub-lease, whether or not forming part of a series of options, is exercised, and that any option to terminate a lease or sub-lease is not exercised.

(5) A relevant disposal is exempted by this sub-paragraph if—

(*a*) it is a disposal of the whole of the dwelling-house and an assignment of the lease and the person or each of the persons to whom it is made is a qualifying person;

(*b*) it is a vesting of the whole of the dwelling-house in a person taking under a will or on an intestacy;

(*c*) it is a disposal of the whole of the dwelling-house in pursuance of an order under section 24 of the Matrimonial Causes Act 1973 or section 2 of the Inheritance (Provision for Family and Dependants) Act 1975;

(*d*) the property disposed of is acquired compulsorily or by a person who has made or would have made, or for whom another person has made or would have made, a compulsory purchase order authorising its compulsory purchase for the purposes for which it is acquired; or

(*e*) the property disposed of is land included in the dwelling-house by virtue of section 3(4) or 50(2) of the 1980 Act.

(6) For the purposes of sub-paragraph (5)(*a*) above a person is a qualifying person in relation to a disposal if he—

    (*a*) is the person or one of the persons by whom it is made;

    (*b*) is the spouse or a former spouse of that person or one of those persons; or

    (*c*) is a member of the family of that person or one of those persons and has resided with him throughout the period of twelve months ending with the disposal.

(7) Where there is a relevant disposal which is exempted by sub-paragraph (5)(*d*) or (*e*) above—

    (*a*) the covenant required by sub-paragraph (1) above shall not be binding on the person to whom the disposal is made or any successor in title of his; and

    (*b*) that covenant and the charge taking effect by virtue of sub-paragraph (10) below shall cease to apply in relation to the property disposed of.

(8) The reference in sub-paragraph (4) above to a lease or sub-lease does not include a mortgage term.

(9) For the purposes of this paragraph and paragraphs 7 to 9 below the grant of an option enabling a person to call for a relevant disposal which is not exempted by sub-paragraph (5) above shall be treated as such a disposal.

(10) Subsections (4) to (6) of section 8 of the 1980 Act shall apply in relation to the liability that may arise under the covenant required by sub-paragraph (1) above and that required by paragraph 7(1) below as they apply in relation to the liability that may arise under the covenant required by subsection (1) of that section.

Payment for outstanding share on disposal

7.—(1) The lease shall contain a covenant binding on the tenant and his successors in title to pay to the landlord on demand for the outstanding share an amount determined in accordance with sub-paragraph (2) below if, at a time when the tenant's total share is less than 100 per cent., there is—

    (*a*) a relevant disposal which is not exempted by sub-paragraph (5) of paragraph 6 above; or

    (*b*) a relevant disposal which is exempted by sub-paragraph (5)(*d*) of that paragraph (in this paragraph and paragraph 8 below referred to as a "compulsory disposal").

(2) The amount payable under the covenant shall be determined by the formula—

$$P = \frac{V(100 - S)}{100}$$

where—

    P = the amount payable under the covenant;

    V = the amount agreed between the parties or determined by the district valuer as the amount which, under this paragraph, is to be taken to be—

        (*a*) except in the case of a compulsory disposal of part of the dwelling-house, the value at the time of the disposal of the dwelling-house; or

        (*b*) in the said excepted case, the value at the time of the disposal of the part of the dwelling-house disposed of;

    S = the tenant's total share expressed as a percentage.

(3) The value at the time of the disposal of the dwelling-house or the part of the dwelling-house disposed of shall be taken to be the price which, at that time, the interest of the tenant therein would realise if sold on the open market by a willing vendor on the assumption that any mortgages of that interest and any liability under the covenants required by paragraph 6(1) and sub-paragraph (1) above would be discharged by the vendor and disregarding—

    (*a*) any interests in or rights over the dwelling-house created by the tenant;

    (*b*) any improvements made by the tenant or any of the other persons specified in section 6(5) of the 1980 Act; and

    (*c*) any failure by the tenant or any of those persons—

        (i) where the dwelling-house is a house, to keep the dwelling-house in good repair (including decorative repair);

        (ii) where the dwelling-house is a flat, to keep the interior of the dwelling-house in such repair.

(4) The lease shall also provide that, on the discharge of a liability arising under the covenant required by sub-paragraph (1) above,—

    (*a*) except in the case of a compulsory disposal of part of the dwelling-house, the rent payable under the lease shall be £10 per annum; and

    (*b*) in the said excepted case, the rent payable under the lease so far as relating to the part of the dwelling-house disposed of shall be £10 per annum.

(5) Where the dwelling-house is a house and the landlord owns the freehold, the lease shall also provide that on the discharge of a liability arising under the covenant required by sub-paragraph (1) above,—

(*a*) except in the case of a compulsory disposal of part of the dwelling-house, any person in whom the tenant's interest in the dwelling-house is vested; or

(*b*) in the said excepted case, any person in whom the tenant's interest in the part of the dwelling-house disposed of is vested,

shall be entitled to require the freehold thereof to be conveyed either to himself or to such other person as he may direct; and a right so conferred on any person shall be exercisable at any time during the term of the lease on that person serving written notice on the landlord.

(6) As soon as practicable after such a right as is mentioned in sub-paragraph (5) above has become exercisable by any person, the landlord shall serve on that person a written notice—

(*a*) informing him of the right; and

(*b*) stating the provisions which, in the opinion of the landlord, should be contained in the conveyance.

(7) A conveyance executed in pursuance of such a right as is mentioned in sub-paragraph (5) above—

(*a*) shall conform with Parts I and II of Schedule 2 to the 1980 Act (terms of conveyance); and

(*b*) where the lease contains any such covenant as is mentioned in section 19(1) of the 1980 Act, shall preserve the effect of that covenant.

(8) A notice required by sub-paragraph (5) above may be withdrawn at any time by notice in writing served on the landlord.

No disposals of part while share outstanding

8.—(1) The lease shall contain a covenant binding on the tenant and his successors in title that there will be no relevant disposal of part of the dwelling-house, other than a compulsory disposal, at any time when the tenant's total share is less than 100 per cent.

(2) Any disposal in breach of the covenant required by sub-paragraph (1) above shall be void.

Supplemental

9.—(1) The lease shall provide that, in the event of a relevant disposal which is exempted by sub-paragraph (5)(*a*), (*b*) or (*c*) of paragraph 6 above, references to the tenant in the provisions of the lease required by this Schedule shall include references to the person to whom the disposal is made.

(2) The lease shall also provide that, in the event of a relevant disposal which is exempted by sub-paragraph (5)(*d*) of that paragraph, being a disposal of part of the dwelling-house, references to the dwelling-house in the provisions of the lease required by this Schedule shall be construed as references to the remaining part of the dwelling-house.

10.—(1) Any power to make an order under this Schedule shall be exercisable by statutory instrument which shall be subject to annulment in pursuance of a resolution of either House of Parliament.

(2) Any order under this Schedule—

(*a*) may make different provision with respect to different cases or descriptions of case, including different provision for different areas; and

(*b*) may contain such transitional provisions as appear to the Secretary of State to be necessary or expedient.

GENERAL NOTE

This Schedule governs the terms of a shared ownership lease, the right to acquire which is introduced by ss.12–17 and s.37 above. See also Sched. 11, para. 1, for the rights acquired by a shared ownership lessee under the Leasehold Reform Act 1967.

Para. 1: When claiming the right to a shared ownership lease, the tenant must state how much equity he seeks to acquire. This must be a multiple of 12·5 per cent., and not less than 50 per cent.: it must, accordingly, be 50 per cent., 62·5 per cent., 75 per cent. or 87·5 per cent. However, the Secretary of State may by order prescribe different percentages for 50 per cent. and 12·5 per cent. The 50 per cent. minimum is called the "minimum initial share", and the 12·5 per cent. factor is the "prescribed percentage". That which the tenant opts for is the "tenant's initial share".

Para. 2: The "tenant's initial contribution" is the price which the tenant must pay for the initial share. The contribution is to be the same percentage of what the tenant would have to pay were the full right to buy exercised, calculated (and determined) in all other respects as if it was a full exercise.

Para. 3: The shared ownership lease is to contain a provision enabling the tenant to acquire further shares—in tranches of the prescribed percentage or a multiple thereof. The right is to be exercisable on written notice, stating how much more of the equity the tenant wants (his "additional share"). The landlord is to respond with a notice stating consideration due, and how much discount has been allowed for in that calculation. This consideration is known as the "additional contribution".

The lease is also to contain a provision entitling conveyance to a tenant who has acquired 100 per cent. of the equity of the freehold of a house of which the landlord owns the freehold. This right is exercisable at any time, also by service of notice. The conveyance may be to the tenant, or to a person nominated by the tenant. Where what is in issue is a lease, because the property is a flat or the landlord has only a leasehold interest, the tenant's "100 per cent. entitlement" is to a lease of five days less than the landlord's interest *cf.* Sched. 1, para. 10 adding a new 1980 Act Sched. 2, para. 11 (see notes above).

Para. 4: The price for additional shares is calculated on the same basis as the initial share, *save* that the valuation of the property is as at the date when the notice seeking an additional share is served. The tenant thus buys subsequent tranches at later valuations, which will normally mean at a higher price. Discount entitlement also continues, however, to the date of the notice seeking the subsequent slice. It would seem that this is at the full rate, rather than "further discounted" to reflect the fact that occupation since the initial grant has been as shared owner. That is to say, the tenant continues to acquire a full discount for each year of occupation, even though he is occupying "half" (for example) as owner; see sub-para. (2)(*a*). The discount is, though, only a percentage, and of course is now to be applied to a share that will be at most 50 per cent.

Sub-paragraph (3) "adapts" the normal assumptions for calculation of value of a lease to the particular circumstance of the "shared owner" seeking a further tranche of the equity, *i.e.* a circumstance which is neither wholly future (as on a normal grant of a lease) nor wholly past (as under, *e.g.* an option to purchase a superior interest). The amount payable will not be affected, *i.e.* reduced, either by a mortgage, or by rights over or interests in the property which have been created by the shared owner.

Para. 5: Rent is to be the appropriate proportion of what would otherwise be a "normal" secure tenant's rent (see sub-para. (3)). The purpose of sub-para. (3) is clearly to prevent penally high rents being set in respect of properties subject to an exercise of the right to a shared ownership lease.

Local authorities have a discretion to set their own "reasonable" rent levels (Housing Act 1957, s.111). They may charge differential rents for similar properties (see *Leeds Corporation* v. *Jenkinson* [1935] 1 K.B. 168; *Summerfield* v. *Hampstead Borough Council* [1957] 1 W.L.R. 157; see also *Mandeville* v. *Greater London Council, The Times*, January 28, 1982). Sub-para. (3) does not *prohibit* the use of rent differentials where shared ownership leases are involved, but it does *require* consideration of other rent levels, and this, in effect, places a burden on authorities to show that their decision to use the rent-differential discretion has been properly reached.

The "rent base" is to exclude rates (including water rates; see sub-para. (5)) and services, which will of course be charged separately under the lease. But the Secretary of State may prescribe an "adjustment" to the base rent, or to charges for repairs, maintenance or insurance: sub-paras. (2) and (5). Once the tenant acquires 100 per cent. of the equity, the rent is to become £10 per annum, as with a conventional lease under the right to buy (see 1980 Act Sched. 2, para. 11, as substituted by Sched. 1, para. 10 above).

Para. 6: Both on the acquisition of an initial share, and on the acquisition of additional shares, the landlord's notice stating the contribution has to identify the "effective discount" to which the tenant was entitled (see s.14(1)(*b*), and para. 3(4)(*b*) above). This paragraph provides for repayment of the discount on early disposal, in line with the provisions governing a full exercise (1980 Act s.8, as amended by s.5 above; see notes thereto; note, however, the additional burdens of para. 7 and 8 below).

The requirement lasts for five years from the initial acquisition, *or* from the acquisition of additional shares. Under sub-para. (2) 20 per cent. is deducted from (a) the initial effective discount, for each year of occupation following the initial acquisition, and (b) subsequent effective discounts, for each year of occupation following each subsequent acquisition.

Para. 7: In the case of a disposal—whether or not within the period for recoupment of discount (see last paragraph)—which is *not* in the class of "exempt disposal" (*i.e.* one which would not attract the requirement to repay the discount; see s.5 above) the landlord is entitled to require the tenant to buy out any residual equity: sub-para. (1)(*a*). This provision also arises in the case of an exempt disposal which is a compulsory purchase, or a purchase by agreement by a body which could have purchased compulsorily (see notes to s.5(2) above): sub-para. 1(*b*).

Disposals *not* within this category (*i.e.* "exempt disposals" excluding the compulsory purchase cases) are prohibited outright at any time when the tenant owns less than 100 per cent. of the equity; see para. 8 below.

The remaining provisions of para. 7 put into effect the same consequences for this "counter-notice purchase" as would arise on the tenant's voluntary acquisition of the balance of the equity.

Para. 8: This paragraph prohibits disposals of the class which would not attract repayment of the discount (excluding compulsory purchase cases, *i.e.* actual or by agreement where compulsory purchase could have been effected; see notes to s.5 and paras. 6 and 7 above) at any time when the tenant owns less than 100 per cent. In effect, then, the repayment of discount provisions (para. 7) bite only once the tenant has bought 100 per cent., and only if the appropriate (five-year) period is still running. Disposals contrary to this prohibition are void.

Section 18.   SCHEDULE 4

SERVICE CHARGES IN RESPECT OF CERTAIN HOUSES

Service charge and relevant costs

1.—(1) In this Schedule "service charge" has the meaning given by section 18(1) of this Act.

(2) For the purposes of this Schedule relevant costs are costs or estimated costs (including overheads) incurred or to be incurred in any period (whether the period for which the service charge is payable or an earlier or later period) by or on behalf of the payee or (in the case of a lease) a superior landlord in connection with the matters for which the service charge is payable.

(3) Other expressions used in this Schedule are to be construed in accordance with paragraphs 11 to 13 below.

Limitation of service charges

2. The extent to which relevant costs are taken into account in determining the amount of a service charge payable for any period shall be limited in accordance with paragraph 3 below, and the amount payable shall be limited accordingly; and where the service charge is payable before the relevant costs are incurred—

(*a*) no greater amount shall be so payable than is reasonable; and

(*b*) after the relevant costs have been incurred any necessary adjustment shall be made by repayment, reduction of subsequent charges or otherwise.

3. Costs are to be taken into account only to the extent that they are reasonably incurred, and costs incurred on the provision of services or the carrying out of works only if the services or works are of a reasonable standard.

Information as to relevant costs

4.—(1) If the payer requests the payee in writing to supply him with a written summary of the costs incurred in the relevant period defined in sub-paragraph (4) below which are relevant to the service charges payable or demanded as payable by the payer in that or any other period, the payee shall do so within six months of the end of the period or within one month of the request, whichever is the later.

(2) The summary shall set out those costs in a way showing how they are or will be reflected in demands for service charges, and must be certified by a qualified accountant as in his opinion a fair summary complying with this requirement and as beng sufficiently supported by accounts, receipts and other documents which have been produced to him.

(3) Where the payer has obtained such a summary as is referred to in sub-paragraph (1) above (whether in pursuance of this paragraph or otherwise) the payer may, within six months of obtaining it, require the payee in writing to afford him reasonable facilities for inspecting the accounts, receipts and other documents supporting the summary and for taking copies or extracts from them, and the payee shall then make such facilities available

to the payer for a period of two months beginning not later than one month after the request is made.

(4) The relevant period mentioned in sub-paragraph (1) above is—

    (*a*) if the relevant accounts are made up for periods of twelve months, the last such period ending not later than the date of the request; and

    (*b*) if none are made up for such a period, the period of twelve months ending with the request.

Information held by superior landlord

5.—(1) If a request made under paragraph 4(1) above relates in whole or in part to relevant costs incurred by or on behalf of a superior landlord, and the payee is not in possession of the relevant information—

    (*a*) he shall in turn make a written request for the relevant information to the person who is his landlord (and so on if that person is not himself the superior landlord) and the superior landlord shall then comply with the request within a reasonable time; and

    (*b*) it shall be the duty of the payee to comply with the payer's request, or that part of it which relates to the relevant costs incurred by or on behalf of the superior landlord, within the time allowed by paragraph 4 above or within such further time, if any, as is reasonable in the circumstances.

(2) If a request made under paragraph 4(3) above relates to a summary of costs incurred by or on behalf of a superior landlord, the payee shall forthwith inform the payer of that fact and the name and address of the superior landlord, and paragraph 4(3) above shall then apply as if the superior landlord were the payee.

Service of requests under paragraph 4

6. A request under paragraph 4 above shall be deemed to be served on the payee if it is served on a person who receives the service charge on behalf of the payee; and a person on whom a request is so served shall forward it as soon as possible to the payee.

Effect of disposal

7. A disposal of the dwelling-house by the payer shall not affect the validity of a request made under paragraph 4 above before the disposal, but a person shall not be obliged to provide a summary or make the facilities available more than once for the same dwelling-house and for the same period.

Determination of reasonableness.

8. Any agreement made by the payer, other than an arbitration agreement within the meaning of section 32 of the Arbitration Act 1950, shall be void in so far as it purports to provide for a determination in a particular manner or on particular evidence of any question whether any amount payable before costs for services, repair, maintenance, insurance or management are incurred is reasonable, whether such costs were reasonably incurred or whether services or works for which costs were incurred are of a reasonable standard.

Offences

9.—(1) If any person without reasonable excuse fails to perform any duty imposed on him by this Schedule he shall be guilty of an offence and liable on summary conviction to a fine not exceeding level 4 on the standard scale (as defined in section 75 of the Criminal Justice Act 1982).

(2) Where an offence under this paragraph which has been committed by a body corporate is proved to have been committed with the consent or connivance of, or to be attributable to any neglect on the part of, a director, manager, secretary or other similar officer of the body corporate, or any person who was purporting to act in any such capacity, he, as well as the body corporate, shall be guilty of an offence and be liable to be proceeded against and punished accordingly.

(3) Where the affairs of a body corporate are managed by its members, sub-paragraph (2) shall apply in relation to the acts and defaults of a member in connection with his functions of management as if he were a director of the body corporate.

Exceptions

10.—(1) Where the payee is a body mentioned in sub-paragraph (2) below—
  (*a*) paragraph 9 above does not apply, and
  (*b*) the persons who are qualified accountants include a member of the Chartered Institute of Public Finance and Accountancy and paragraph 11(2)(*b*) below does not apply.
(2) The bodies referred to in sub-paragraph (1) above are—
  (*a*) a local authority or development corporation (as defined in section 50(1) of the 1980 Act),
  (*b*) the council of a county,
  (*c*) the Commission for the New Towns,
  (*d*) the Development Board for Rural Wales.

Definitions

11.—(1) Subject to sub-paragraph (2) below, a person is a qualified accountant if he is either a member of one of the following bodies—
  (*a*) the Institute of Chartered Accountants in England and Wales;
  (*b*) the Institute of Chartered Accountants of Scotland;
  (*c*) the Association of Certified Accountants;
  (*d*) The Institute of Chartered Accountants in Ireland;
  (*e*) any other body of accountants established in the United Kingdom and recognised by the Secretary of State for the purposes of section 161(1)(*a*) of the Companies Act 1948,
or a person who is for the time being authorised by the Secretary of State under section 161(1)(*b*) of that Act as being a person with similar qualifications obtained outside the United Kingdom.
(2) None of the following is a qualified accountant—
  (*a*) a body corporate;
  (*b*) an officer or employee of the payee or, where the payee is a company, of a company which the payee's holding company or subsidiary (within the meaning of section 154 of the Companies Act 1948) or a subsidiary of the payee's holding company; and
  (*c*) a person who is a partner or employee or any such officer or employee.
(3) A Scottish firm is a qualified accountant, notwithstanding sub-paragraph (2)(*a*) above, if each of the partners in it is a qualified accountant.
12. "Payee" means the person who is entitled to enforce payment of the service charge.
13. "Payer" means the person liable to pay the service charge.

GENERAL NOTE

The provisions of s.18 apply both to right to buy transactions and to voluntary sales. They are applicable *only* in relation to houses (*i.e.* not flats) where the freehold is conveyed, or a lease granted, by specified public landlords; see notes to s.18 above. They concern the recovery of "service charges" from the purchaser, *i.e.* under the terms of a lease or conveyance, "for services, repairs, maintenance or insurance or the vendor's or lessor's costs of management", and which costs do or may vary according to expenditure (s.18(1)(*b*)). They are aimed at leases of houses, and sales on estates where there may be a number of common facilities, communal areas, estate management and maintenance, etc.
The provisions are modelled very closely on those contained in Sched. 19 of the 1980 Act applicable to service charges in flats. The principal omissions are: requirements for prior estimates (1980 Act Sched. 19, paras. 4–6); express jurisdiction in the county court to determine questions such as reasonableness of costs, or standard of works (*ibid.* para. 12— but such power exists under (i) this Act, Sched. 11, para. 24 below, and (ii) County Courts Act 1984, s.22, provided the rateable value of the dwelling-house is within the limits for the time being applicable to county court jurisdiction); and provision for the recognition of tenants' associations (1980 Act Sched. 19, paras. 20 and 21—some occupiers will, of course, no longer be tenants).
Paras. 2 and 3: Service charges are to be based on actual costs only to the extent that they are reasonably incurred and provide services or work to a reasonable standard, and estimated costs only to a reasonable amount and subject to provision for subsequent adjustment.
Para. 4: Within six months of a written demand, the payee (see para. 12) must provide a written summary of the costs incurred during either (a) the last 12-month period ending before the request, if accounts are made up in 12-monthly periods, or (b) if no accounts are made up for 12-monthly periods, the last 12 months ending with the request. The accounts

must show how costs are or will be reflected in service charges, and must be certified by a qualified accountant (as defined in para. 11, subject in the case of public authorities to para. 10, *i.e.* by the inclusion of CIPFA members and their own employees). There is also provision for inspection and copying of accounts, receipts and other supporting documentation.

Para. 5: The landlord must relay requests for information to superior landlords, where the superior landlord possesses the relevant information and, if the relevant information cannot be obtained within the time allowed in para. 4, within such time as is reasonable in the circumstances.

Para. 9: Local and other public authorities (see para. 10(2)) are not subject to criminal sanctions. Other landlords affected, *e.g.* housing associations, may be.

Section 19.   SCHEDULE 5

VESTING OF MORTGAGED DWELLING-HOUSE IN
LOCAL AUTHORITY ETC.

Vesting of dwelling-house with leave of court

1.—(1) In any case where this Schedule applies, the authority may, if the county court gives it leave to do so, by deed vest the dwelling-house in itself—

(a) for such estate and interest in the dwelling-house as is the subject of the mortgage or as it would be authorised to sell or convey on exercising its power of sale; and

(b) freed from all estates, interests and rights to which the mortgage has priority,

but subject to all estates, interests and rights which have priority to the mortgage.

(2) Where application for leave under this paragraph is made to the county court, the court may adjourn the proceedings or postpone the date for the execution of the authority's deed for such period or periods as the court thinks reasonable.

(3) Any such adjournment or postponement may be made subject to such conditions with regard to payment by the mortgagor of any sum secured by the mortgage or the remedy of any default as the court thinks fit; and the court may from time to time vary or revoke any such condition.

Effect of vesting

2.—(1) On the vesting of the dwelling-house the authority's mortgage term or charge by way of legal mortgage, and any subsequent mortgage term or charge, shall merge or be extinguished as respects the dwelling-house.

(2) Where the dwelling-house is registered under the Land Registration Acts 1925 to 1971, the Chief Land Registrar shall, on application being made to him by the authority, register the authority as proprietor of the dwelling-house free from all estates, interests and rights to which its mortgage had priority, and he shall not be concerned to inquire whether any of the requirements of this Schedule were complied with.

(3) Where the authority conveys the dwelling-house, or part of it, to any person—

(a) he shall not be concerned to inquire whether any of the provisions of this Schedule were complied with; and

(b) his title shall not be impeachable on the ground that the dwelling-house was not properly vested in the authority or that those provisions were not complied with.

(4) A dwelling-house vested under this Schedule in a local authority (as defined in section 50 of the 1980 Act) shall be treated as acquired under Part V of the 1957 Act.

Compensation and accounting

3.—(1) Where, under paragraph 1 above, the authority has vested the dwelling-house in itself it shall appropriate a fund equal to the aggregate of—

(a) the amount agreed between the authority and the mortgagor or determined by the district valuer as being the amount which under sub-paragraph (2) below is to be taken as the value of the dwelling-house at the time of the vesting; and

(b) interest on that amount for the period beginning with the vesting and ending with the appropriation at the rate or rates prescribed for that period under section 32 of the Land Compensation Act 1961.

(2) The value of the dwelling-house at the time of the vesting shall be taken to be the price which, at that time, the interest vested in the authority would realise if sold on the

open market by a willing vendor on the assumption that any prior incumbrances to which the vesting is not made subject would be discharged by the vendor.

(3) The fund shall be applied—

    (a) first, in discharging, or paying sums into court for meeting, any prior incumbrances to which the vesting is not made subject;

    (b) secondly, in recovering the costs, charges and expenses properly incurred by the authority as incidental to the vesting of the dwelling-house;

    (c) thirdly, in recovering the mortgage money, interest, costs, and other money (if any) due under the mortgage; and

    (d) fourthly, in recovering any amount which falls to be paid under the covenant required by section 104B(2) of the 1957 Act, section 8(1) of the 1980 Act or paragraph 6(1) or 7(1) of Schedule 3 to this Act or any provision of the conveyance or grant to the like effect;

and any residue then remaining in the fund shall be paid to the person entitled to the mortgaged dwelling-house, or who would have been entitled to give receipts for the proceeds of sale of the dwelling-house if it had been sold in the exercise of the power of sale.

(4) Section 107(1) of the Law of Property Act 1925 (mortgagee's written receipt sufficient discharge for money arising under power of sale) applies to money payable under this Schedule as it applies to money arising under the power of sale conferred by that Act.

GENERAL NOTE

This Schedule contains the provisions ancillary to the vesting power contained in s.19 above, which are equivalent to those applicable to vesting orders under the 1980 Act s.112, contained in *ibid.* ss.112 and 113.

Para. 1: Note the powers of the county court in sub-paras. (2) and (3). They may be compared with the powers of the court in the Administration of Justice Act 1970, s.36: there is no requirement in this Schedule to show that in the event of the court exercising its powers, the mortgagor is likely to be able to pay any sums due under the mortgage within a reasonable period.

Para. 2: Note the protection for purchasers contained in sub-para. (3). Property vested in the authority is treated as acquired under the Housing Act 1957, Pt. V (*i.e.* the principal housing stock ownership powers): sub-para. (4).

Para. 3: The authority must set up a fund equal to the amount which it would have had to pay in exercise of its rights of pre-emption, together with interest thereon. This money is to be applied in the discharge of any interests *prior* to the mortgage, which are discharged by the vesting; next in recovering the costs, charges and expenses incidental to the vesting; thirdly, in recovering principal, interest, costs and other monies due under the mortgage; finally, the residue—if any—is to be paid to the person entitled to the mortgaged property, or who would have been entitled to the receipts had it been sold.

Section 23.   SCHEDULE 6

AMENDMENTS OF SECTIONS 104B AND 104C OF 1957 ACT

Section 104B

1.—(1) In subsection (2) of section 104B of the 1957 Act (repayment of discount on early disposal) for the words "disposal falling within subsection (4)" there shall be substituted the words "relevant disposal which is not exempted by subsection (4A)".

(2) For subsection (4) of that section there shall be substituted the following subsections—

    "(4) A disposal is a relevant disposal for the purposes of this section if it is—

        (a) a conveyance of the freehold or an assignment of the lease; or

        (b) the grant of a lease or sub-lease for a term of more than twenty-one years otherwise than at a rack rent,

whether the disposal is of the whole or part of the house; and for the purposes of paragraph (b) above it shall be assumed that any option to renew or extend a lease or sub-lease, whether or not forming part of a series of options, is exercised, and that any option to terminate a lease or sub-lease is not exercised.

    (4A) A relevant disposal is exempted by this subsection if—

        (a) it is a disposal of the whole of the house and conveyance of the freehold or an assignment of the lease and the person or each of the persons to whom it is made is a qualifying person;

   (b) it is a vesting of the whole of the house in a person taking under a will or on an intestacy;

   (c) it is a disposal of the whole of the house in pursuance of an order under section 24 of the Matrimonial Causes Act 1973 or section 2 of the Inheritance (Provision for Family and Dependants) Act 1975;

   (d) the property disposed of is acquired compulsorily or by a person who has made or would have made, or for whom another person has made or would have made a compulsory purchase order authorising its compulsory purchase for the purposes for which it is acquired; or

   (e) the property disposed of is land falling within paragraph (a) of the definition of 'house' in section 189(1) of this Act.

(4B) For the purposes of subsection (4A)(a) above a person is a qualifying person in relation to a disposal if he—

   (a) is the person or one of the persons by whom it is made;

   (b) is the spouse or a former spouse of that person or one of those persons; or

   (c) is a member of the family of that person or one of those persons (within the meaning of Chapter II of Part I of the Housing Act 1980) and has resided with him throughout the period of twelve months ending with the disposal.

(4C) Where there is a relevant disposal which is exempted by subsection (4A)(d) or (e) above—

   (a) the covenant required by subsection (2) above shall not be binding on the person to whom the disposal is made or any successor in title of his; and

   (b) that covenant and the charge taking effect by virtue of subsection (5) below shall cease to apply in relation to the property disposed of."

(3) In subsection (5) of that section for the words "specified in" there shall be substituted the words "falling within".

(4) After that subsection there shall be inserted the following subsection—

"(5A) The local authority may at any time by written notice served on a body falling within subsection (6) below postpone the charge taking effect by virtue of subsection (5) above to any legal charge securing any amount advanced or further advanced to the purchaser by that body."

(5) For subsection (6) of that section there shall be substituted the following subsection—

"(6) The bodies referred to in subsections (5)(b) and (5A) above are—

   (a) any building society;

   (b) any body falling with paragraphs 6 to 9 of the Schedule to the Home Purchase Assistance and Housing Corporation Guarantee Act 1978; and

   (c) any body specified or of a class or description specified in an order made under section 8(5) of the Housing Act 1980."

(6) In subsection (9) of that section, for the words "disposal falling within subsection (4) above" there shall be substituted the words "relevant disposal which is not exempted by subsection (4A) above".

(7) Where any conveyance, grant or assignment executed under section 104 of the 1957 Act or section 122 of the 1980 Act before the commencement date contains the covenant required by section 104B(2) of the 1957 Act, then, as from that date, that covenant shall have effect with such modifications as may be necessary to bring it into conformity with the amendments made by this paragraph.

Section 104C

2.—(1) In subsection (1) of section 104C of the 1957 Act (houses in National Parks and areas of outstanding natural beauty etc.) for the words "by order of the Secretary of State" there shall be substituted the words "under section 19 of the Housing Act 1980" and for the words "and his successors in title" there shall be substituted the words "(including any successor in title of his and any person deriving title under him or any such successor)".

(2) In subsection (2) of that section for the words "or his successors in title" there shall be substituted the words "or a successor in title of his" and for the words "disposal falling within subsection (4) below" there shall be substituted the words "relevant disposal which is not exempted by section 104B(4A) of this Act".

(3) Subsection (4) of that section shall be omitted.

(4) For subsection (7) of that section there shall be substituted the following subsections—

"(7) Where there is a relevant disposal which is exempted by section 104B(4A)(*d*) or (*e*) of this Act, the covenant mentioned in subsection (1) above shall cease to apply to the property disposed of.

(7A) In this section 'relevant disposal' has the same meaning as in section 104B of this Act."

(5) In subsection (9) of that section for the words from "means" onwards there shall be substituted the words "has the same meaning as in section 19 of the Housing Act 1980".

(6) In subsection (10) of that section for the words "disposal falling within subsection (4) above" there shall be substituted the words "relevant disposal which is not exempted by section 104B(4A) of this Act".

(7) Where any conveyance, grant or assignment executed under section 104 of the 1957 Act or section 122 of the 1980 Act before the commencement date contains such a covenant as is mentioned in section 104C(1) of the 1957 Act, then, as from that date, that covenant—

(*a*) shall be binding not only on the purchaser and any successor in title of his but also on any person deriving title under him or any such successor; and

(*b*) shall have effect with such modifications as may be necessary to bring it into conformity with the amendments made by this paragraph.

GENERAL NOTE

This Schedule amends the Housing Act 1957 provisions for voluntary disposals, to bring them into line with the 1980 Act right to buy provisions, as amended by this Act; see ss.5 and 8 above.

Section 26.   SCHEDULE 7

SCHEDULE INSERTED AFTER SCHEDULE 4
TO 1980 ACT

SCHEDULE 4A

GROUNDS FOR WITHHOLDING CONSENT TO ASSIGNMENT
BY WAY OF EXCHANGE

Ground 1

The tenant of the proposed assignee is obliged to give up possession of the dwelling-house of which he is the secure tenant in pursuance of an order of the court, or will be so obliged at a date specified in such an order.

Ground 2

Proceedings have been begun for possession of the dwelling-house of which the tenant or the proposed assignee is the secure tenant on one or more of grounds 1 to 5A as set out in Part I of Schedule 4 to this Act or there has been served on the tenant or the proposed assignee a notice under section 33 of this Act which specifies one or more of those grounds and that notice is still in force.

Ground 3

The accommodation afforded by the dwelling-house is substantially more extensive than is reasonably required by the proposed assignee.

Ground 4

The extent of the accommodation afforded by the dwelling-house is not reasonably suitable to the needs of the proposed assignee and his family.

Ground 5

The dwelling-house either forms part of, or is within the curtilage of, a building to which sub-paragraph (2) of paragraph 1 of Part I of Schedule 1 to this Act applies or is situated in a cemetery and (in either case) the dwelling-house was let to the tenant or to a predecessor in title of his in consequence of the tenant or predecessor being in the employment of the landlord or of a body specified in sub-paragraph (3) of that paragraph.

Ground 6

The landlord is a charity within the meaning of the Charities Act 1960 and the proposed assignee's occupation of the dwelling-house would conflict with the objects of the charity.

Ground 7

The dwelling-house has features which are substantially different from those of ordinary dwelling-houses and which are designed to make it suitable for occupation by a physically disabled person who requires accommodation of the kind provided by the dwelling-house and, if the assignment were made, there would no longer be such a person residing in the dwelling-house.

Ground 8

The landlord is a housing association or housing trust which lets dwelling-houses only for occupation (alone or with others) by persons whose circumstances (other than merely financial circumstances) make it especially difficult for them to satisfy their need for housing and, if the assignment were made, there would no longer be such a person residing in the dwelling-house.

Ground 9

The dwelling-house is one of a group of dwelling-houses which it is the practice of the landlord to let for occupation by persons with special needs and a social service or special facility is provided in close proximity to the group of dwelling-houses in order to assist persons with those special needs and, if the assignment were made, there would no longer be a person with those special needs residing in the dwelling-house.

GENERAL NOTE

This Schedule contains the grounds on which a landlord may object to an assignment under the new "right to exchange"; see s.26 above. Many of the grounds cross-refer to grounds for possession, or to circumstances in which the right to buy cannot be exercised.
Ground 1: see Sched. 1, Pt. II, para. 1 of the 1980 Act.
Ground 2: Possession proceedings begin with a notice of intended proceedings, or notice of seeking possession, which must specify the ground (under Sched. 4 of the 1980 Act) on which possession is sought: 1980 Act s.33. The grounds for possession fall into three classes: those requiring proof of ground and that it is reasonable to make the order sought; those requiring proof of ground and the provision of suitable alternative accommodation; and, those requiring proof of ground and both reasonableness and suitable alternative accommodation; see 1980 Act s.34; see also notes to s.26 above. (Some of those within the *second* and *third* class are covered by Grounds 6–9 below.)
Grounds 1–5B are within the first class, *i.e.* ground plus reasonableness only. The first class also includes a Ground 6, covering a secure tenancy granted to a person while works were carried out to another property of which he was, hitherto, the secure tenant. This Ground is not within this provision. However, this provision applies whether proceedings have actually been commenced, or a mere notice of seeking possession has been served. (Such a notice may survive for more than a year; see 1980 Act s.33).
Ground 3: Note that the accommodation afforded by the property must be *substantially* more extensive than that reasonably required by the proposed assignee.
Ground 4: This Ground would appear to cover the case where a family seeks to move into accommodation which is too *small* for them, *e.g.* for reasons of economy. It is hard to see how otherwise it differs from Ground 3, because the distinction between accommodation substantially more extensive than reasonably required by assignee (which must surely import the assignee's family) and an *extent* of accommodation not reasonably suitable to the needs of proposed assignee and family, is in no other respect of such significance that it could not have been met by, *e.g.* alternative wording within the same Ground.
It is the word "extent" to which attention must be paid. If it was not present, the Ground might be construed as permitting refusal of, *e.g.* a flat, to a family with young children, or a property with difficult access to an elderly or disabled person. ("Special" accommodation—for the physically handicapped—is covered by Ground 7 below; accommodation adapted for the elderly is left wholly uncovered but might have been within the present Ground, again were it not for the word "extent"). But "extent" clearly refers to the

amount of accommodation, as distinct from its nature or quality, or indeed its special facilities.

The debates give no clue to any other reason why the separate Ground was thought necessary, a fact not wholly unrelated to the introduction of the provisions for the first time at about 11 o'clock in the evening, in the House of Lords in Committee Stage ("An earful to take in so late at night"—Baroness Birk, *Hansard*, H.L. Vol. 448, col. 1268 (February 28, 1984)).

Ground 5: See note to s.2 above.

Ground 6: This refers to the 1980 Act, Sched. 4, Ground 9. If the assignment took place, Sched. 4, Ground 9 would be available.

Ground 7: This refers to the 1980 Act, Sched. 4, Ground 10. Sched. 4, Ground 10, would be available if the assignment took place.

Ground 8: This refers to the 1980 Act, Sched. 4, Ground 11. Sched. 4, Ground 11 would be available if the assignment took place.

Ground 9: This refers to the 1980 Act, Sched. 4, Ground 12. Sched. 4, Ground 12 would be available if the assignment took place.

Section 46.	SCHEDULE 8

PROVISIONS CONSEQUENTIAL UPON PUBLIC BODY'S NOTICE

Duration of notice

1.—(1) A public body's notice shall come into force when it is accepted by the local authority, either by notice given within the prescribed period to the public body by which it was given or by virtue of section 46(3) of this Act and, subject to paragraph 3(3) below, shall continue in force until the occurrence of, or the expiry of a prescribed period of time beginning on the date of, such event as may be prescribed.

(2) Building regulations may empower a local authority to extend (whether before or after its expiry) any such period of time as is referred to in sub-paragraph (1) above.

Public body's plans certificates

2.—(1) Where a public body—
    (*a*) is satisfied that plans of the work specified in a public body's notice given by it have been inspected by a servant or agent of the body who is competent to assess the plans, and
    (*b*) in the light of that inspection is satisfied that the plans neither are defective nor show that work carried out in accordance with them would contravene any provision of building regulations, and
    (*c*) has complied with any prescribed requirements as to consultation or otherwise, the body may give to the local authority a certificate in the prescribed form (in the enactments relating to building regulations referred to as a "public body's plans certificate").

(2) Building regulations may authorise the giving of a public body's notice combined with a certificate under sub-paragraph (1) above and may prescribe a single form for such a combined notice and certificate; and where such a prescribed form is used,—
    (*a*) any reference in this Schedule or in any other provision of Part II of this Act to a public body's notice or to a public body's plans certificate shall be construed as including a reference to that form; but
    (*b*) should the form cease to be in force as a public body's notice by virtue of paragraph 1(1) above, nothing in that paragraph shall affect the continuing validity of the form as a public body's plans certificate.

(3) A public body's plans certificate—
    (*a*) may relate either to the whole or to part only of the work specified in the public body's notice concerned; and
    (*b*) shall not have effect unless it is accepted by the local authority to whom it is given.

(4) A local authority to whom a public body's plans certificate is given—
    (*a*) may not reject the certificate except on prescribed grounds; and
    (*b*) shall reject the certificate if any of the prescribed grounds exists.

(5) Unless, within the prescribed period, the local authority to whom a public body's plans certificate is given give notice of rejection, specifying the ground or grounds in question, to the public body by which the certificate was given, the authority shall be conclusively presumed to have accepted the certificate.

(6) If it appears to a local authority by whom a public body's plans certificate has been accepted that the work to which the certificate relates has not been commenced within the period of three years beginning on the date on which the certificate was accepted, the authority may rescind their acceptance of the certificate by notice, specifying the ground or grounds in question, given to the public body.

Public body's final certificates

3.—(1) where a public body is satisfied that any work specified in a public body's notice given by it has been completed, the body may give to the local authority such certificate with respect to the completion of the work and compliance with building regulations as may be prescribed (in the enactments relating to building regulations referred to as a "public body's final certificate").

(2) Sub-paragraphs (3) to (5) of paragraph 2 above shall have effect in relation to a public body's final certificate as if any reference to those sub-paragraphs to a public body's plans certificate were a reference to a public body's final certificate.

(3) Where a public body's final certificate has been given with respect to any of the work specified in a public body's notice and that certificate has been accepted by the local authority concerned, the public body's notice shall cease to apply to that work, but the provisions of section 40(1) of this Act, as applied by section 46(4), shall, by virtue of this sub-paragraph, continue to apply in relation to that work as if the public body's notice continued in force in relation to it.

Effects of public body's notice ceasing to be in force

4.—(1) The provisions of this paragraph apply where a public body's notice ceases to be in force by virtue of paragraph 1(1) above.

(2) Building regulations may provide that, if—

    (a) a public body's plans certificate was given before the day on which the public body's notice ceased to be in force, and

    (b) that certificate was accepted by the local authority (before, on or after that day), and

    (c) before that day, that acceptance was not rescinded by a notice under paragraph 2(6) above,

then, with respect to the work specified in the certificate, such of the functions of a local authority referred to in section 40(1) of this Act as may be prescribed for the purposes of this sub-paragraph either shall not be exercisable or shall be exercisable only in prescribed circumstances.

(3) If, before the day on which the public body's notice ceased to be in force, a public body's final certificate was given in respect of part of the work specified in the notice and that certificate was accepted by the local authority (before, on or after that day), the fact that the public body's notice has ceased to be in force shall not affect the continuing operation of paragraph 3(3) above in relation to that part of the work.

(4) Notwithstanding anything in sub-paragraphs (2) and (3) above, for the purpose of enabling the local authority to perform the functions referred to in section 40(1) of this Act in relation to any part of the work not specified in a public body's plans certificate or final certificate, as the case may be, building regulations may require the local authority to be provided with plans which relate not only to that part but also to the part to which the certificate in question relates.

(5) In any case where this paragraph applies, the reference in subsection (4) of section 65 of the 1936 Act (twelve month time limit for giving certain notices) to the date of the completion of the work in question shall have effect, in relation to a notice under subsection (1) of that section, as if it were a reference to the date on which the public body's notice ceased to be in force.

(6) Subject to any provision of building regulations made by virtue of sub-paragraph (2) above, if, before the public body's notice ceased to be in force, an offence under section 4(6) of the 1961 Act (contravention of provisions of building regulations) was committed with respect to any of the work specified in that notice, summary proceedings for that offence may be commenced by the local authority at any time within six months beginning with the day on which the functions of the local authority referred to in section 40(1) of this Act became exercisable with respect to the provision of building regulations to which the offence relates.

(7) Any reference in the preceding provisions of this paragraph to section 40(1) of this Act is a reference to that section as applied by section 46(4) thereof.

Consultation

5. Building regulations may make provision for requiring, in such circumstances as may be prescribed, a public body which has given a public body's notice to consult any prescribed person before taking any prescribed step in connection with any work specified in the notice.

GENERAL NOTE

This Schedule makes provision in respect of a public body's notice parallel to the provisions which appear in Pt. II which relate to initial notices.

Section 57(1).   SCHEDULE 9

SECTIONS INSERTED AFTER SECTION 65 OF THE 1936 ACT

Obtaining of report where section 65 notice given

65A.—(1) In any case where—

    (*a*) a person to whom a section 65 notice has been given gives to the local authority by whom the notice was given notice in writing of his intention to obtain from a suitably qualified person a written report concerning work to which the section 65 notice relates, and

    (*b*) such a report is obtained and submitted to the local authority and, as a result of their consideration of it, the local authority withdraw the section 65 notice,

the local authority may pay to the person to whom the section 65 notice was given such amount as appears to them to represent the expenses reasonably incurred by him in consequence of their having given that notice including, in particular, his expenses in obtaining the report.

(2) Subject to subsection (3) of this section, if a person to whom a section 65 notice has been given gives notice under subsection (1)(*a*) of this section then, so far as regards the matters to which the section 65 notice relates, the reference to twenty-eight days in section 65(3) of this Act shall be construed as a reference to seventy days.

(3) Notice under subsection (1)(*a*) of this section shall be given before the expiry of the period of twenty-eight days referred to in subsection (3) of section 65 of this Act or, as the case may be, within such longer period as a court allows under that subsection; and where such a longer period has been so allowed before notice is given under subsection (1)(*a*) of this section, subsection (2) of this section shall not apply.

(4) In this section and in section 65B of this Act a "section 65 notice" means a notice under subsection (1) or subsection (2) of section 65 of this Act.

Appeals against section 65 notices

65B.—(1) Any person aggrieved by the giving of a section 65 notice may appeal to a magistrates' court acting for the petty sessions area in which is situated land on which has been carried out any work to which the notice relates.

(2) Subject to subsection (3) below, on an appeal under this section the court shall,—

    (*a*) if they determine that the local authority were entitled to give the notice, confirm the notice; and

    (*b*) in any other case, give the local authority a direction to withdraw the notice.

(3) If, in a case where the appeal is against a notice under subsection (2) of section 65 of this Act, the court is satisfied that—

    (*a*) the local authority were entitled to give the notice, but

    (*b*) in all the circumstances of the case the purpose for which was enacted the section of this Act by virtue of which the notice was given has been substantially achieved,

the court may give a direction under subsection (2)(*b*) of this section.

(4) An appeal under this section shall be brought—

    (*a*) within twenty-eight days of the giving of the section 65 notice; or

    (*b*) in a case where the person to whom the section 65 notice was given gives notice under subsection (1)(*a*) of section 65A of this Act, within seventy days of the giving of the section 65 notice.

(5) The procedure on appeal to a magistrates' court under this section shall be by way of complaint for an order and the Magistrates' Courts Act 1980 shall apply to the proceedings.

(6) Where an appeal is brought under this section—

    (*a*) the section 65 notice shall be of no effect pending the final determination or withdrawal of the appeal; and

    (*b*) subsection (3) of section 65 of this Act shall have effect in relation to that notice as if after the words "twenty-eight days" there were inserted the words "(beginning, in a case where an appeal is brought under section 65B of this Act, on the date when the appeal is finally determined or, as the case may be, withdrawn)".

(7) If, on an appeal under this section, there is produced to the court a report which has been submitted to the local authority under subsection (1) of section 65A of this Act, the court, in making any order as to costs, may treat the expenses incurred in obtaining the report as expenses incurred for the purposes of the appeal.

GENERAL NOTE

S.65 of the Public Health Act 1936 provides that if any work to which the building regulations are applicable contravenes any of those regulations the authority may by notice require the owner to pull down or alter the work. The new provision s.65A enables a person upon whom a notice has been served to obtain a report from a suitably qualified person concerning the work to which the notice relates. If the authority withdraw the s.65 notice after having considered the report the authority may meet the expense of obtaining the report.

S.65B confers a right of appeal to the Magistrates' Court against a s.65 notice, and the Court may confirm the notice or direct the authority to withdraw the notice. The Court may direct an authority to withdraw a notice if the purposes of s.65 have been substantially achieved. If a report has been submitted to the authority under s.65A(1) the Court may include the expenses incurred in obtaining the report in any order as to costs.

Section 59(3).   SCHEDULE 10

SECTION 64(4) OF THE 1936 ACT AND SECTION 6 OF THE
1961 ACT, AS AMENDED

Public Health Act 1936

64.—(4) For the purposes of this Part of this Act, the expression "the prescribed period", in relation to the passing or rejection of plans, means five weeks or such extended period (expiring not later than two months from the deposit of the plans) as may before the expiration of the five weeks be agreed in writing between the person depositing the plans and the local authority.

Public Health Act 1961

6.—(1) Subject to the provisions of this section, if the Minister, on an application made in accordance with the provisions of this Act, considers that the operation of any requirement in building regulations would be unreasonable in relation to the particular case to which the application relates, he may, after consultation with the local authority, give a direction dispensing with or relaxing that requirement.

(2) If building regulations so provide as regards any requirement contained in the regulations, the power to dispense with or relax that requirement under subsection (1) of this section shall be exercisable by the local authority (instead of by the Minister after consultation with the local authority):

Provided that any building regulations made by virtue of this subsection may except applications of any description.

(2A) If—

    (*a*) building regulations so provide as regards any requirement contained in the regulations, and (*b*) a public body considers that the operation of any such requirement would be unreasonable in relation to any particular work carried out or proposed to be carried out by or on behalf of the public body,

the public body may give a direction dispensing with or relaxing that requirement.

(2B) In subsection (2A) above "public body" means—

    (*a*) a local authority;

    (*b*) a county council;

    (*c*) any other body which is prescribed for the purposes of section 52 of the Housing and Building Control Act 1984.

(3) Building regulations may provide as regards any requirement contained in the regulations that the foregoing subsections of this section shall not apply.

(4) An application under this section shall be in such form and shall contain such particulars as may be prescribed.

(5) The application shall be made to the local authority and, except where the power of giving the direction is exercisable by the local authority, the local authority shall at once transmit the application to the Minister and give notice to the applicant that it has been so transmitted.

(6) An application by a local authority in connection with a building or proposed building in the area of that authority shall be made to the Secretary of State except where the power of giving the direction is exercisable by that authority.

(7) The provisions of Part I of the First Schedule to this Act shall have effect as regards any application made under this section for a direction which will affect the application of building regulations to work which has been carried out before the making of the application.

Section 64.   SCHEDULE 11

Minor and Consequential Amendments

Interpretation

1. In this Schedule expressions used in Part I of this Act have the same meanings as in that Part.

The Leasehold Reform Act 1967

2.—(1) Part I of the Leasehold Reform Act 1967 (enfranchisement and extension of long leaseholds) shall not apply where, in the case of a tenancy or sub-tenancy to which this sub-paragraph applies, the landlord is a housing association and the freehold is owned by a body of persons or trust established for charitable purposes only.

(2) Where a tenancy of a dwelling-house which is a house is created by the grant of a lease in pursuance of Chapter I of Part I of the 1980 Act, the tenancy shall be treated for the purposes of Part I of the said Act of 1967 as being a long tenancy notwithstanding that the lease is granted for a term not exceeding 21 years.

(3) Where a tenancy of a dwelling-house which is a house is created by the grant of a lease in pursuance of Part I of this Act, the tenancy shall be treated for the purposes of Part I of the said Act of 1967—

    (*a*) as being a long tenancy notwithstanding that the lease is granted for a term not exceeding 21 years; and

    (*b*) as being a tenancy at a low rent notwithstanding that rent is payable under the tenancy at a yearly rate equal to or more than two-thirds of the rateable value of the dwelling-house on the first day of the term.

(4) Notwithstanding anything in sub-paragraph (3) above, where a tenancy of a dwelling-house which is a house is created by the grant of a lease in pursuance of Part I of this Act, then, so long as the rent payable under the lease exceeds £10 per annum, neither the tenant nor the tenant under a sub-tenancy directly or indirectly derived out of the tenancy shall be entitled to acquire the freehold or an extended lease of the dwelling-house under Part I of the said Act of 1967.

(5) Where, in the case of a tenancy or sub-tenancy to which this sub-paragraph applies, the tenant exercises his right to acquire the freehold under Part I of the said Act of 1967, the price payable for the dwelling-house shall be determined in accordance with section 9(1A) of that Act notwithstanding that the rateable value of the dwelling-house does not exceed £1,000 in Greater London or £500 elsewhere.

(6) Sub-paragraphs (1) and (5) above apply to—
   (a) a tenancy of a dwelling-house which is a house which is created by the grant of a lease in pursuance of Chapter I of Part I of the 1980 Act or Part I of this Act and any sub-tenancy directly or indirectly derived out of such a tenancy; and
   (b) where in any case Part I of the said Act of 1967 applies as if there had been a single tenancy granted for a term beginning at the same time as the term under a tenancy falling within paragraph (a) above and expiring at the same time as the term under a later tenancy, that later tenancy and any sub-tenancy directly or indirectly derived out of that later tenancy;
and sub-paragraph (5) above also applies to a tenancy which is granted in substitution for a tenancy or sub-tenancy falling within paragraph (a) or (b) above in pursuance of Part I of the said Act of 1967.

3. In section 3(1) of the said Act of 1967 (meaning of "long tenancy") in paragraph (b) of the proviso after the word "assignment" there shall be inserted the words "otherwise than by virtue of section 37A of the Housing Act 1980 (assignments by way of exchange)".

The Health and Safety at Work etc. Act 1974

4. Subsection (3) of section 69 of the Health and Safety at Work etc. Act 1974 (appeals against certain decisions of the Secretary of State) shall be amended as follows—
   (a) for paragraph (b) there shall be substituted the following paragraph—
      "(b) on a reference under section 64 of the 1936 Act or section 42 of the Housing and Building Control Act 1984;";
   (b) after the words "local authority", in the second place where they occur, there shall be inserted the words "or, as the case may be, the person approved for the purposes of Part II of the said Act of 1984"; and
   (c) in the definition of "the relevant person" for paragraph (ii) there shall be substituted the following paragraph—
      "(ii) as regards a reference under the said section 64 or the said section 42, means the person on whose application the reference was made;".

The Airports Authority Act 1975

5. In section 19(2) of the Airports Authority Act 1975 (application of enactments relating to statutory undertakers) for the words "shall apply in relation to the Authority as it applies" there shall be substituted the words "and section 71 of that Act (which exempts such buildings from building regulations) shall apply in relation to the Authority as they apply" and for the words "(which excludes" there shall be substituted the words "and the proviso to the said section 71 (which exclude".

The Housing Act 1980

6. Subsections (4) and (4A) of section 3 of the Housing Act 1980 (meaning of "house", "flat", "dwelling-house" etc.) shall have effect as if any reference to the right to buy included a reference to the right to be granted a shared ownership lease.

7. Section 4(3) of that Act (joint tenants and members of family occupying dwelling-house otherwise than as joint tenants) shall have effect as if the reference to Chapter I of Part I of that Act included a reference to Part I of this Act.

8.—(1) After subsection (1) of section 5 of that Act (notice claiming to exercise the right to buy) there shall be inserted the following subsection—
      "(1A) A landlord's notice under subsection (1) above shall inform the tenant of any application for a determination under paragraph 5 of Part I of Schedule 1 to this Act and, in the case of a notice admitting the tenant's right, shall be without prejudice to any determination made on such an application."

(2) In subsection (2) of that section for the words "three years" there shall be substituted the words "two years".

(3) The amendment made by sub-paragraph (1) above shall not apply where the tenant's claim to exercise the right to buy was made before the coming into force of Part I of this Act; and the amendment made by sub-paragraph (2) above shall not apply where the landlord's notice under section 5(1) of that Act was served before the coming into force of Part I of this Act.

9. At the end of section 6 of that Act (purchase price) there shall be added the following subsection—
      "(6) Where the secure tenant's tenancy has at any time been assigned by virtue of section 37A of this Act, the persons specified in subsection (5) above shall not include any person who under that tenancy was a secure tenant before the assignment.".

10.—(1) In subsection (1) of section 10 of that Act (notice of purchase price etc.) for the words "as soon as practicable" there shall be substituted the words "within eight weeks or, where the right is that mentioned in section 1(1)(*b*) above, twelve weeks".

(2) In subsection (2) of that section for the words "section 7(5)" there shall be substituted the words "section 7(1)" and for the words "section 7(2) or (4)" there shall be substituted the words "section 7(1A), (2) or (4).".

(3) After subsection (2) of that section there shall be inserted the following subsection—

"(2A) Where the notice states provisions which would enable the landlord to recover from the tenant service charges within the meaning of Schedule 19 to this Act or section 18(1) of the 1984 Act, the notice shall also state—

(*a*) the landlord's estimate of the average annual amount (at current prices) which would be payable in respect of each head of charge; and

(*b*) the aggregate of the estimated amounts stated under paragraph (*a*) above;

but there shall be disregarded for the purposes of any such statement any estimated amount stated under paragraph 17 of Schedule 2 to this Act."

(4) In subsection (3) of that section after the word "mortgage", in the first place where it occurs, there shall be inserted the words "and the effect of Part I of the 1984 Act so far as relating to the right to be granted a shared ownership lease", for the words "section 16(4)" there shall be substituted the words "section 16(2) to (4), (6) and (6b)" and for the word "exercising" there shall be substituted the words "claiming to exercise".

(5) The amendments made by this paragraph shall not apply where the notice under section 10(1) of that Act was served before the coming into force of Part I of this Act.

11. In section 11(6) of that Act (right of tenant to have value determined by district valuer) for the word "exercising" there shall be substituted the words "claiming to exercise".

12. In section 12 of that Act (claim to a mortgage) after subsection (5) there shall be inserted the following subsection—

"(5A) Where the amount which, in the opinion of the landlord or Housing Corporation, the tenant is entitled to leave outstanding, or have advanced to him, on the security of the dwelling-house is less than the aggregate mentioned in section 9(1) above, the notice shall also inform the tenant of the effect of Part I of the 1984 Act so far as relating to the right to be granted a shared ownership lease and shall be accompanied by a form for use by the tenant in claiming, in accordance with section 13(1) of that Act, that right."

13.—(1) In subsection (1) of section 13 of that Act (change of secure tenant after notice claiming right to buy) for the words from "becomes the secure tenant" to the end of paragraph (*b*) there shall be substituted the following paragraphs—

"(*a*) becomes the secure tenant under the same secure tenancy otherwise than on an assignment made by virtue of section 37A of this Act; or

(*b*) becomes the secure tenant under a periodic tenancy arising by virtue of section 29 of this Act on the coming to an end of the secure tenancy;".

(2) In subsection (2) of that section for the word "exercising" there shall be substituted the words "claiming to exercise".

14.—(1) Section 18 of that Act (right to a mortgage—terms of mortgage deed) shall have effect as if any reference to the deed by which a mortgage is effected in pursuance of Chapter I of Part I of that Act included a reference to the deed by which a further mortgage is effected in pursuance of section 16 of this Act.

(2) Where that section applies in relation to such a deed by virtue of sub-paragraph (1) above, it shall also have effect as if any reference to the term of a lease were a reference to the unexpired term of that lease.

15.—(1) Section 19 of that Act (dwelling-houses in National Parks and areas of outstanding natural beauty etc.) shall have effect as if any reference to Chapter I of Part I of that Act included a reference to Part I of this Act.

(2) Where that section applies in relation to the grant of a shared ownership lease by virtue of sub-paragraph (1) above, it shall also have effect as if—

(*a*) in subsections (2), (4) and (12) for the words "section 8(3A) of this Act" there were substituted the words "paragraph 6(5) of Schedule 3 to the 1984 Act";

(*b*) in subsection (6) for the words "section 8(1) of this Act" there were substituted the words "paragraph 6(1) or 7(1) of Schedule 3 to the 1984 Act";

(*c*) in subsection (7) for the words "subsection (3A) of section 8 of this Act" there were substituted the words "sub-paragraph (5) of paragraph 6 of Schedule 3 to the 1984 Act" and for the words "subsection (1) of that section" there were substituted the words "sub-paragraph (1) of that paragraph or paragraph 7(1) of that Schedule";

(*d*) in subsection (11) for the words "section 8(3A)(*d*) or (*e*) of this Act" there were substituted the words "paragraph 6(5)(*d*) or (*e*) of Schedule 3 to the 1984 Act"; and (*e*) in subsection (12), in the definition of "relevant disposal" for the words "section 8 of this Act" there were substituted the words "paragraph 6 of Schedule 3 to the 1984 Act."

16. Section 20 of that Act (registration of title) shall have effect as if—

(*a*) the reference to the conveyance of a freehold in pursuance of Chapter I of Part I of that Act included a reference to the conveyance of a freehold in pursuance of such a right as is mentioned in paragraph 3(5) or 7(5) of Schedule 3 to this Act; and

(*b*) the reference to the grant of a lease in pursuance of that Chapter included a reference to the grant of a lease in pursuance of Part I of this Act.

17.—(1) For section 21 of that Act (costs) there shall be substituted the following section—

   "Costs

     21.—(1) Any agreement between—

       (*a*) a tenant claiming to exercise the right to buy and the landlord; or

       (*b*) a tenant claiming to exercise the right to a mortgage and the landlord or, as the case may be, the Housing Corporation,

shall be void in so far as it purports to oblige the tenant to bear any part of the costs incurred by the landlord or Housing Corporation in connection with the tenant's exercise of that right.

     (2) Where a tenant exercises the right to a mortgage, the landlord or, as the case may be, the Housing Corporation may charge to him the costs incurred by it in connection with the tenant's exercise of that right, but only on the execution of the deed by which the mortgage is effected and to the extent that those costs do not exceed such amount as the Secretary of State may by order specify."

(2) That section as so substituted shall have effect as if—

(*a*) the reference to the right to buy included a reference to the right to be granted a shared ownership lease and to such rights as are mentioned in paragraphs 3(1) and (5) and 7(5) of Schedule 3 to this Act; and

(*b*) the reference to the right to a mortgage included a reference to such a right as is mentioned in section 16(1) of this Act.

18.—(1) After subsection (1) of section 22 of that Act (notices) there shall be inserted the following subsection—

     "(1A) Where the form of and the particulars to be contained in a notice under this Chapter are so prescribed a tenant who proposes to claim or has claimed to exercise the right to buy may request the landlord to supply him with a form for use in giving such a notice, and the landlord shall do so within seven days of the request."

(2) That section shall have effect as if any reference to Chapter I of Part I of that Act included a reference to Part I of this Act.

19.—(1) Subsection (5) of section 23 of that Act (Secretary of State's power to intervene) shall be omitted.

(2) In subsection (9) of that section for the words "on demand" onwards there shall be substituted the words "on a date specified in the certificate, together with interest from that date at a rate so specified".

(3) In subsection (11) of that section for the words "subsections (5) to (10)" there shall be substituted the words "subsections (6) to (10)".

(4) That section shall have effect as if any reference to Chapter I of Part I of that Act included a reference to Part I of this Act and any reference to the right to buy included a reference to the right to be granted a shared ownership lease.

20.—(1) In subsection (2) of section 24 of that Act (vesting orders) for the words "the landlord and the tenant and their successors in title" there shall be substituted the words "both the landlord and its successors in title and the tenant and his successors in title (including any person deriving title under him or them)".

(2) That section shall have effect as if any reference to Chapter I of Part I of that Act included a reference to Part I of this Act.

21. The following provisions of that Act, namely—

     section 24A (Secretary of State's power to give directions as to covenants and conditions);

     section 24B (effect of directions on existing covenants and conditions);

     section 24C (Secretary of State's power to obtain information etc.);

     section 24D (Secretary of State's power to give assistance); and

     section 25 (statutory declarations),

shall have effect as if any reference to Chapter I of Part I of that Act included a reference to Part I of this Act and any reference to the right to buy included a reference to the right to be granted a shared ownership lease.

22. In section 27(3) of that Act (interpretation of Chapter I), for the words "Chapter II", in the first place where they occur, there shall be substituted the words "Part I of the 1984 Act", after the words "Chapter II", in the second place where they occur, there shall be inserted the words "and that Part" and for paragraphs (*a*) and (*b*) there shall be substituted the following paragraphs—

"(*a*) a predecessor of a local authority within the definition in section 50(1) shall be deemed to have been such an authority;

(*b*) a predecessor of a county council shall be deemed to have been such a council; and

(*c*) a housing association shall be deemed to have been registered under Part II of the 1974 Act if it is or was so registered at any later time".

23. In subsection (1) of section 31 of that Act (meaning of successor) for the words from "but a tenant" onwards there shall be substituted the words "but subject to subsection (1A) below" and after that subsection there shall be inserted the following subsection—

"(1A) A tenant to whom the tenancy was assigned in pursuance of an order under section 24 of the Matrimonial Causes Act 1973 is a successor only if the other party to the marriage was himself a successor; and a tenant to whom the tenancy was assigned by virtue of section 37A below is a successor only if he was a successor in relation to the tenancy which he himself assigned by virtue of that section.".

24. In section 50(1) of that Act (interpretation of Chapter II of Part I) immediately before the definition of "development corporation" there shall be inserted the following definition—

"'cemetery' has the same meaning as in section 214 of the Local Government Act 1972;".

25.—(1) In subsection (2) of section 86 of that Act (jurisdiction of county court and rules of procedure) there shall be inserted after paragraph (*a*) the following paragraph—

"(*aa*) whether any consent required by section 37A was withheld otherwise than on one or more of the grounds set out in Schedule 4A to this Act;".

(2) That section shall have effect as if any reference to any question arising under Part I of that Act or Chapter I of Part I of that Act included a reference to any question arising under Part I of this Act or any lease granted in pursuance of it.

26. In section 110(1) of that Act (local authority mortgage interest rates) at the end of paragraph (*c*) there shall be inserted the words "or section 20 of the 1984 Act".

27. In subsection (1) of section 127 of that Act (registration of housing associations) for the words from the beginning to "its objects" there shall be substituted the words "Section 13 of the 1974 Act (the register of housing associations) shall have effect as if the additional purposes or objects mentioned in subsection (3) of that section included" and the words from "without" onwards shall be omitted.

28. In section 137(1) of that Act (avoidance of certain unauthorised disposals) after the words "section 128(2) of the Local Government Act 1972" there shall be inserted the words ", section 29 of the Town and Country Planning Act 1959".

29. At the end of section 150 of that Act (interpretation) there shall be inserted the following definition—

"'the 1984 Act' means the Housing and Building Control Act 1984".

30. In section 151(1) of that Act (regulations and orders) after the word "section", in the second place where it occurs, there shall be inserted the word "8(5)".

31. Part II of Schedule 1A to that Act (qualification and discount) shall have effect as if "previous discount" included a discount which was given, before the relevant time, in pursuance of the provision required by paragraph 3 of Schedule 3 to this Act or any other provision to the like effect.

32. Part IV of Schedule 2 to that Act (charges and other matters) shall have effect as if any reference to the right to buy included a reference to the right to be granted a shared ownership lease and to such rights as are mentioned in paragraphs 3(5) and 7(5) of Schedule 3 to this Act.

33.—(1) Paragraph 1 of Schedule 3 to that Act (tenancies which are not secure tenancies) shall have effect as if the reference to a tenancy granted in pursuance of Chapter I of Part I of that Act included a reference to a tenancy granted in pursuance of Part I of this Act.

(2) In paragraph 2(1) of that Schedule for paragraphs (*a*) to (*e*) there shall be substituted the words "a body specified in paragraph 1(3) of Schedule 1 to this Act".

(3) In paragraph 8 of that Schedule for the words "or his predecessor in title", in the first place where they occur, there shall be substituted the words "(or a predecessor in title of his)" and for the words "(or his predecessor in title)", in the second place where they occur, there shall be substituted the words "or predecessor".

34. In Part I of Schedule 4 to that Act, in ground 6, for the words "or his predecessor in title", in the first place where they occur, there shall be substituted the words "(or a

predecessor in title of his); and for the words "he (or his predecessor in title)", in both places where they occur, there shall be substituted the words "the tenant or predecessor".

The Civil Aviation Act 1982

35. In paragraph 1(1) of Schedule 2 to the Civil Aviation Act 1982 (application of enactments relating to statutory undertakers etc.) for the words "shall apply in relation to the CAA as it applies" there shall be substituted the words "and section 71 of that Act (which exempts such buildings from building regulations) shall apply in relation to the CAA as they apply" and for the words "(which excludes" there shall be substituted the words "and the proviso to the said section 71 (which exclude".

GENERAL NOTES

This Schedule contains "minor and consequential amendments".

Para 2: It is hard to perceive this as a "minor"—or indeed necessarily consequential— amendment. Sub-leases of houses may be for 21 years or less. This provision applies to such a lease the full benefit of the right to enfranchise or extend for 50 years, binding not only on the immediate landlord, but of course also on intervening interests and the freeholder, to be found in the Leasehold Reform Act 1967, although normally the 1967 Act applies only to terms of more than 21 years (see 1967 Act ss.1 and 3). Excluded, however, are leases or subleases under which the landlord is a housing association, and the freeholder is a body of persons or trust established for charitable purposes only.

Shared ownership leases would also seem to be within sub-paras (2) and (3), which means that they obtain *some* rights under the 1967 Act. The provision allows tenants under shared ownership leases to acquire residential qualifications under the 1967 Act, notwithstanding that the lease may be for 21 years or less, and that the rent payable is two-thirds or more of the rateable value of the property (see 1967 Act, ss.1 and 4). However, this does not confer upon the tenant the right to enfranchise or extend: in order to enfranchise or extend, the rent must have fallen to £10 per annum, *i.e.* the tenant must have acquired 100 per cent. of the equity.

Note that under the 1980 Act s.140, some shared ownership leases granted after August 8, 1980, which comply with certain conditions, are exempt from the operation of the 1967 Act altogether (*i.e.* even to the extent of acquiring residential qualifications prior to acquisition of 100 per cent. of equity). If granted by a district council, London Borough Council, the Greater London Council, the Common Council of the City of London, the Council of the Isles of Scilly, a development corporation, the Commission for the New Towns or the Development Board for Rural Wales, the conditions are (a) that the lease provides for the tenant to acquire the freehold for a consideration to be calculated in accordance with the terms of the lease and which is reasonable, having regard to the premium paid by the tenant, and (b) that the lease contains a statement of the landlord's opinion that by virtue of s.140 the 1967 Act will not apply. If granted by a registered housing association, the conditions are somewhat different. They are that (a) the lease is granted at a premium calculated by reference to a percentage of the value of the house or the cost of providing it, (b) at the time of grant, it complies with regulations made by the Secretary of State for the purposes of s.140, and (c) that the lease contains a statement of the landlord's opinion that by virtue of s.140 the 1967 Act will not apply.

The purpose of s.140 was to prevent the occupier enfranchising under the 1967 Act at a *lower* price than he would have to pay to complete the purchase under the lease. It would not seem that shared ownership leases granted under this Act will fall within s.140 because the maximum entitlement will be to sub-lease of five days less than the landlord's interest: see Sched. 1, para. 10 above.

The provision applying s.9(1A) of the 1967 Act, regardless of whether or not the rateable value exceeds £1,000 (in Greater London, or £500 elsewhere) affects the price payable for enfranchisement. In a normal case, lower rated housing is to be valued according to the presumptions set out in the 1967 Act, s.9(1) (which assumes in the tenant's favour the fifty-year extended lease to which the tenant is entitled as an alternative to enfranchisement under the 1967 Act) and only the higher rated housing is valued in accordance with the presumptions set out in the 1967 Act s.9(1A) (added by the Housing Act 1974, s.118(4), which does not presume the 50-year extension).

Para. 3: The amendment to s.3 of the 1967 Act concerns tenancies terminable by notice on death or marriage. Such tenancies are not long tenancies for the purposes of that Act if granted before April 18, 1980, or—in relation to later tenancies—if (a) the notice may be given at any time after death or marriage, (b) the length of notice is not more than three months, and (c) the terms of the tenancy preclude both subletting of the whole of the premises *and* assignment—to which last proviso must now be added, other than under the right to exchange, *i.e.* a tenancy terminable on death or marriage need not preclude a right to exchange assignment in order to preserve its exemption from the 1967 Act.

Para. 8: As to sub-para. (1); see notes to s.2(3) above. As to sub-para. (3), note that the reduction in qualifying time needed before an exercise of the right to buy does not apply if the landlord has served the s.5 notice (admitting or denying the right to buy) before this Act comes into force.

Para. 9: Improvements carried out by the tenant, his predecessor under the same tenancy, or another member of his family who was a secure tenant of the same property but under another tenancy, are to be disregarded in the calculation of the purchase price: 1980 Act, s.6(5). Those carried out by a former secure tenant who assigned the tenancy under s.37A of the 1980 Act, introduced by s.26 above, are *not* disregarded.

Para. 10: An offer notice under s.10 of the 1980 Act (a) now has to be served within eight weeks, save where the right is to be a lease, in which case it must be served within twelve weeks, (b) must provide an estimate relating to service charges which will be payable—if any, but whether in respect of flats or houses, and (c) inform the tenant about the right to a shared ownership lease, in addition to other matters already required.

Para. 17: The substantive part of this amendment—aside from its applicability to shared ownership leases—is the limitation contained in the new s.21(2), restricting properly chargeable costs to those "on the execution of the deed by which the mortgage is effected . . ." It was thought that s.21 as formerly drafted could—albeit to the limit prescribed by the Secretary of State (£50: S.I. 1980 No. 1390)—cover such costs as surveying work by the mortgagee. The properly chargeable costs are now clearly limited to legal costs.

Para. 18: Yet another new right: this time, the right to a form from the landlord! S.22 of the 1980 Act gives the Secretary of State a general power to prescribe forms of, and particulars to be contained in, any notice under the right to buy provisions as a whole.

Para. 19: S.23(5) of the 1980 Act contained the power of the Secretary of State to require the production of documents or information, and is now replaced by s.24C, added by s.10 above.

Para. 21: The Secretary of State's powers of intervention (see ss.9–11 above) are as exercisable in relation to shared ownership as full exercise.

Para. 23: The first part of the amendment repeats the present words of s.31(1), *i.e.* a party to whom a tenancy is assigned under s.24 of the Matrimonial Causes Act 1973 is only a successor if the party from whom it was assigned was a successor. Where there is an exchange of tenancies under the 1980 Act s.37A, added by s.26 above, the assign*ing* tenant is the one who remains a successor or non-successor, *i.e.* if Tenant A is a successor and exchanges with Tenant B, a non-successor, Tenant A remains a successor in his new property, while Tenant B remains a non-successor.

Para. 28: This fills an omission in the 1980 Act. See notes to s.22 above.

           SCHEDULE 12

REPEALS

PART I

REPEALS RELATING TO BUILDING CONTROL

Chapter	Short title	Extent of repeal
1966 c.27.	The Building Control Act 1966.	The whole Act.
1966 c.34.	The Industrial Development Act 1966.	In Schedule 3, Part I.
1968 c.73.	The Transport Act 1968.	In Schedule 16, paragraph 9.
1969 c.35.	The Transport (London) Act 1969.	In Schedule 3, paragraph 9(2)(*a*).
1969 c.48.	The Post Office Act 1969.	In Schedule 4, paragraph 80.
1971 c.78.	The Town and Country Planning Act 1971.	In Schedule 23, in Part II, the entry relating to the Building Control Act 1966.
1972 c.5.	The Local Employment Act 1972.	In Schedule 3, the entry relating to the Building Control Act 1966.
1972 c.52.	The Town and Country Planning (Scotland) Act 1972.	In Schedule 21, in Part II, the entry relating to the Building Control Act 1966.
1975 c.64.	The Iron and Steel Act 1975.	In Schedule 6, paragraph 7.
1977 c.49.	The National Health Service Act 1977.	In Schedule 14, in paragraph 13(1)(*b*), the words "107 to". In Schedule 15, paragraph 38.
1978 c.44.	The Employment Protection (Consolidation) Act 1978.	In Schedule 16, paragraph 32.
1981 c.38.	The British Telecommunications Act 1981.	In Schedule 3, paragraph 45.

PART II

FURTHER REPEALS

Chapter	Short title	Extent of repeal
26 Geo. 5 & 1 Edw. 8. c.49.	The Public Health Act 1936.	Section 67.
5 & 6 Eliz. 2. c.56.	The Housing Act 1957.	Section 104C(4).
1974 c.37.	The Health and Safety at Work etc. Act 1974.	Section 61(5). Section 62(3). Section 63(6) and (7). In section 69, in subsection (1) the words "section 64 of the 1936 Act". In Schedule 6, in Part I, paragraphs 1, 2, sub-paragraphs (*a*), (*d*) and (*e*) of paragraph 5, and paragraphs 6 and 7, and Part II except in so far as it sets out section 4 of the Public Health Act 1961. In Schedule 10, in the third column of the entry relating to the Public Health Act 1936, the words "Section 71", the entry relating to the Education Act 1944 and, in the third column of the entry relating to the Public Health Act 1961, the words "Section 7(3) to (6)", "Section 10(1) and (2)" and "and 71".
1975 c.78.	The Airports Authority Act 1975.	Section 25(10).
1980 c.51.	The Housing Act 1980.	In section 2, in subsection (4) the words "Subject to subsection (5) below" and subsection (5). In section 7, subsections (5) to (11). Section 15. In section 18(1), the words from "but the Secretary of State" onwards. Section 19(8). Section 23(5). In section 24, in subsections (3) and (5) the word "land". In section 28(2), paragraph (*d*) and the word "or" immediately preceding that paragraph. In section 127(1), the words from "without" onwards. In Schedule 2, in the provision renumbered as paragraph 15(1), paragraph (*b*) and the words "and paragraph 16 below". In Schedule 3, paragraph 3.
1980 c.65.	The Local Government, Planning and Land Act 1980.	In section 156, subsection (1) and in subsection (2)(*b*), the words from "and" onwards.

1. The repeal of section 2(5) of the Housing Act 1980 has effect subject to section 2(4) of this Act.

2. The repeals of sections 7(5) to (11) and 15 of that Act have effect subject to section 3(6) of this Act.